Voice of the Democracy

Other Writings in History and Literature by Louis Filler

Books

Appointment at Armageddon: Muckraking and Progressivism in the American Tradition (1976)
Randolph Bourne (1965 ed.)
The Crusade against Slavery, 1830–1860 (1960 ff.)
A Dictionary of American Social Reform (1963; Greenwood ed, 1970)
The Unknown Edwin Markham (1966)
Muckraking and Progressivism: an Interpretive Bibliography (1976)

Edited Works

The New Stars: Life and Labor in Old Missouri, Manie Morgan (1949)
Mr. Dooley: Now and Forever, Finley Peter Dunne (1954)
From Populism to Progressivism (1978), anthology
The Removal of the Cherokee Nation: Manifest Destiny or National Dishonor? (1977 ed.)
The World of Mr. Dooley (1962)
The Anxious Years (1963), anthology of 1930s literature
Horace Mann and Others, Robert L. Straker (1963)
A History of the People of the United States, John Bach McMaster (1964)
The President Speaks (1964), major twentieth-century addresses
Horace Mann on the Crisis in Education (1965; Spanish translation, 1972)
Wendell Phillips on Civil Rights and Freedom (1965)
The Ballad of the Gallows-Bird, Edwin Markham (1967)
Old Wolfville: the Fiction of A.H. Lewis (1968)
Slavery in the United States of America (1972)
Abolition and Social Justice (1972)
A Question of Quality (1976)

Introductions

Chatterton, Ernest Lacy (1952)
Plantation and Frontier, Ulrich B. Phillips, in new edition, John R. Commons et al., A Documentary History of American Industrial Society (1958)
The Acquisition of Political, Social and Industrial Rights of Man in America, John Bach McMaster (1961)
My Autobiography, S.S. McClure (1962)
A Modern Symposium, G. Lowes Dickinson (1963)
A Statistical History of the American Presidential Elections, Svend Petersen (1963)
Samuel Gompers, Bernard Mandel (1963)
The Political Depravity of the Founding Fathers, John Bach McMaster (1964)
Democrats and Republicans, Harry Thurston Peck (1964)
A Political History of Slavery, W.H. Smith (1966)
Georgia and States Rights, Ulrich B. Phillips (1967)
The Pantarch: a Biography of Stephen Pearl Andrews, Madeleine B. Stern (1968)
Forty Years of It, Brand Whitlock (1970)

VOICE OF THE DEMOCRACY

A Critical Biography
of David Graham Phillips:
Journalist, Novelist, Progressive

Louis Filler

> Others will come after me,
> Others, when my race is run,
> Sing my song in softer guise,
> With more delicate surprise,
> I am but the pioneer,
> The voice of the democracy. . . .
>
> —Vachel Lindsay

The Pennsylvania State University Press

University Park and London

Library of Congress Cataloging in Publication Data

Filler, Louis, 1911–
    Voice of the democracy

    Bibliography: p. 191.
    Includes index.
    1. Phillips, David Graham, 1867–1911. 2. Novelists,
American—20th century—Biography. 3. Journalists—
United States—Biography. I. Title.
PS3531.H5Z67   813'.5'2 [B]   77-13893
ISBN 0-271-00528-9

Printed in the United States of America

Contents

Works by David Graham Phillips vii

Introduction: A View from the Bridge 1

1 Hoosier 5

2 The Higher Education 14

3 Midwest 23

4 "That Damned East!" 30

5 "Alice" 40

6 A Brilliant Failure 53

7 Venture in a New Time 60

8 Success Story 77

9 Fiction and the Senate Blast 95

10 Harvest 109

11 Legends 124

12 Art and Social Change 136

13 Murder in Gramercy Park 155

14 Afterglow 164

15 Susan Lenox: An American Odyssey 171

16 Phillips: Queries and Conjectures 182

Bibliographic Note 191

Notes 195

Index 203

Works by David Graham Phillips Discussed in This Book

"The Assassination of a Governor." *Cosmopolitan*, April 1905
"The 'Beat' on the Victoria Disaster." *Saturday Evening Post*, May 26, 1900
"The Bowery at Night." *Harper's Weekly*, September 19, 1891
"The Business Organization of a Church." *Harper's Weekly*, July 1903
The Conflict. New York 1911
The Cost. Indianapolis, 1904
Degarmo's Wife and Other Stories. New York, 1913
The Deluge. New York, 1905
"The Delusion of the Race Track." *Cosmopolitan*, January 1905
"The Empire of Rothschild." *Cosmopolitan*, March 1905
The Fashionable Adventures of Joshua Craig. New York, 1909
"The First Born." *Harper's Weekly*, May 23, 1891
The Fortune Hunter. Indianapolis, 1906
George Helm. New York, 1912
Golden Fleece. New York, 1903
The Grain of Dust. New York, 1911
The Great God Success. New York, 1901
"Great Magazines and Their Editors." *Success*, VI (May 1903)
Her Serene Highness. New York, 1902
The Hungry Heart. New York, 1909
The Husband's Story. New York, 1910
Light Fingered Gentry. New York, 1907
"Literary Folk." *Saturday Evening Post*, April 12, 1902
"The Making of a Billionaire." *Saturday Evening Post*, October 4, 1902
The Master Rogue. New York, 1903
"The Millionaires." *Saturday Evening Post*, July 26–August 23, 1902
The Mother Light. New York, 1905
"The Novelist—Theoretically Speaking." *Book News Monthly*, March 1907
Old Wives for New. New York, 1908
"Painter of the Joy of Life." *Pearson's*, April 1911

"Phillips's Methods." *Bookman,* XXXIII (1911)

The Plum Tree. Indianapolis, 1905

"A Point of Law." In *The Worth of a Woman*

The Price She Paid. New York, 1912

"The Race for Circulation." *Saturday Evening Post,* February 8, 1902

"The Real Boss of the United States." *Saturday Evening Post,* February 14, 1903

The Reign of Gilt. New York, 1905

The Second Generation. New York, 1907

The Social Secretary. Indianapolis, 1905

"The Story of the City Daily." *Saturday Evening Post,* February 8, 1902

Susan Lenox, Her Fall and Rise. New York, 1917

"Thursday at Three." *McClure's,* December 1902

"The Treason of the Senate." *Cosmopolitan,* March–November 1906

"The Union of Sixth Avenue and Broadway." *Harper's Weekly,* March 21, 1891

White Magic. New York, 1910

A Woman Ventures. New York, 1902

The Worth of a Woman. New York, 1908

Introduction

A View from the Bridge

Upton Sinclair, good man, once suggested to me that I forget about Phillips's critics and about his background and influences, and concentrate on telling his story. In general, I found the long-time muckraker an admirable person and his views worth heeding. In the present instance, I concluded that Sinclair's advice was worth qualifying—not ignoring, just qualifying.

For Sinclair's vision of a proper tale assumed a readership with background for appreciating the broad cultural expectations of Phillips's time, and empathetic to a good tale. The first condition is readily met. Everybody goes to college, though fewer now than yesterday. Most people, including those in high schools, have heard of the muckrakers, Upton Sinclair, "Teddy" Roosevelt, even Phillips. His "The Treason of the Senate" series has been echoed again and again in textbooks, and can be put in italics; there have been three book printings of it in modern times. Phillips's novel *Susan Lenox: Her Fall and Rise* has been continuously in print, though, until the recent rash of reprints, bowdlerized, and mostly for copyright purposes.

But, Sinclair to the contrary, readers will not necessarily respond to a good story, unless it is supported by relevant-sounding information and ideas. Both get dim with time, are soiled and misused. One writer thinks, or thinks he thinks, that Phillips was a hasty scribbler, and this foolish lie, consoling to impotent "researchers," becomes a stubborn part of his ghostly legend. Another critic has him confused, or insincere, or whatever else it is that rationalizes the critic's own or imposed bias.

That bias may itself deteriorate under the pressure of events, as Twenties egotistical writing did when the Great Depression of 1929 took over, giving way to "Marxist" pieties, themselves destined to obsolescence. Nonetheless, insubstantial opinion lingers and vibrates in classrooms and out. Glib phrases always accompany shallow impressions. It sounds weak to say: "I don't know why; I just don't like the thing." So we add something like: "—because he sounds like a fascist," or like a mere photographer, or like something else we find offensive. And quite rightly. Someone having been a fascist or a photographer or whatever else will not dull our appreciation of his virtues, when we have it to give. The first condition did not prevent the honoring of Ezra Pound when the time came for humanists to protect him from unesthetic military and court authorities. And neither the first, nor the second—nor a third; Theodore Dreiser had a sort of communist period—interfered with Dreiser's success, when the hour struck for him to achieve success. Nor did his success prevent his literary status from melting away into literary history when new conditions undermined his prestige.

Phillips is in a more complex state than Dreiser or many other writers, and a "good story" cannot suffice for him. Good things said about Phillips in old essays and wrinkled reviews are irrelevant and may be cited only when they illuminate some point. And the same is true of antipathetic comments about him. Aside from that, my main concern is indeed with the story. One might wonder why it has to be reconstructed from disparate and even obscure materials. Phillips was not unknown or unregarded. I have already considered some parts of this puzzle in my essay "The Reputation of David Graham Phillips" (Antioch Review, Winter 1951–52) and in book form in connection with another author, The Unknown Edwin Markham (1966).

Our civilization is complex and should be our major study. It isn't, always. We permitted Herman Melville to slip away from us for some sixty years, before "rediscovering him" in the 1920s. After that, he became a gilt-edged, certified classic, though he continues to need rediscovery as a human being who strove and doubted as we do, and whose profound failures want understanding as much as does the "success" he has enjoyed since his death.

I have pondered for some time what seems to be a social law. All opinions originate at home. Only they sound different abroad. For instance, Americans like to think of themselves as "young," and Europeans also think of us as "young." Only "young" sounds different in their mouths and ours. We think we are "friendly," and so do the English who pride themselves on their "reserve." And so with other words which mean one thing to us, intended to be self-flattering, and something else to others.

Similarly, we have not been proud of Upton Sinclair. He is more honored abroad than at home, but as a mere critic of capitalism, that is, of America. We *have* been proud of Ernest Hemingway, and for-eigners have agreed that he is the best we can produce. Emerson bores them as he does us, though once Emerson had represented the emer-gence of a fine, native American spirit. And so with others. As for Phillips, he is as dead abroad as he is at home; but in addition, he is dead in Indiana.[1] No favorite son, he, and he never was. Indeed, it is a social phenomenon that Phillips's generation of liberals, socialists, and reformers of every stripe, with newspapers and magazines as outlets, should have done so little for their own in memoirs, pub-lished letters, and the like. And not only about Phillips, but about Lincoln Steffens, the cowboy chronicler A.H. Lewis, Jack London, Finley Peter Dunne, Brand Whitlock, and others whose writings should persist in recollection and influence new creativity. What, for example, relates the writings of any of the above to the writings of Norman Mailer or Saul Bellow?

There are many things we do not know about this process of ne-glect and best-sellerdom. But it is more important to consider what of the past we *need* to know. This applies to the old among us as well as the young. I recall an American Legionnaire who cheerfully remem-bered having been among those who in 1917 raided the Dayton, Ohio, Public Library, pulled out its books in German, and burned them in the street. Looking at my face he hastened to add, "Of course, I was only twelve years old." It did not occur to him that he stood, retrospectively, in full responsibility for the actions of his elders as well as his own.

How do we stand on World War I? For it has probably been more responsible for our view of Phillips and his fellows than anything that happened during his stormy years as a novelist and social critic. By now, Phillips's entire world is as remote from us as Leo Tolstoi's, and its transitional character is much less understood. In the end, the problem is one of art, but also of some high view which penetrates the humanity of people who did not have to cope with atom bombs and television, but who had the same essential dilemma that we have, of living effectively within their time.

Indeed, it is not quite accurate to equate obscurity or reputation with readership. For one thing, we need to know more about what people read for duty's sake—say, for academic classes—as compared to what they read by choice. Ben Hecht, for example, subtitled a section of the introduction to his autobiography, *Child of the Century* (1954), "My Lack of Fame." Yet his book probably sold half a million copies and capped a career of famous and distinguished books and stage and screen scripts. What must one do to be famous? Dreiser complained in 1939 that he was not famous, and all his books were at one point out of print. Sherwood Anderson stopped writing novels because, he said, no one was reading novels—or at least reading *his* novels.

But aside from such considerations, Phillips is far from buried. I have mentioned the constant reference to, and probably some use of, his "The Treason of the Senate" articles and *Susan Lenox*. In addition, many of his books are "in print," issued at ridiculous prices as a by-product of Lyndon B. Johnson's determination to do something for all his people, including librarians, though they could have, with the slightest effort, obtained any of Phillips's books for modest to trifling prices at large city bookstores and Goodwill establishments. The interesting point is that almost none of these reprinted writings represent Phillips's best work. More of that later.

My intention is to pass on to readers some of the pleasure and understanding I have found in Phillips's life and work. A clarification of Phillips's qualities as artist must be basic. I will insist on his humanity, believing that literature without life is meaningless. But it is futile to review him in terms of the rise of realism and naturalism, the psychological effect on authors of the Darwinian hypothesis, or the hopes and concerns inspired by the Progressive era. Phillips's novels and essays serve our psychological needs today, or we ought to consider why they do not.

The tragedy has been that we have permitted ossified generalizations about Phillips—and others, as will be seen—to pass as good enough. The tragedy has been that such inappropriate writings as Phillips's first sketch of a novel, *The Great God Success*, have passed and been reprinted as typical of his maturity. There has also been tragedy in deeming the image of a busy scribbler sufficient for a world which needs an understanding of past societies, and needs adequate portraits of its predecessors for rejection or emulation. It is a long time since my essay "Murder in Gramercy Park" told the tale of a man who knew how to live and how to die. Readers of poetry and fiction preferred to make much more of another man to whom they gave everything they had in honor and regard, and who, in return, blew his head off with a rifle. And they have preferred to endorse the life and work of a woman who found little more to seek than a convenient form of suicide. One can only hope that for their own well-being, readers may wish to reconsider just what goals their interests comprehend. Literature is no idle pursuit. It affects life.

1

Hoosier

On a November afternoon—it must have been November, although he long after recalled it had been summer-warm, with the windows open and many men in the streets in shirt-sleeves—David Graham Phillips was on his way home from school. As he neared the county court-house, he saw a crowd in the yard and was reminded that it was election day, and that his father was running for reelection. He ran across the street to his father's office. Graham wanted news of the election. In Indiana in the late 1870s, he later observed, and particu-larly in such a quiet riverport town as Madison, politics and law formed the chief subjects for general discussion. Even the children understood when their elders argued current issues.

Graham found his father standing by the window, looking out at the polling place so intently that he did not notice his son standing beside him. And so Graham also looked out of the window:

> I can shut my eyes and see that courthouse yard, the long line of men going up to vote, single-file, each man calling out his name as he handed in his ballot, and Tom Weedon—who shot an escaping pris-oner when he was deputy sheriff—repeating the name in a loud voice. Each oncoming voter in that curiously regular and compact file was holding out his right arm stiff so that the hand was about a foot clear of the thigh; and in each one of those thus conspicuous hands was a conspicuous bit of white paper—a ballot. As each man reached the polling window and gave in his name, he swung that hand round with a stiff-armed circular motion that kept it clear of the body and in full view until the bit of paper disappeared in the slit in the ballot box.
>
> I wished to ask my father what this strange spectacle meant; but as I glanced up at him to begin my question, I knew I must not, for I felt that I was seeing something that shocked him so profoundly that he would take me away if I reminded him of my presence. I know now that I was witnessing the crude beginnings of the money-machine in politics,—the beginnings of the overthrow of the people as a political power. Those stiff-armed men were the floating members of that ward. . . . They had been bought up by a rich candidate of the opposi-

> tion party, which was less scrupulous than our party, then in the flush
> of devotion to "principles" and led by such old-fashioned men as my
> father with old-fashioned notions of honor and honesty. Those
> "floaters" had to keep the ballot in full view from the time they got it
> of the agent of their purchaser until they deposited it beyond the
> possibility of substitution—he had to see them "deliver the goods."
>
> (*The Plum Tree*, pp. 12–13)

There were those who, almost thirty years later, were startled by the
fury with which Phillips blasted Senate corruptionists in a series of
exposés that captured the attention of the country. It gave half a million readers to *Cosmopolitan Magazine* and reverberated through the
entire West in agitational speeches and election campaigns. It gave
form to the popular protest which finally brought about passage of the
Seventeenth Amendment to the Constitution providing for direct election of Senators, previously chosen by state assemblies. All this made
Phillips more notorious than famous, and it jeopardized his literary
hopes.

Phillips's public career before 1906 did not make it clear that he
was prepared to step outside established opinion and contemporary
standards of literature. Some of his magazine writing had taken a
recognizably antiboss, antimonopoly position, and his early tales contained harsh portraits of politicians and businessmen. But his pen
belonged to no political party. He wrote articles for the *Saturday
Evening Post,* no Populist forum. He was primarily interested in fiction, and his articles reflected the times, not a hard-and-fast radical
program. Phillips was evidently ambitious. Editors and critics could
reasonably suppose that he was no more dangerous than any one of a
score of writers who had been made prominent by the new Progressive upheaval: no more, for example, than Jack London, who called
himself a socialist, but wrote restlessly of men and women who confronted animals and human brutes in uncivilized places.

As George Horace Lorimer of the *Saturday Evening Post* himself
jocundly wrote of Phillips:

> No long hair sweeps Phillips's collar, and no flowing tie encircles
> his neck. . . . Some of Phillips's friends are saying of him that he has a
> "message" to deliver, and that is pretty tough, for when an author gets
> an idea he has a message to deliver, usually he finds the wires are
> crossed. Phillips is sane and level-headed—barring a tendency now
> and then to enthusiasms that have not so many piles driven under
> them as would be well—and it is quite likely he will get over the
> message business.[1]

What then possessed Phillips to denounce the United States Senate in terms and with effect that all but isolated him on the Progressive scene? The easy answer was that he was a "Hearst writer," and so ready to do his employer's bidding. This was the gross canard of Mark Sullivan, another muckraker of the time. "The Treason of the Senate" articles, however, were the one job Phillips did, not for the master journalist, but for his editor Bailey Millard. Phillips had not sought the assignment. He had protested that it would be infringing on the time he needed for his fiction. He did the work, he said, because it ought to be done.

Phillips had not consciously been biding his time while making his place with the reading public. Tall, capable, conscientious, he had previously stirred speculation only on the score of his legendary capacity for work and his eccentrically modish wardrobe. Now, with publication of "The Treason of the Senate" articles, he seemed an embarrassment to conscientious muckrakers who were exposing politicians of the second and third rank, but not raising questions about the basic social establishment. Some of Phillips's critics now branded him a socialist, others, more confidently, a sensationalist. It was significant that it fell to H.L. Mencken, then a literary enthusiast contemptuous of reform, to call Phillips "the leading American novelist." Phillips himself remained as unpredictable as he had been in less famous days. He had come a long way before trusting himself to speak his mind.

He had, for example, never forgotten the crude election fraud he had witnessed in boyhood; and there were other experiences in his life which helped make him the stern-faced critic of contemporary manners with which the public had become acquainted.

It would have been news that Phillips loved his father and revered his principles, if only because so little was known of his personal life. The several articles written in praise of his midwestern upbringing did not circulate widely and did not catch on as explaining his character and views. As late as six years after his death, when his novel *Susan Lenox* was finally published, it was denounced as pornographic and as a fierce attack on tradition. The elder David Graham Phillips was anything but an iconoclast, but there is reason to believe he would have recognized the honest intent in his son's long-bruited fiction, if he had lived to read it.

Phillips Senior was the son of a farmer, a descendant of Scotch-Irish immigrants who, generations before, had left Pennsylvania to move down the Ohio River and settle in southern Indiana. It was said he was the first of his family in generations to leave the farm for the city. He came to Madison to attend one of the "private" schools of the time when he was sixteen years old, and when Madison still bustled with expectations of becoming a great riverport. In 1848 Phillips entered Asbury College, a Methodist institution in Greencastle, not far from Indianapolis, where he remained several years without graduating. He returned to Madison, and after working as a clerk entered the local bank, in which he rose to become a leading citizen of the town.

For a moment in time Madison had been Indiana's largest city, replete with shipyards, foundries, and all the means for becoming a major outlet for products of the wilderness farms. Madison acquired its first elaborate mansion as early as 1818, and in a few decades contained no fewer than 130 blocks of nineteenth-century architecture, "including the most impressive collection of Federal, Classic Revival and American-Italianate houses to be found in the Midwest." It was "a collection which would recommend it to fanciers of the past more than a hundred years after."[2]

It is of interest that neither the elder Phillips nor his son made much of this distinction. The younger Phillips would have better approved the views of a fellow Indianan who, like his father and himself, was to attend what became DePauw University, and who made of his heritage a criterion for the quality of American life:

> In these Western states there arose a type of economic society such as had never before appeared in the history of the world, at least on a large scale. A vast region was settled by hardy and restless pioneers who crossed the mountains, cut down the forests, built houses and founded homes. In the possession of this world's goods, they were, for the most part, substantially equal; it was easy to acquire land; any thrifty and industrious farmer with his family could readily secure the comforts of a rude but healthful and independent life. Practically every white man could vote. In the log cabins were developed political ideas fundamentally different from those entertained by the rich merchants of the East or the aristocratic land-holders in the manors along the Hudson.
>
> In the West, the leveling theories of Jefferson were fairly realized. Owing to the simple life which farmers lived, government was to them a simple thing; anyone could hold the office of sheriff, county clerk, road supervisor, state auditor or governor.[3]

Madison settled down to second-rate status, closer to the Hannibal of Mark Twain's youth thirty years earlier than to Cincinnati up the Ohio River from Madison, or St. Louis down the Mississippi from Hannibal. Still, Madison was no backwater of civilization. It had a population of some ten thousand, libraries and schools, and a railroad connection with Indianapolis. The elder Phillips built his life in a vital town boasting lovely hills and waterfront, in the American way he believed ideal, and which he defended with some bitterness as he read the trends of the post-Civil War affluent years. He was a strong, kindly man who, before he retired from politics, had served as deputy auditor, sheriff, and clerk of the Jefferson County court. He taught Sunday School for many years and, though he kept the best private library in Madison, read the Bible more than any other book.

He had joined the Republican Party when, as one nostalgic reformer, B.O. Flower—himself the son of famous settlement raisers—put it:

> It stood for human freedom and lofty moral idealism. . . . When the spirit of Lincoln dominated, or perhaps it would be more correct to say, permeated it. . . . Few men in those days would have dreamed that the great party would soon become a bond slave of privileged interests and corporate greed.[4]

Phillips's son was born October 31, 1867, when his father was thirty-eight years old. The fourth of five children, the first boy, he grew up in conditions of comfort and love which not a few children of similar homes would remember when they set themselves to assessing their experiences. Those circumstances influenced Phillips's ultimate career with the same finality that Theodore Dreiser's more distraught youth, also laid in Indiana, influenced him.[5]

Phillips remembered his mother "when her face was smooth and had the shallow beauty that the shallow dote upon," but he was also to write of her when time had made changes:

> I have heard it said of those markings in human faces, "How ugly!" But it seems to me that, to anyone with eyes and imagination, line and wrinkle and hollow always have the somber grandeur of tragedy. . . . Her face whereon was written the story of fearlessness, sacrifice, and love—that is the face beautiful of my mother for me.
> (*The Plum Tree*, p. 11)

Phillips in boyhood gave few hints of the energetic career with which he was to be identified. Boys of his upbringing displayed aptitudes which foreshadowed the financier, the farmer, the intellectual. Graham was a dreamer; the scowl he later assumed before strangers was defensive and intended to protect him from careless associates who might obtrude into his high sensitivity and separateness. He was also shielded by his large frame and vigorous constitution, which hid the fact that he was a reader and visionary.

Here in Madison, he was to write, "the sky seemed near, and its awful problems of the eternal verities: life and death, right and wrong—thrust at everyone every moment of day and night" (*The Hungry Heart*, p. 339). They thrust, at any rate, at Phillips. He later summarized his young career:

> My mother had the idea of education with its usual strong mother[']s energy so we were all started in young—I used to read the Bible in family prayers when I was between three & four years old— And as I had a passion for reading, I never played much at games etc[.] but read and studied—it was fortunate for me that I had the constitution to stand the hours & hours of reading, reading, reading year in and year out—
>
> I went to the public schools in Madison—I think I had a tutor in Greek when I was nine or ten—some Hebrew too, [t]hough not much as I neglected it for novels and history.[6]

His father had early introduced him to his library and particularly urged him to read American history. Graham watched the Tom Sawyers of Madison from a distance "swimming and sledding, orchard-looting and fighting, [and engaged in] raft-boat and raft races." He played his pranks in the family circle, consorted with his younger brother, Harrison, and with his sisters, especially the eldest, Carolyn, who was to be a leading influence in his life.

Hardly a boy one would have picked to cope with surrounding American customs and ideals. Unlike Dreiser, Phillips was not at odds with his environment. He enjoyed his boyhood, loved his quiet home town, found nothing to criticize in its pleasant industrial life. The mass herding of workers into concentrated areas was under way in New York, in Pittsburgh, as far away as Denver. Here, Graham could see sunlight in the mills, labor and capital only as diffused terms. In time, Phillips would learn of more pitiful circumstances, but it would be as a reporter and student of American life, none of which made any less gracious the scenes of his youth.

But Graham had eyes which told him that much had happened to the nation since the brave days of the Revolution of which he could read in his father's books, and even of the Civil War, only a few short years behind. He caught no more than hints of the changes signaled by "Boss" William Marcy Tweed in New York . . . the Whisky and "Star Route" postal frauds of the Grant Administration . . . the Crédit Mobilier railroad scandal . . . the bloody Railroad Strikes of 1877. But it was because his youth was a happy one that the actual chaos of modern life struck him with full force.

For in the meantime, shrewd, determined youths had trained themselves in mean and distinguished capacities and looked for the main chance. Unlike the elder Phillips, they looked for results first and found the principles later. And if Thomas A. Edison typified the genius of the new era as well as John D. Rockefeller, Sr., it was no less true that it was the industrialists, the railroad builders, the trust-makers rather than the technicians who set their ultimate seals on the politics and economics of the new time. Culture and the humanities no more touched them than they did the workers who struggled with their masters for a livelihood. They were unmoved by the moral issues of the Civil War, except to the extent that they added up to untrammeled free enterprise. They overran industrial America at an all but unbelievable pace.

One of Phillips's characters later phrased the situation shockingly—his own character will be separately viewed—but his concept merits quotation:

> To find a class approaching [the financiers] in frank savagery of will and action, you would have to descend through the social strata until you came to the class that wields the blackjack and picks pockets and dynamites safes. The triumphant class became triumphant not by refinement and courtesy and consideration, but by defiance of those fundamentals of civilization—by successful defiance of them. It remained the triumphant class by keeping that primal savagery of nature. As soon as any member of it began to grow tame—gentle, considerate, except where consideration for others would increase his own wealth and power, became really a disciple of the sweet gospel he professed and urged upon others—just so soon did he begin to lose his wealth into the strong, unscrupulous hands ever reaching for it—and with waning wealth naturally power and prestige waned.
>
> (*The Husband's Story*, p. 143)

There were several approaches a midwestern boy of Phillips's upbringing could take to such a state of affairs. He could adjust himself to this main tendency of American life, perhaps mildly deplore its excesses as William Dean Howells was doing. Or he could follow the example of Henry Demarest Lloyd, a journalist who was also interested in literature, but turned by his fear of an unbridled industry to the study of their workings and prospects. As early as 1881, when Graham was fourteen years old, Lloyd published in the *Atlantic Monthly* his "The Story of a Great Monopoly," a first and ominous report for the literate public on the rise of the Standard Oil Company. Thirteen years later Lloyd's *Wealth against Commonwealth* linked facts with eloquence in its quest for controls on John D. Rockefeller's business genius and accumulation of power.

Those who believed with Graham's father that an antidote would have to be found for the unqualified political amorality and cultural muddle which accompanied the rise of the trust and the big-city Democratic machines tried variously to combat them. The swiftly growing metropolises were not close to the lives they had known and to an extent still knew, and the cities' problems of boss-ruled constituents were remote from their thoughts and affections. Older Americans required to cope with boss rule focused on vice, crime, and corruption as intolerable agencies of society. Especially in the Midwest, the threat to freedom seemed the trusts, and solutions took direct forms. Old stock Americans sponsored free trade and greenback panaceas, and more or less approved Populist agitation. They produced a legion of social messiahs who at least reflected their dissatisfaction, at most displayed the power and insight of a Henry George, an Edward Bellamy, a General James B. Weaver.

They failed to hedge around the new masters of American life. Corporation battles succeeded the battles of the individual titans. Refiners and processors—of sugar, oil, ores—as well as designers and salesmen stepped into the shoes of the great inventors.

It remained for the sons of old-fashioned Americans to prove whether industry could be harnessed, and whether democratic means were adequate to social needs. Graham lived a sheltered life, but he was never far away from awareness of large social questions. A love of literature might have seemed poor preparation for dealing with them. But it was still in living memory that literature had earlier produced a Wendell Phillips, an Emerson, a Harriet Beecher Stowe, and others whom practical men had been unable to ignore. Culture might become significant again—a force, rather than a diversion—in the world which was molding Graham.

It is noteworthy that although Phillips's youth was spent among books, no single work of his ever showed the full dimensions of the images and ideas he had assimilated. He never bandied quotations about or studded his pages with literary conversation. This was one of the reasons why the common people whom he idealized read him. He challenged them, he excited them. Ultimately, they abandoned him for what seemed to them more modern fare. But some readers remain, and whether they, and his work, warrant a still more modern reconsideration remains the question.

2

The Higher Education

"A dazed boy from a quiet Indiana town." So Phillips recalled himself coming to Asbury, soon to be DePauw University, in the first term of the 1882–83 college year. He was not quite fifteen years old, a fat, rosy-cheeked boy in the traumas of slimming and rapid growth. He came chaperoned by his mother; with him came his younger brother William Harrison, who was placed in the school's academy, Graham was neatly dressed, with an air of assurance, even sternness, which belied his inner turmoil.

It was his first substantial contact outside his own society. Here, though the atmosphere was still that of school, although he still had the defenses of family and finances, he sensed differences. He lacked father and sisters, for one thing, and he soon lost the companionship of his brother, who went elsewhere. He roomed and had to keep regular hours and attend classes.

The changes impressed him more than he willingly confessed. It is an open question whether boys then, even boys such as Phillips, of large physical build and precocious mind, were able to think more maturely at an earlier age than the average of those in following generations. The age of adolescence lengthened, so that students could stay on in school for lack of a reason to leave it. In Phillips's time, young and not so young adults filled out the college rosters because they had often spent years gathering the funds to support their education. So Phillips sat in classes with men well into their twenties, even in their thirties, mature in ways impressive to a sensitive lad.

Asbury College was adjusting to its university prospects:

> It has classical courses and scientific courses and a preparatory school [boasted a Phillips puppet, Olivia]—and a military department for the men and a music department for the women. And it's going to have lots and lots of real university schools—when it gets the money. And there's a healthy, middle-aged wagon-maker who's said to be thinking of leaving it a million or so—if he should ever die and if they should change its name to his.

(The Cost, p. 23)

At this time Asbury was a leisurely Indiana college community surrounded by fields and woods, and Phillips was pleased with it. He was entered as a sophomore, a tribute to his private tutoring, though his work was sufficiently up and down to cause variations in his standing. He elected the usual course of belles-lettres and history, mathematics, Latin, and Greek; the well-known historian John Clark Ridpath taught him the first of these courses. Asbury was too much for him at first, and after three months he left to register for courses at the new young University of Cincinnati, while living with his sister Carolyn, now Mrs. Frevert, and her husband at their Auburn Avenue address. Phillips completed the first term of the academic year, taking French, mathematics, Latin, and Greek toward the Bachelor of Arts degree.[1] Following a further pause for maturation, he returned to Asbury.

There were no dormitories on campus. Phillips lived in one of the hundred or more Greencastle boardinghouses, in a large frame house kept by a Mrs. Sheridan, whose own boys were intelligent and varied in temperament. Phillips enjoyed the dual sense of private living and college discipline. What impressed him was that the majority of the student body came from farms, and that its bucolic nature and even bumptiousness did not detract from its sound quality.

> [Their] bodies and brains . . . were strong but awkward. Almost all were working their way through—as were not a few of the women. They felt that life was a large, serious business impatiently waiting for them to come and attend to it in a large serious way better than it had been attended to before. They studied hard; they practiced oratory and debating. Their talk was of history and philosophy, religion and politics. They slept little; they thought—or tried to think—even more than they talked.
>
> (*The Cost,* p. 27)

All this helped modify the suspicions and fears of his growing years. There were morning prayers. There were assignments. There were "grinds," and there was

> a small fast set—there were not many spoiled sons. . . . But its pace was rapid; for every one of them had a constitution that was a large reservoir of animal spirits and western energy. They cribbed their way through recitations and examinations—as the faculty did not put the students on honor but matched them, they reasoned that cribbing was not dishonorable provided one did barely enough of it to pull him through. They drank a great deal—usually whisky, which they disliked but poured down raw, because it was the "manly" drink and to take it undiluted was the "manly" way. They made brief excursions to

Indianapolis and Chicago for the sort of carousals that appeal to the strong appetites and undiscriminating tastes of a robust and curious youth.

(The Cost, p. 101)

Phillips, then, saw enough and remembered well what Owen Wister's bland *Philosophy 4* (1903) and other college chronicles of his time did not for the most part care to recall.[2] Among the rakes and serious ones Phillips made his tentative way. Even then, his peers noticed, he dressed well and preserved personal cleanliness in marked degree: a courteous, somewhat reticent, and friendly boy. His fraternity connection is the one recorded notice of his participation in extracurricular activities. He was no more than a fair student; at least one instructor recalled him as having done poor work.

What was remarked was that he read much more than he studied, and argued more than he contributed to campus activities. His roommate for several terms, J.W. Piercy, later a journalist and professor of journalism, saw him as constantly engrossed in a book. He preferred the realists and carried about paperbacked editions of Emile Zola's writings in tiny print.[3] There is no record of his having read E.W. Howe's *The Story of a Country Town* (1883), a pioneer study in country pessimism, or the fiction of John W. DeForest, a Civil War veteran whose *Miss Ravenal's Conversion* (1869) and *Honest John Vane* (1875) made brave efforts to fight their way past William Makepiece Thackeray's Olympian vision to realistic accounts of American sex and politics in postwar decades.

Here at Asbury Phillips met a young man who was to be one of his few friends of long acquaintance, and who was to make a deep impress on his life. Albert J. Beveridge had known poverty, had worked hard since boyhood, and was older by five years than Phillips. By efforts accounted desperate he had won his way to college. On review, he seems merely to have worked hard and to have taken himself most seriously. The contrast between himself and Beveridge was in Phillips's mind, he not having had to earn money in his young years. In any case, Beveridge was indeed the campus star. Phillips, fearful of his own lack of direction, was deeply struck by Beveridge's rigid efforts and ambitions. He planned his days and hours relentlessly, all but robbing himself of sleep to tramp through woods to practice oratory, earn his living, and be "the man" at school. "We all knew [he was]," Phillips later recalled; and others also bore testimony about the young Indianan who took Lincoln as literally as legend had averred.

Oratory was still one of the most serious of college pursuits, the key to law and politics, more important to ambitious youth than mathematics or science. Those who experienced Beveridge's brusque ways were empathetic to his goals. The state oratorical prize which he took in 1885, and the interstate contest at Columbus, Ohio, in which he also triumphed, which Phillips elaborately reported in his early novel *The Cost,* were only two of the honors Beveridge acquired.

It was a measure of Phillips's anxious search for goals that he not only endured a vast amount of Beveridge's self-absorption and egotism, but justified it in terms of idealism and results. Beveridge's conceit was disarming in its naiveté. As he wrote to Phillips more than twenty years later, he had taken his new wife for a visit to Greencastle, with horse and buggy:

> Showed Catherine where you and I roomed at De Mott[e]'s, showed her where I had roomed from the time I entered college to the time I left; showed her where you roomed when I took the state oratorical— showed her everything, in fact.[4]

Beveridge fascinated his wife further by leading her to "the beautiful little valley where I used to go out and practice my voice." They then walked over the old hills until he

> found the tree on which every day for four years after I graduated I went down and carved the letter "S," one letter above the other, standing for the word success; had the superstition, you remember, that if I did not do that I wouldn't be successful.

Phillips did not fail to notice his friend's lack of humor. But on one level he himself saw no humor in a Darwinian world of life or destruction, and on another level he perceived Beveridge's authentic sense of honor. For example, he one season signed a contract for a summer's work as a door-to-door book salesman. Such "contracts" had little reality, and Beveridge prepared to drop the work as uncongenial. His father, however, reminded him that a contract was "sacred," and as a result Beveridge not only carried through with it, but did so with such success that he was the next season given command of a whole corps of youths.

A truly inspiring success story, and one which Phillips later displayed in his novel *The Cost,* with due admiration which first readers

gave lip-service, and later properly forgot. There is more to the incident than is here stated (see pp. 81–83), but the point was that Phillips could not fail to see the will to honest success behind the sometimes annoying single-mindedness of his austere friend. It made him
wistful for a comparable conviction.

The thought of girls first seriously entered his life. Being coedu-
cational, Asbury offered opportunities for freer speculation on the
matter than would be generally realized by later generations. The
college put no restraints on its young women, any more than on its
young men. They all lived separate lives beyond the campus, without
supervision. "In theory and practice it was democratic, American,
western"—again one hears in his reminiscent pages the leitmotif of
Phillips's life.

Young man and woman friendships were part of the regular
round at Asbury:

> They were usually brief and strenuous. A young man and a young
> woman would be seen together constantly, would fall in love, would
> come to know each other thoroughly. Then with the mind and char-
> acter and looks and moods of each fully revealed to the other, they
> would drift or fly in opposite directions, wholly disillusioned. Occa-
> sionally they found that they were really congenial, and either love
> remained or a cordial friendship sprang up. The modes of thought,
> inconceivable to Europeans, or Europeanized Americans, made catas-
> trophe all but impossible.
>
> (*The Cost*, pp. 50–51)

It is likely that Phillips in such a passage was being more rational
than his own actual circumstances would have reflected. According to
one of the Sheridan boys, he himself fell in love with a local Greencastle girl, and though no more than seventeen years of age, urged her
to marry him.[5] Her refusal may well have been his reason for leaving
Asbury for Princeton. The boy he was, who now entered into the
intemperate ways of love, is well described in one of the passages of
his mature fiction:

> August shone hot and clear upon the hills of Southern Indiana.
> The grain had been cut, and quail were gleaning in the stubble, with a
> pause now and then to whistle from the grey, zigzag fence. But the
> timothy were still standing, waist deep; the full blown blossoms of
> clover, white and pink, were scenting the air; and down where the
> now shallow creek bustled along, over and among the stones of its

rocky bed, the cornstalks were rustling like so many ladies in stiff green Sunday silk.

There was a path through the great hillside meadow. It began at the barnyard, where the threshing machine was making the sweat pour from a score of workers, to trickle and glisten upon their sun-scorched faces and bared, hairy chests. It clove the sea of gold-tinted grass straight to an island where a clump of pear trees reveled in the western sun; thence it wound down the slope to emerge into the road along the creek bottom. On that midway island, in the shade of the pear trees, sprawled in graceful idleness a boy of seventeen, like a young corn and wine god. His eyes were full of dreams; upon his handsome features lay a faint smile of content that it was summer and the free open air, with youth rollicking through his veins, and all the world before him in the glory of its veil of illusion and hope. His carelessly roving glance spied and paused upon a pale-blue sunbonnet far away, down toward the creek fence. The little bonnet, so blue, so airily light, suggested a quaint boat adrift upon that bright, bronze sea; its occupant was a small sweet face, like a flower afloat in an azure shell.

In this boy, just then somewhat tardily awakening to the sense of sex, all faces feminine aroused vague confused minglings of wonder and awe and longing—now an impetuous impulse to push through the veil of the temple's divine mystery, now a timid and even fearful shrinking. But he was a reader and a dreamer, this boy with the quick, blue-grey eyes and the tawny skin and the splendid shock of auburn hair; thus, no sooner would he look at a woman than his glance would turn impatiently away; he had compared her with some composite dream-woman, evolved from his picturings of the women who lived for him in history and in romance—Cleopatra and Aspasia, Theodora and a boy's version of Messalina; the two Catherines, she whom Florence gave to France, and she who set upon her own head the crown of great Peter's crazy, impish grandson; Dickens's Agnes, and Thackeray's Becky, the woman who ran away from her master in Second Judges, and the burning eyed roadside preacher, who finally taught Adam Bede the meaning of love. She was tall, this composite woman of the boy's dreams; and she had masses of golden hair, and a white robe and a purple cord at the waist, a robe that was flowing yet clung to her figure. A proud, haughty woman, one he would be afraid to approach; yet she would somehow hearten and compel him to—to—he did not know just what; some restrained kind of worship, for he had not got so far as to venture to think of touching, of kissing her.

The tiny, pale-blue boat with its interesting passenger was floating nearer and nearer on the surface of that sea of emerald and gold.

(*Old Wives for New*, pp. 1–3)

Phillips did not play football at college, as his inadequate "biographer" Marcosson ventured to note for posterity. Nor was Phillips instrumental in introducing the game to the school. There was no college team, nor did intercollegiate sports begin for some years. Nor was Phillips a member of any military company at Asbury. He talked well, a fact noticed by many of his acquaintances, who called him "Duke." Beveridge, his biographer Claude G. Bowers claimed, turned his young friend's hand to writing, observing that if he wrote as well as he talked he would succeed brilliantly. If true, Graham may well have been pleased, needing something to put up against his friend's prestige. . . . Nevertheless, when the time came for him to indicate a possible future, Phillips wrote "Banking."[6]

His face showed remarkably firm lines for so young a man. And though he was friendly and esteemed as a friend, he evidently harbored somber thoughts. One day in his sophomore year a classmate found him in his room upset. He had the night before had a dream in which an old man in a long white beard had said, "You will have a short life." Phillips had replied: "Short, but merry!" The old man had answered: "No—short and not merry."[7]

Transferring to the College of New Jersey—Princeton University, as it became, where Phillips matriculated in the fall of 1885—was in some ways as traumatic an experience as his earlier Asbury venture had been. This was his first trip East—Far East, as he and countless others from the Midwest saw it.

> When I was a schoolboy in a western town [he later wrote], I had the habit—I and many of my schoolmates—of reading these romances of the adjective and the exclamation point behind a geography tilted high, to conceal the novel from the teacher. As my favorite writers divided their attention pretty evenly between the far west and the New York Bowery, I got, or imagined that I got, a clear idea of life in both these places.
>
> To me the Bowery was a wonderful place—fascinating, full of romance, yet terrible and most dangerous.
>
> ("The Bowery at Night")

The sight of the pleasant Princeton college grounds and buildings was reassuring, and on that level created some identity between his Asbury career and his new life. However, he quickly noted with displeasure a caste system at Princeton which had been unknown to him in his native state, and which affected the outlook of some of his classmates. He was particularly resentful of the effect of class ideas on others from the Midwest. Oddly enough, his viewpoint was superficially like one which an older Princetonian, Woodrow Wilson, was to develop when he returned to the campus as a professor in 1890 and

noted the presence of exclusive student clubs which retarded democratic relations among students. But Phillips increasingly emphasized
in his thought the democratic potential of Americans on campus and
off. Wilson sought the Jeffersonian ideal of a class raised for leadership, but democratic in its choice of leaders within that class.[8]

Phillips had yet to discriminate between the undemocratic tendencies he imputed to the East and its cultural and social wealth. He
enjoyed his Princeton stay. He was now an imposing figure, grown to
a fine height, friendly and interesting. "La Bouche," they called him;
Phillips did not always take pleasure in the implications of this
phrase. He later insisted, as one sensitive on the subject, that the
thinker was always a talker. "As if there ever lived a thinker who did
not overflow with torrents of talk like a spring fed from a glacier; but
of course, the spring flows only when the conditions are favorable,
not when it is ice-bound (*The Husband's Story*, p. 273).

Moreover, there were urgent topics to debate. The depression of
1883 was still running its course. . . . The Haymarket Riot of May 1886
produced its martyred anarchists; William Dean Howells denounced
the court sentences of death in terms severe for a genteel novelist and
was active in the anarchists' behalf. . . . John Hay's anonymously published *The Bread Winners* (1883), an antilabor novel, could be discussed as social commentary and as fiction. . . . The student body at
Princeton, with its strong and traditional contingent of young southern gentlemen, showed little interest in the Civil War, although many
readers were bemused by General William T. Sherman's *Memoirs* in
1875, or were now turning attention to General U.S. Grant's *Personal
Memoirs*.

Phillips seems to have increased his efforts to write better, and he
confided to a few friends that he intended to be a writer. Yet he
avoided campus journalism and made no other attempts to sound out
responses to his ambitions. All his later steps taken in their direction
pointed to his intention to learn what to write about, and how. His
actual work showed no significant influences, either American or
British. What is certain is that he was determined to find a mode of
expression which was his own.

He may well have learned something from the English novelist
George Gissing respecting the social question: the troubles of the
poor, their own corruption through envy of the gains they professed
to despise, the dilemmas they posed to the middle classes and the
rich. At least, Phillips read the English realist's just released *Demos*.

His college paper's response to it was puerile, expressing disgust with the greedy and confused "socialist" types of Gissing's fancy. One of Gissing's moderating characters voiced equal repugnance for the crasser commercial Victorians, sufficiently so for young Phillips to join him in unspecific generalizations about their sordid qualities.[9] But Phillips himself would later be accused of "socialistic" ideas, and he would be a close friend and companion of socialists. Indeed, he himself would perpetrate a novel of socialism, one of his less happy efforts. It suffices that the dilemma of defending both individualism and the need for social cooperation early beset Phillips, and, in a first fling, with less than memorable results.

Phillips remembered Princeton with delight. In later years it was "the beautiful little town" to him. He kept up with Princeton's affairs and counted old classmates as friends. He belonged to the Princeton Club of New York and was about to enter it on the day he was shot and mortally wounded.

But it was DePauw which stirred his consciousness and moved him to write, though it was apprentice work. Princeton was culture and light, but DePauw was the hope. It produced the Beveridges of America. He looked back to the West, but afterwards he returned, if not to Princeton, to New York.

Phillips was almost twenty in 1887, and a Bachelor of Arts. He was tall—over six feet three, and still inclined to heaviness. He was a full-fledged dandy in dress, strikingly handsome and intense, and with an air of confidence which verged on brashness. It hid his anxiety and drew not a little antagonism. Those who knew him found him, if anything, overkind. But in the Darwinian world he perceived, his main goal was to earn a living, to be independent, and if possible, to be something more.

3

Midwest

Henry Adams tells readers of his autobiography that he and young men like himself—wealthy, well-connected, and intellectual—turned away from newspaper life as beneath them. It offered too few opportunities for worthwhile work, they felt, and its "venality" repelled them.

It did not help Adams's perspective to idealize older eras, those of *The Federalist Papers* and the *North American Review*. Decisive changes had taken place in communication since their proud editors had imposed their views on a social elite. The days of great newspaper proprietors and their editorial pages were fast coming to an end. The Civil War had begun their downfall. An anxious public had learned to look for the news first of all, and a wider readership demanded vivid writing and eye-catching leads rather than editorial opinion.

Between 1869 and 1879 died those who had built the journalism of an older time: in New York, Henry Raymond of the *Times*, Horace Greeley of the *Tribune*, the elder James Gordon Bennett, rabble-rouser of the *Herald*, and the dignified and distinguished poet—recalled as a poet, not as New York's first citizen and great *Post* editor—William Cullen Bryant. To succeed them came men of power, able and willing to support the tradition of "personal journalism." New York boasted Charles A. Dana of the *Sun*, shorn of his Brook Farm idealism but brilliant in his scorn of bosses and labor unionists. There were also Whitelaw Reid of the *Tribune* and Manton Marble of the *World*. And others elsewhere, such as Henry Watterson, "Marse Henry," florid editor of the Louisville *Courier-Journal*. Samuel Bowles of the Springfield, Massachusetts, *Republican* was a spearhead of liberalism to whom right and wrong were clear and unequivocal. Still others included Murat Halstead of the Cincinnati *Commercial-Gazette* and the vibrant emigré from Hungary, Joseph Pulitzer of the St. Louis *Westliche-Post* (later the *Post-Dispatch*), and, as of 1883, the *New York World*.

The times were against them as arbiters of opinion, and they bent to the new conditions. Dana, assuming the *Sun* editorship in 1868, promised it would study "condensation, clearness, point . . . in the most luminous and lively manner." But despite his high standards of clarity and good English, his stature and that of editors generally was down. The press was popular, but it had been decentralized. The rise of the Associated Press diminished the great chiefs further. Reporting the news, getting scoops, assumed a new importance in the journalistic race, but not the kind of importance to attract a Henry Adams. What talents other than spryness and inquisitiveness did the New Journalism require? What use would it make of a dreamer, a man of opinions?

Phillips, who was both, was well aware that he was seeking entry into a harsh and unsympathetic milieu. He was also aware that journalism might be a school for teaching him what to write about. But first of all it might enable him to earn a living. He turned away from New York as too formidable, and returned "west" to enter newspaper work.

There are two versions of Phillips's beginnings in journalism. One he told himself, in support of his contention that college courses in English were of negative value as training for a writer.[1]

He had looked for work alone, "on the leading daily in a western city"—evidently the Cincinnati *Commercial-Gazette*. Finally he obtained a chance to show what he could do, by offering his services for nothing. It was cold and the temperature in the office was somewhere below sixty degrees, yet hour after hour Phillips sat at his desk with sweat rolling from his brow, struggling to make news items of the bits of information given him.

On the tenth day, the chief editor happened to pass through the sitting room and stood for some minutes watching him. "Who is that man?" he finally asked the city editor. The latter explained.

"Get rid of him!" his chief said curtly.

"But we're getting him for nothing!"

"I don't care if he is paying for the privilege," the other retorted. "Get rid of him at once. I can't bear to see any human being work so hard!"

The other and separate version merely tells that Phillips applied to Halstead's *Commercial-Gazette* and was rejected by "Deacon"

Smith, who was not interested in his posture or approach. It tells further how Phillips then asked Marshall Halstead, his college mate, to introduce him to James A. Green, city editor of the rival *Times-Star*, and how he obtained an introduction.

The truth is probably in Phillips's version. He did not make up stories about himself. And he had a reason for trying to find work without introductions and by dint of hard work and native talents. Phillips feared his own languor and tendency toward dreaminess. A child of Darwinism, he believed life was struggle or failure; and this conviction was to dominate his work and put it on the scales for judgment. His effort at free labor unrequited was almost certainly on Halstead's *Commercial-Gazette,* and his turning to his friend for an introduction to Green a counsel of last resort.

This insistence of Phillips on being independent and self-initiating is at the base not only of his life but of his writings, and may do much to explain what his work may or may not offer to the 1970s. To the extent that independence is an outmoded idea in a world of interdependence and social security, one can understand how his social outlook might appear old-fashioned to modern readers. Yet though conditions for self-identity and social status may have changed, the problem of attaining them persists.

Phillips himself recognized the dilemma in his own condition in that, while he struggled for independence, he was constrained to take orders from a variety of editors and proprietors, orders which essentially directed his opinions. The shadow of independence, if it was to be attained, had to be found in the interstices of social controls. Phillips later transmuted the challenge in his portrayal of Susan Lenox, who rejected the position of a kept woman individually owned, only to engage in prostitution, which put her at the command of a variety of impersonal clients, to whom, however, she could be equally impersonal. There were dilemmas in either case involving independence; the question for readers was whether or not they found those dilemmas profitable to consider, in terms of their own prospects.

Phillips's approach to job-getting contrasts strikingly with that of Theodore Dreiser who, aged twenty-one, dreamed of finding a newspaper job in Chicago. Ill-read, a turgid intellectual, and from a broken and divided family, Dreiser fantasized vainly of wealth, longed indiscriminately for women, and sought work on newspapers with no preparation or plan. He saw himself plainly as without dignity, "a homeless cat [hanging] about on doorsteps for days and days meowing to be taken in."[2] In 1892 he landed a job on the Chicago *Daily Globe* because it was the least regarded sheet in the metropolis; and not before he had sold at a dollar each 120 copies of a novel the city editor had written in collaboration, and which was selling poorly.[3]

As a journalist Dreiser did evince successful qualities of fact-finding and conventional phrasing. But this was a philosophical stance directly opposite to Phillips's, and one which would ultimately triumph over Phillips's. Dreiser was a journalist solely for money and yearned to write or advance in ways having nothing to do with the services journalism provided. Phillips sought constantly to improve his journalistic skills, so that his reports might be consistently better.

His ideals did not help him to make a start. Green, like the others, was impressed by Phillips's manner, but on the wrong side. There was no opening, he said. Phillips then asked for the privilege of visiting the office and reading the exchange newspapers, and Green consented.

Every morning, then, early in the morning, Phillips appeared at the *Times-Star* office, read newspapers diligently, smoked innumerable cigarettes, and learned as best he could the ways of journalism. The staff disliked him on sight, and Green's distaste deepened.

This went on for weeks. Phillips, sensitive and unused to the rough and ready of social intercourse, must have hated those days of humiliation. Perhaps he felt a footing in his petty victory over Green, and certainly an inner challenge. His opportunity came one time when there was a dearth of reporters and a story which had to be covered. Green in despair sent Phillips out to get the facts and be back by 12:30; he himself would write the story. Phillips was back before his deadline, and not only with the facts: he had written the story himself, in the *Times-Star* manner, and with none of the college flourishes Green had imagined Phillips's style contained.

Green printed the story as it stood, gave Phillips other chances, and soon knew he had an excellent newspaperman in hand. Phillips "went on space," receiving a weekly stipend of twenty dollars no matter how much of his work saw print. And so he had a job.

His sister Carolyn, married to a wealthy businessman, provided her brother with a home during his three years of work in the city. He and Carolyn had always been congenial, and it was preference, not convenience, which dictated the arrangement.

Phillips not only began the conscientious system of responsible work which became his trademark, he set out to acquaint himself with the details of Cincinnati life. He talked with barmen, and with policemen and politicians. He visited theaters and the waterfront. Far from interfering with his reading habits, his job intensified them. He was soon not only well-known in newspaper circles but well-liked, or at least respected. Close relations did not add much to other journalists' knowledge of Phillips's aims and predilections. He was "secretive," one associate noted, and he had few friends and no confidants other than his sister.

Phillips later showed himself to have been a student of journalism, and he wrote articles describing its ways and directors. He does not seem to have realized that he was one of many who had entered the field for a living, but also as an avenue to literature. Journalism was to him a graveyard for literary talent, saved from ignominy only when it operated in the interests of "the people." Yet only a few years earlier the exotic Lafcadio Hearn had lived in Cincinnati and worked on its *Enquirer*.[4] And soon a movement of new writers would appear, all journalists who wrote essays, fiction, even poetry. Of them all Stephen Crane would emerge as the manifest genius, though their number also included Frank Norris, Harold Frederic, and Abraham Cahan.

Phillips himself, in those early days, worked over sketches and short stories, skits and quips, which were sometimes printed, sometimes discarded, according to the editors' whims. "Worked over"—for it was something new he was attempting on his own time and for no additional pay. Not the genteel writing of a Henry James. Not imitations of Fitz-James O'Brien, Poe, and Gautier, in the manner of the bohemians. Phillips also abjured the major literary movement of his period, that of local color, working to capture the thought and language of the various regions of the nation, mostly rural, before they were washed over and diluted by urban and technological tides. Local color was producing notable fiction in the significant tales of George Washington Cable, Edward Eggleston, Sarah Orne Jewett, Joel Chandler Harris, and others from Maine to Iowa and beyond. But Phillips would have none of it. His subject was neither western, nor decadent, nor yet Bostonian. It was common. Phillips was writing, or trying to write, of the ordinary man and woman at their characteristic work, doing things which peculiarly interested them or were required of them: shaking hands, rouging, drinking beer. So far journalism: lively, but little directed. Nevertheless, it was intimate knowledge; and what Phillips intended to do with it, he himself hardly knew.

Within the year the *Commercial-Gazette* editors wrote Green, thanking him for "training the young man" and asking for him back. Green thought this rather cool; but Murat Halstead offered Phillips twice his salary on the *Times-Star*. Money was the main consideration. Phillips became a reporter on the *Commercial*.

He was soon on the top rung in reportorial circles. His constant work, sharp newspaper style, and willingness to write feature pieces for nothing gave him a species of distinction. But Phillips had learned the evanescent quality of newspaper fame. If one was not an editor, one was nothing. Who could remember a newspaper "beat" a week after it had been achieved?

But though Carolyn urged her brother to go to New York, he stayed in Cincinnati. Self-support had become the breath of life in his lungs. He had none of the softness and weakness which enabled other artists to take loans, receive favors, truckle for bread and friendship while somehow preserving their essences of art. In Phillips, pride and art would have to be one. Yet earning daily bread could itself become an enslavement. All about him were men of talent and hope who had been caught up in newspaper work as by an undertow. Phillips, with his need to be clean and well-dressed, was not too sure of his own will to avoid decline. He developed a sense of pessimism and depression which would accompany him for years, until the tide of Progressivism would give him a new faith and conviction.

He experienced problems with the sordid scenes and poverty which some of his work involved, and for which he was not constitutionally fitted. He overcame their effect by will and by conviction that journalism was either a school or a cemetery. Yet the shadow remained:

> Always that note of despair; always that pointing to the motto over the door of the profession: "Abandon hope, ye who enter here." What was the explanation? Were these men right? Was he wrong in thinking that journalism offered the most splendid of careers: the sharpening of all the faculties; the service of truth and right and human betterment, in daily combat with injustice and error and falsehood; the arousing and stimulating of the drowsy minds of the masses of mankind?
>
> (*The Great God Success*, p. 17)

Three years of work in Cincinnati, and he had had enough. He knew the streets and the people, the tone of the river city and its work. He was one of its foremost journalists, and being that, was nothing more. He was twenty-three years old, and already the craft he had mastered had become a treadmill.

Phillips, in deciding to go to New York, was obeying an inner pressure which told him he must. He had not come down since leaving Princeton. He was even better dressed than he had been before; dress was a shield against being assimilated by others. Yet he was no longer the young man with "a great shock of black hair," as Green had remembered him, with extreme clothes and wide trousers and a cigarette in his mouth. More mature, better controlled, Phillips was not going East; he was returning to it.

He had good introductions now, introductions which he might have used, as anyone would. But it gives some insight into his frame of mind that he made no effort to do so. Whatever are the final facts of how he won the rank and position that were soon his, it is certain he won it alone.

4

"That Damned East!"

> "We send it most of our money, and our
> best young men; and what do we get from it
> in return? Why, sneers and snob ideas."
> *The Second Generation*

Lincoln Steffens observed that New York in the Nineties was about like what Tennessee had become by 1930 when he wrote his autobiography: provincial, with a conscience willing to accept such a reformer as the Reverend Charles H. Parkhurst, repelled by vice and police corruption, whose campaign against both sparked the once-famous Lexow Investigation of 1894.

Steffens himself, following an exceptionally happy California boyhood, following an extensive and expensive Berkeley-Heidelberg-Sorbonne education, having married and cherished dim literary ambitions, returned from abroad in 1892, aged twenty-six. In New York he was met by a note from his father, a successful businessman, telling him he had received the best of education according to his own will and desires, and that he was now on his own. After a shock of panic, Steffens, in English tweeds, made the round of newspaper offices seeking work, and leaving his card wherever possible. Nobody wanted him. Meanwhile he was living on his wife and mother-in-law. Pride and wifely insistence finally prodded him into the use of his father's introductions, the elder Steffens knowing influential California editors. His son settled upon the New York *Post*, made a sensational success, and became known as a newspaper reporter.

Phillips before and Dreiser a little after Steffens came to New York with much less assurance and, once they had established themselves in jobs, with none of Steffens's satisfaction. It needs emphasis that all three among numerous others aspired to write fiction, and of the three Steffens looked most the artist, with his goatee, string tie, and quizzical eyes. Although he never wrote the novel of which he dreamed, and wrote muckraking journalism which was more contrived than his admirers realized, he would ultimately write memoirs which were literature more than they were history.

Dreiser was different from both Steffens and Phillips, though more in life-development than in essence. His father had been a successful woolens manufacturer in Indiana who to the end of life spoke with a German accent. Moreover, Dreiser's father had been of rigid Lutheran persuasion, wholly dominating with his somber principles his timid wife and many children. His permanent bankruptcy not only broke up but demoralized his family, the girls and men drifting off in varied ways, from Chicago to New York. One sister became the original for "Sister Carrie": a kept woman who did not achieve the success which Dreiser improbably portrayed in his first novel. Dreiser's older brother Paul Dresser for a while was the successful one, writing sentimental songs, the best known one being "On the Banks of the Wabash." It is typical of Dreiser's undiscriminating outlook in cultural matters as well as other social areas that he should have worked earnestly to make his case for the right to credit for the absurd words of the song.

Dreiser learned the newspaper trade in Chicago and St. Louis, contemplated settling down in Ohio as a small town editor, then, driven by restless fancies and a yearning for wealth, as well as by erotic compulsions which were not appeased by marriage, he made his way among newspaper men, fiction writers, and editors in New York. His own life told him that people were essentially flotsam, that victories were illusory, love and ideals no more than an evasion of the reality of death. He sincerely admired the rich, who had at least conquered material pain and harassment. And he expressed compassion for weak, aimless people—people like himself who were driven by sexual hungers for which they had no responsibility.

Dreiser claimed not to have read Zola, whose naturalistic principles his work illustrated. It was curious that life taught him those principles. Phillips had read Zola, but he could not accept degradation as a valid norm. Dreiser and Phillips were both New York journalists of the 1890s, but they represented opposed outlooks.

Dreiser wandered into City Hall Square, on his entry to New York. He sat on the public benches with others, the odds and ends of the city, who were whiling away a few hours there. Sitting among them, feeling as lost as they were, with the specter of failure and need to haunt him, Dreiser knew that never, no matter what he might achieve, could he feel secure. Something broke in him which could not be mended by journalistic successes or literary triumphs. He read Herbert Spencer, he tells us, and it destroyed the cosmos for him. But this no more than rationalized for a muddled thinker what psychically had already happened to him.

Phillips too felt the force of the city, knew that it created human debris, and that each day added to it. He knew too that a conviction about the value and meaning of life was difficult to sustain in an age of Darwin and Rockefeller; and that a reason for living would have to be sought, rather than accepted. Phillips felt—the feeling appears often in his letters and responses to the time—tendencies toward weariness, but something of his heritage and desires kept him fighting pessimism, though he felt alone. As he wrote his father, shortly after coming to New York: "Here I am in this great city, and no man [,] woman or child cares whether I am dead or alive, but I will make them care before I am done with them."[1]

Darwinism—and Rockefeller—told Phillips that his first need was to be strong, and he consistently admired strength; it was a quality which would in time confuse would-be critics who noted the apparent "contradiction" between Phillips's reform attitudes and his printed views of J. Pierpont Morgan and the elder Rockefeller. Phillips differed from Dreiser in rejecting weakness as a major subject for attention. And though he voiced compassion, and felt it more than he made evident, he would not treat weakness as a fit topic for imperial consideration. One did not build a civilization on weakness. Phillips vowed to succeed, to be a figure in life; and if he could do it, others could.

In sum, he became partisan to planned work and victory. In time, after he was dead, his program would be stereotyped in the phrase: *You too can do it!* Here was a catchword which, in the anxious years of the 1930s, when jobs and social opportunities wasted to a shadow, became a byword for satirists and malcontents of every kind. Still later their experiences with the welfare state raised questions about the validity of their own views that better security cushions and governmental matrices would create permanent happiness and civic achievements.

But it was 1890 when Phillips came to New York and found work, briefly on the *Tribune*, and then on Dana's *Sun*. There were ten years left before the twentieth century. Politics were real, art was real. But most real was the necessity for work and a more secure hold on life. Phillips continued to test himself, repeating his earlier feat of obtaining newspaper work on his own merits. He was treated as a neophyte and given a neophyte's assignment: covering the Jefferson Market police court in Greenwich Village, along with the sordid tales which he followed up from the court record. Phillips continued his private war by overcoming his repugnance for dreary poverty and debasement, while persisting in his adherence to elegant clothing.

Phillips stuck with his job until an opportunity came which formed a legend in newspaper annals. A child was said to be lost in the Catskill Mountains, and a skeptical editor sent Phillips to investigate. He returned and handed the astonished editor a story which rang with drama and emotion, and to which, when it was printed, Phillips's name was attached.[2] Phillips was put on space, and so once more had rooted himself in life.

He corresponded with Cincinnati friends, and with Beveridge, Piercy, and others of Asbury days, and made acquaintances on the Sun and with other newspapermen. There were seemly people to know on the *Sun*: Jacob Riis, reformer of slums, whose use of the camera for revelations would be better appreciated as art by a later generation; Julian Ralph, the best and most admired of contemporary reporters; Samuel Hopkins Adams, whose exposures of patent medicine frauds would in time become classic. The Sun's leading spirit, Dana, believed only in literacy and himself and was skeptical of immigrants, labor, and progress. But he believed also in attracting readers, and he opposed the crass civic cheating which served some rich and poor of the growing cities, though at a frightful cost. The *Sun* was varied and exciting, and it attracted artists and personalities. Richard Harding Davis was a star who became a symbol of physical splendor and, moreover, the envy of journalists who hoped also to write fiction successfully.

There were in the small circles of newspaper offices downtown interesting journalists on other papers who would make greater marks on literature, though they were too perplexed by inner conflicts of style and personality to realize that they were part of a general impulse toward realism which questioned life as well as society. Stephen Crane of the *Herald* and *Tribune* and Harold Frederic of the *Times* were two among many capital reporters who hungered to generalize their views of war, of religion, of love. For the most part they

worked alone, on a literary scene imbued with overabundant reverence for Emerson and James Russell Lowell.

Phillips prided himself on his inner resources, his independence,
and his reading, but his essential uprootedness and acute attacks of
loneliness cannot be missed. A letter to his father covers a spectrum of
topics. He thanks the old gentleman for a continuing subscription to a
religious paper and avers that he enjoys Dr. Brickley's editorials,
gently regretting "that he is not a real journalist with the wider fields
of all subjects and all sects" at his command. He thanks his mother for
the beautiful gloves; she made Christmas merry with her dear name
attached:

> Well, another year has gone and the world is still whirling and the
> stars still keeping up their endless procession—and all us poor mortals
> are fretting and preening—I as much as any in proportion to my abil-
> ity—which, for fretting and preening, is truly great, I assure you.[3]

He reads histories and biographies: lives of Voltaire, Franklin, and
Andrew Jackson by the essayist-biographer James Parton. He finds
Draper's *Intellectual Development of Europe* good, and Buckle's *History of Civilization in England*, now reread, superb. McMaster's *History of the People of the United States* he finds magnificent: a work
every American ought to read. Phillips wishes he could give all his
time to reading instead of a few hours a day.

1891 was significant for him in bringing important newspaper
assignments and an outburst of magazine publication, apparently
promising important work to come. Not the least of Phillips's exploits
was his signal job of reporting a bloody strike in the mountains of East
Tennessee. "Miniature civil war broke out," so Charles Edward Russell phrased it. A huge mining company tried the experiment of convict labor, and the labor that was not convict rebelled and emphasized
its protest with guns. The situation appeared critical, and New York
papers sent correspondents to cover the battle. Phillips, dressed in his
usual style, stepped off the Pullman and was carefully appraised by
strikers and soldiers. He went about his business, and it was only
when the New York papers arrived with his reports that he was properly assessed:

> It appeared that this young man going quietly about in white
> flannels, and mostly concerned with his lost pajamas had been every-
> where, seen and noted everything, absorbed every salient fact and
> detail, and then with skill and compelling power had pictured all
> visibly to the utmost comprehension of the dullest reader. Still more

he had dealt with the well-springs and causes of action as well as with their superficial results; he had analyzed and weighed and humanized the elements of the conflict so that instead of a thing temporary and insignificant, it had touches homeric and universal.[4]

Thus Charles Edward Russell, a fellow-journalist who became a life-long friend: like Phillips from the Midwest, of old-family stock, and with literary ambitions. Russell was to become the leading muckraker and one of the most highly admired of socialists. But he made too small a distinction between journalism and art. He wrote books of verse committed to forms which had no future. More important, he was unresponsive to new forms, derogating Walt Whitman as an orator rather than a poet, and adoring Swinburne at the expense of less "musical" artists. Russell's dilemma was that he hungered for art, but would not face the conditions which produced an artist. Swinburne, for example, was not normal sexually, and required whippings to achieve sexual euphoria. Russell's code forced him to ignore such matters and created frames of mind which would forever separate his thought from Phillips's, who, without joining in empathy the more psychically distressed artists like Oscar Wilde, could distinguish their art from their peccadilloes.

On March 7, 1891, Phillips broke into Harper's Weekly, one of the most influential of publications of the time, with a rewrite of an article he had done for the Sunday feature section of the Sun. It told of the rescue of the Jeansville, Pennsylvania, miners and gave a moving story of their courage while trapped in a cave-in.

Here was an opening away from journalism, and on and off into that year and the next Phillips contributed other pieces on a variety of themes: city scenes, the Revenue Marine, the strange vanishing of a military guard in Siberia, Sioux Indians, the funeral train of General William T. Sherman, a famous robbery of 1890, another disaster in the oil regions of Pennsylvania—in all, some fifteen articles. And then, no more. It is not easy to say just why Phillips did not persist in this mode of expression. Regular newspaper work took a great deal out of him. All his life he complained that writing was hard work for him and rarely satisfying.

The articles did give pleasure to his father, who imparted news about them to Beveridge. He expressed his own particular satisfaction with the Jeansville piece, probably because of the religious faith which had sustained the miners in their trouble.[5]

The times had created enormous opportunities for the production and publication of articles and tales of every kind, so that they availed writers little, unless they were able to create some such sensation as did Stephen Crane's *The Red Badge of Courage* in 1895. In the end, Phillips apparently concluded that he was accomplishing too little with his articles and gave up trying.

Yet the articles tell a reader much about their author. A general bleakness pervades them which contrasts markedly with the warm and positive tone Phillips achieved a decade later. Such an article as "The Union of Sixth Avenue and Broadway" in *Harper's Weekly* is less interesting in itself than expressive of a certain bareness in Phillips's style of that time, an inability to offer more than descriptive statements, without gusto or variety.

Although literary people who had served as journalists were to complain that certified litterateurs too often scorned them unreasonably because of their newspaper background, the journalistic fraternity contributed its own quota of myopia to a literary scene which sought vainly to distinguish "journalism" from "literature." Thus one of the admirers of "great" journalists kept stressing the power which enabled Julian Ralph of the *Sun* to be continuously "interesting." The fugleman was able to give some sense of Ralph's endless search for news, but not of its quality:

> Some one said of Ralph that he "could write five thousand words about a cobblestone." If he had done that, it would have been an interesting cobblestone. He had a passion for detail, but it was not the lifeless and wearisome detail of the realistic novelist.[6]

All of this and more said something of journalistic goals, but little of what the novel could or ought to contain. Phillips was to a degree victimized by his numerous associates who complimented him by insisting that he had been first and foremost a "good reporter," but who were dim on what he had had in mind while writing novels.

One of Phillips's pieces was a story, or rather a sketch, "The First Born," which twenty years later would become part of the vivid pages of "Degarmo's Wife" itself a spin-off from his novel *Old Wives for New* (1908). Its persistence in Phillips's thought is a comment upon those critics who casually referred to his "hasty" writing. Aside from that, the sketch reveals how much Phillips had yet to learn in control of his pen, how little reason he had for writing at all in this early time. His sketch contained, too, pessimistic overtones which lacked the catharsis of tragedy. In the absence of struggle and enthusiasm, "The First Born" suggests that Phillips was closer to artistic death than life.

His was, after all, an abnormal life for a normal young man. He worked mostly at night, and his schedule was liable to disarrangement. It left him often alone with himself. It stifled his opportunities to see people not on assignments but as individuals. There were compensations: the sharp excitement of the newspaper world, its constant high-tensioned expectancy. Yet:

> The office-boy came with a bundle of papers, warm, moist, the ink brilliant.
> "And now for the inquest."
> "The inquest?"
> "Yes—viewing the corpse. It was to give birth to this that there was all that intensity and fury—that and a thousand times more. For, remember, this paper is the work of perhaps twenty-thousand brains, in every part of the world, throughout civilization and far into the depths of barbarism. Look at these date-lines—cities and towns everywhere in our own country, Canada, Mexico, Central America, South America. You'll find most of the capitols of Europe represented; and Africa, north, south and central, east and west coast. Here's India and here's the heart of Siberia. This is China, and there is Japan and there Australia. . . .
> "There it lies, a corpse. Already a corpse, its life ended before it was fairly born. There it is, dead and done for—writ in water, and by anonymous hands. Who knows who did it? Who cares?"
>
> (*The Great God Success*, p. 210)

Phillips remained on the *Sun* three years. In the spring of 1893 he moved over to the *World*, another plum plucked by a nervous and incessantly active Joseph Pulitzer, who had fought a desperate duel with the cruel and brilliant Dana to establish himself in New York. It was not only that Pulitzer had made Phillips a handsome offer; Phillips was also in sympathy with Pulitzer's ideal of vivid news-making. The tide was toward the *World* autocrat, who not only got the news but created it, and who maintained a tone of reform that the cynic Dana had long lost.

A famous example was "Nellie Bly's" 1889 race around the globe to the accompaniment of *World* reports, to beat the report set in Jules Verne's *Eighty Days Around the World*. More noteworthy, though less remembered by a fickle public which prized entertainment at least as much as public service, was "Nellie's" enterprise in feigning insanity in order to enter Blackwell's Island hospital and expose the sad conditions of its inmates. But Phillips as well as Pulitzer felt that the public deserved to be wooed as well as instructed.

Important to Phillips in his shift from the *Sun* to the *World* was his salary increase. He could save nothing, and money was his one security. He never seemed to be living better, and yet he could not account for the money's flow. "A more extensive wardrobe, a little better food, a more comfortable suite of rooms, an occasional dinner to some friends, loans to broken down reporters . . . " (*The Great God Success*, p. 31).

Phillips was assigned to London as foreign correspondent. It was his first trip abroad, and one of many to come, not only for vacations and foreign scenes, but on assignment. Thus in 1897 he as well as Richard Harding Davis and Stephen Crane were in Greece to witness a Greek-Turkish confrontation, especially at Velestinos where a battle took place.[7] The remarkable fact, there as in Phillips's other experiences abroad, was that he felt no need to exploit these exotic situations as part of his fictional strategy. If anything, Phillips's impulse was the other way, toward concentrating on individuals in an American place, and determining their character there. He even, as will be seen, created a town which he saw as representative of the nation and its inhabitants as a whole. Phillips's love of home, though seemingly parochial in a later era which felt constrained to cope with world and even cosmic affairs, had the potential, at least in his own time, of appealing to people who felt that they lost nothing by loving their homeland.

On this, his first trip to London, Phillips set his office in order and telegraphed reports on Gladstone and other major leaders of Great Britain. He visited Paris, which he learned to love, and traveled elsewhere on the Continent. Phillips built up a hatred of the snobbery and political repression which he observed everywhere, and felt renewed in faith that his own country had little to apologize for.

In June of that same year of 1893, Phillips scored one of the historical scoops of the decade. It has been brought up in every review of Phillips. True, the collision of the two great British battleships, the *Victoria* and the *Camperdown*, was one of the worst of sea tragedies, and still receives notices and comment.[8] True, too, Phillips's feat was extraordinary, since he received reports of this remote Middle East catastrophe before the British Admiralty, through enterprise and incredible good fortune. True that he prepared a fine report which reached American readers before it did British.

Yet, with vague reports of Phillips's crucial writings still hung upon the literary scene, it confuses perspective to give more than passing attention to his feat. It was Phillips's literary misfortune to have given his best to journalism, so that its very qualities could be arraigned against him on literary grounds. There was no such problem in Dreiser's career; his twenty years of journalistic scribbling died where it stood. For living purposes, the *Victoria* affair may be discounted.

Work in London did not satisfy Phillips. It was a "lounging" job, he felt, and kept him fearing that he was wasting time. His lack of sympathy with British life, his passionate Americanism added up to a prejudice which muddied his appreciation of the opportunities he enjoyed as a visitor abroad. He asked Pulitzer for permission to return home. Pulitzer liked this valuable young man, but, going blind as he was, he felt compelled to assert his authority. He took a high hand with him, intimating that he was not thoroughly satisfied with Phillips's performance. Phillips would not be coerced. The New York *Herald* liked his work, he informed Pulitzer frankly and at length. Pulitzer opened the way to Phillips's resignation, and Phillips prepared to leave the *World*. Now Pulitzer, opposed, gave way and Phillips returned to New York.

5

"Alice"

This is the story of "Alice," as Phillips himself told it in his first book, *The Great God Success*. How this novelistic incident happens to be biographical now needs to be explained.

After the turn of the century, Phillips set himself almost desperately to the work of finally producing a book—a coherent whole—a step from what, despite all rationalizations, he felt to be his journalistic bondage. The end of a century is a great milestone, and this one impressed American lives inordinately; it may well have speeded up events beyond the ordinary course of nature. In any event, Phillips felt that he must act and act quickly. He was thirty-three years old. Journalism had no more to give him, so far as his ambitions were concerned. There was no more time to waste. It was get out or give up.

Hence, in spare time, at odd hours snatched from his routine, he pressed himself to the writing of pages. There was no time to plan an ambitious book; he would never finish it, he knew. Roughly, he projected the story of a newspaper man who became enslaved by the wealth he imagined would ensure his freedom. Phillips put down whatever came to mind: thumbnail sketches of men and things, hasty chapters and paragraphs skewering together events, bits of observation. . . . But in the matter of "Alice" the pen slowed down and stopped. The vision focused. And what was intended as an incident among larger things grew large itself and overshadowed the "point" of his book.

It included inconsistencies indeed. Yet, as Frank Harris later argued in his *The Man Shakespeare*, inconsistencies can often be revealing. That is, the author's need to say something of personal import may be so intense that he will neglect or forget his larger scheme to describe certain episodes with compulsive detail. In Phillips's case, the contrast between incident and scheme was heightened by his haste.

In thirty-nine pages he made his protagonist over from a jobless college graduate to a Park Row journalistic celebrity. In fact, *half* those few pages were given over to the young man's first day in the newspaper office—gray pages expressing the hopeless, futureless, ephemeral nature of newspaper life as Phillips found it. What followed was a series of notes for the story of the rise of a neophyte to prominence. Then, for over forty pages stares out unwinkingly the story of Alice, the one episode in the book having dimensions, ringing authentic and consistent from beginning to end, far more detailed than the rest of the book. As best he could without bogging his plan of work, Phillips told his story in The Great God Success.

He lived in Washington Square South. He had gone to a "furnished-room house" there because it was cheap. He stayed because he was comfortable and was without motive for moving. . . .

"A new lodger . . . usually took the best rooms that were to be had. Then, sometimes slowly, sometimes swiftly, came the retreat upward until a cubby-hole under the eaves was reached. Finally came precipitate and baggageless departure, often with a week or two of lodging unpaid. The next pause, if pause there was, would be still nearer the river-bed or the Morgue."

This was what the terrors of the city, loneliness, and friendlessness told Phillips as, several years later, it told Dreiser. A contemporary of Stephen Crane, who was also of the New York press and also domiciled in Washington Square, Phillips was unreconciled to pessimism. Yet a need for motives adding value to life plagued him. And he was shy; it was difficult for him to open his heart. His passionate need for freedom inhibited in him the normal search for companionship.

"He had never been gregarious. Thus far he had not had a single intimate friend, man or woman. He knew many people and knew them well. They liked him and some of them sought his friendship. These were often puzzled because it was easy to get acquainted with him, impossible to know him intimately."

This can be readily accepted. For Phillips left no one, not one of his scores of friends, many of them men and women of substance and influence, to interpret him.

"The explanation of this combination of openness and reserve, friendliness and unapproachableness, was that his boyhood and youth had been spent wholly among books. That life had trained him not to look to others for amusement, sympathy or counsel, but to depend upon himself. As his temperament was open and good natured and sympathetic, he was as free from enemies and enmities as he was from friends and friendship.

"Women there had been—several women, a succession of idealizations which had dispersed in the strong light of his common-sense. He had never disturbed himself about morals in what he regarded as the limited sense. He always insisted that he was free, and he was careful only of his personal pride and of taking no advantage of another."

His life was more complicated than he willingly confessed. Phillips left evidence of loneliness and unsatisfied familial instincts, even at the height of his fame and success. His cerebrations on this and related themes varied with changing times and his own maturing, but they never diminished. Even while he wrote, however, he was reliving an experience which explained many of his later attitudes.

"A poor woman, he felt, he could not marry; a rich woman, he felt, he would not marry. And he cared nothing about marriage because he was never lonely, never leaned or wished to lean upon another, abhorred the idea of any one leaning upon him; because he regarded freedom as the very corner-stone of his scheme of life."

"Never" was a large word, one of the "inconsistencies" which an astute critic could notice and ponder.

Into the house one day moved two girls.

" 'They say that they're sisters,' a German boarder commented, 'they say they have run away from home because of a step-mother and that they are going to earn their own living. But they won't. They spend the nights racing about with a gang of the young wretches of this neighborhood. They won't be able to stand getting up early for work. And then—' "

One night he met her.

"She was above the medium-height—tall for a woman—and slender. Her loose wrapper, a little open at the round throat, clung to her, attracting attention to all the lines of her form. Her hair was indeed black, jet black, waving back from her forehead in a line of curving and beautiful irregularity. Her skin was clear and dark. There were deep circles under her eyes, making them look unnaturally large, pathetically weary. In repose her face was childish and sadly serious. When she smiled she looked older and pert, but no happier.

" 'You're in early tonight,' said he, the circles under her eyes reminding him of what the German had told him.

" 'I haven't slept much for a week,' the girl replied. 'I'm nearly dead. But I won't go to bed till Nellie comes. . . . We agreed always to stay together. She broke it tonight. My fellow got too fresh, so I came home. She said she'd come too. That was an hour ago, and she isn't here yet.'

" 'Isn't she rather young to be out alone at this time?' . . . At this remark . . . she laughed with an expression of cunning at once amusing and pitiful.

" 'She's a year older than me,' she said, 'and I guess I can take care of myself. Still she hasn't much sense. She'll get into trouble yet. She doesn't understand how to manage the boys when they're too fresh.' "

The girls were not sisters. Alice had left home and now, running loose, was finding Nellie, a girl of lesser sensitivity, no strong companion in a cold world.

" 'If Nellie doesn't look out, I'll go away and live alone,' she said, and the accompanying unconscious look of loneliness touched him.

" 'You might go back home.'

" 'You don't know my home or you wouldn't say that. You don't know my father. . . . He can't treat me as he treats my mother. Why he goes away and stays for days. Then he goes home and quarrels with her all the time. They never both sit through a meal. One or the other flares up and leaves. He generally whipped me when he got very mad—just for spite.'

" 'But there's your mother.'

" 'Yes. She doesn't like my going away. But I can't stand it. Papa wouldn't let me go anywhere or let anybody come to see me. He says everybody's bad. I guess he's about right. Only he doesn't include himself.'

" 'You seem to have a poor opinion of people.'

" 'Well, you can't blame me.' She put on her wise look of experience and craft. 'I've been away, living with Nellie for four months and I've seen no good to speak of. A girl doesn't get a fair chance.' "

She made six dollars a week as cashier in a restaurant, working from nine to four, and Nellie made three. How a girl could live on such a sum was a question that would interest writers and the gathering social work forces more and more. O. Henry was soon to write a short story on the theme and was to have trouble in placing it for publication.

She entered Phillips's consciousness. He would come upon her at the front door "where a young man was detaining her in a lingering good-bye. Another night as he was passing her room he saw her stretched upon the floor, her head supported by her elbows and an open book in front of her. She looked so childlike that he paused and said: 'What is it—a fairy story?'

" 'No, it's a love story,' she replied, just glancing at him with a faint smile and showing that she did not wish to be interrupted."

But they became acquainted, the troubled, aloof journalist and the lonely girl. She doubtless caused him more thought than he fancied. As for him, he could see that if her clothes and manners were not the most fashionable, "there was yet a certain distinction in her walk and her manner of wearing her clothes; and to a pretty face and graceful form was added the charm of youth, magnetic youth."

They walked in Washington Square, and as they talked he noticed in greater detail features of her face, her eyes "brown with lines of reddish gold raying from the pupils," chin and mouth which were firm, yet—a point which concerned Phillips all his life—suggesting "weakness through the passions." She was now quite alone; her friend had gone definitely "bad," and she was determined not to follow. Why? Phillips asked.

" 'I don't know why,' she replied. 'There doesn't seem to be any good reason. I've thought I would several times. And then—well, I just couldn't.'

" 'And you won't go home?'

" 'Never in the world,' she said with almost fierce energy; then some thought made her laugh. . . . He decided that she had not told him everything about her home life, even though she had rattled on as if there was nothing to conceal. He sat watching her, she looking straight before her, her small bare hands clasped in her lap. He was pitying her keenly—this child, at once stunted and abnormally developed, this stray from one of the classes that keep their women sheltered; and here she was adrift, without any of those resources of experience which assist the girls of the tenements."

He found that she had "an intelligent way of looking at things," that she appreciated more than he had anticipated. He began to spend evenings with her, letting her accompany him on newspaper assignments and taking her to dinner at well-known Village and Second Avenue restaurants. "Late in June she bought a new gown—a pale-grey with ribbons and hat to match. He was amused at the anxious expression in her gold-brown eyes as she waited for his opinion. And when he said: 'Well, well, I never saw you look so pretty,' she looked much prettier with a slight colour rising to tint the usual pallor of her cheeks."

One Sunday he came home to find her helping the maid straighten his room. He lay on the couch smoking and watching her handle his books. From one of them she read aloud a tangle of technical words in political economy. " 'What do you have such stupid things around for?' she asked smiling." . . . Later she flitted about uneasily, taking up various things and noticing a picture. Who was it? she asked. His sister-in-law, he answered. He "did not then understand why she became so gay, why her eyes danced with happiness."

He had thought of her, "or had thought that he thought of her"— this was to become one of Phillips's crucial phrases in his fiction— "only as a lonely and desolate child, to be taught so far as he was capable of teaching and she of learning. He was conscious of her extreme youth and of the impassable gulf of thought and taste between them. He did not take her feelings into account at all. It never occurred to him that the part of friend and patron which he was playing was not safe for him, not just and right toward her."

So Phillips later wrote, with quiet bitterness. He had not thought. . . .

Once he took her to a social affair. "And the next day a reporter for the *Sun* whom he knew slightly said to him with a grin he did not like: 'Mighty pretty little girl you're taking around with you. Where'd you pick her up?'

" 'This must stop,' he said to himself. 'It must stop at once. It is unjust to her. And it is dragging me into an entanglement.'

"But the mischief had been done. She loved him. And with the confidence of youth and inexperience she was disregarding all the obstacles, was giving herself up to the dream that he would presently love her in return, with the end as in the storybooks. Indeed, love stories became her constant companions. Where she once read them with amusement, she now read them as a Christian reads his Bible— for instruction, inspiration, faith, hope and courage."

The accounting came soon.

"One evening—it was in the week of Independence Day. . . . There were steps in the hall, and then, peeping around the door frame was the face of his young neighbor.

" 'Where have you been all evening?'

" 'Oh, I've been up to see a friend. She lives in Harlem, and she wants me to come and live with her.'

" 'Are you going to?' he inquired, noting that he was interested and not pleased. 'The house wouldn't seem natural without you.'

"She gave him a quick, gratified glance and, advancing further into the room, sat upon the arm of the big rocking-chair. 'She gave me a good talking to,' she went on with a smile. 'She told me I ought not to live alone at my age. She said I ought to live with her and meet some friends of hers. She said maybe I'd find a nice fellow to marry.'

"He thought over this as he smoked and at last said in an ostentatiously judicial tone: 'Well, I think she's right. I don't see what else there is to do. You can't live on down here alone always. . . . '

" 'I don't want to get married,' she replied, shaking her head slowly from side to side.

" 'That's what all the girls say,' . . . [he laughed] 'But of course you will. It's the only thing to do.'

" 'Then why don't you get married?' asked Alice, tracing one of the flowers in her wrapper with her slim, brown forefinger.

" 'I couldn't if I would and I wouldn't if I could.'

" 'Oh, you could get a nice girl to marry you I'm sure,' she said, the colour rising faintly toward her long, down cast lashes." . . .

This was strategically the time to end her illusions. He would be very careful, wrote Phillips, very adroit. He would not let her suspect that he had any idea of her thoughts. Indeed, he was not certain he had. . . .

" 'I shall never get married,' he said, sitting up and talking as one who is discussing a case which he understands thoroughly yet has no personal interest in. 'I haven't the money and I haven't the inclination. I am what they would call a confirmed bachelor. I wouldn't marry any girl who had not been brought up as I have been. We should be unhappy together, unsuited each to the other. She would soon hate me. Besides, I wish to be free. I care more for freedom than I ever shall for any human being. As I am now, so I shall always be, a wandering fellow without ties. It is not a pleasant prospect for old age. But I have made up my mind to it and I shall never marry.' "

Had she known, it was Phillips's way to plunge into words to make it difficult for him to draw back. "Better too far than not far enough," was one of his maxims. He played this card and won. Alice left the house, and left him to what relief and perplexity he harbored.

He was amazed to discover what hold she had on him. "The nearest he had come to companionship was with Alice. With the other women whom he had known in various degrees from warmth to white-heat, there had been interruptions, no such constant freedom of access, no such intermingling of daily life. Her he had seen at all hours and in all circumstances. She never disturbed him but was ready to talk when he wished to listen, listened eagerly when he talked, and was silent and beautiful and restful to look at when he wished to indulge in the dissipation of mental laziness."

He longed for her so intensely that he "almost suspected himself of being in love with her." He congratulated himself, thinking that it had not been nearly so one-sided as he had first imagined. While he turned such thoughts over in his mind, there occurred the great strike in the Tennessee mountains previously noted, to which he was assigned by the *Sun;* the time sequence in Phillips's affairs holds up very well in his fictional account. The strike took all his energy and attention for three weeks, and when he returned to New York, "Alice had ceased to tempt him."

"One midnight in the early spring he was in his sitting room, reading and a little bored. There came a knock at the door. He hoped that it was someone bringing something interesting or coming to propose a search for something interesting. 'Come in,' he said with welcome in his voice. The door opened. It was Alice.

"She was dressed much as she had been the first time he talked with her—a loose, clinging wrapper open at the throat. There was a change in her face—a change for the better but also for the worse. She looked more intelligent, more of a woman. There was more sparkle in her eyes and in her smile. But—he saw instantly the price she had paid. As the German had suggested, she had 'got on up town.'

"She was pulling at the long blue ribbon of her negligee. Her hands were whiter and her pink finger nails had had careful attention. She smiled, enjoying his astonishment. 'I have come back,' she said.

"He came forward and took her hand. 'I'm glad, very glad to see you. For a minute I thought I was dreaming.'

" 'Yes,' she went on, 'I'm in my old room. I came this afternoon. I must have been asleep, for I didn't hear you come in.'

" 'I hope that it isn't bad luck that has flung you back here.'

" 'Oh, no. I've been doing very well. I've been saving up to come. And when I had enough to last me through the summer, I—I came.'

" 'You've been at work?'

"She dropped her eyes and flushed. And her fingers played more nervously with her ribbons.

" 'You needn't treat me as a child any longer,' she said at last in a low voice. 'I'm eighteen now and—well, I'm not a child.'

"Again there was a long pause. He, watching her downcast face, saw her steadying her expression to meet his eyes. When she looked it was straight at him—appeal, but also defiance.

" 'I don't ask anything of you,' she said. 'We are both free. And I wanted to see you. I was sick of all those others—up there. I've never had—had—this out of my mind. And I've come. And I can see you sometimes. I won't be in the way.'

"[He] went over to the window and stared out into the lights and shadows of the leafy square. When he turned again she had lighted and was smoking one of his cigarettes.

" 'Well,' he said smiling down at her. 'Why not? Put on a street gown and we'll go out and get supper and talk it over.'

"She sprang up, her face alight. She was almost running toward the door. Midway she stopped, turned and came slowly back. She put one of her arms upon his shoulder—a slender, cool, smooth, white arm with the lace of the wide sleeve slipping away from it. She turned her face up until her mouth, like a rosebud, was very near his lips. There was appeal in her eyes.

" 'I'm very, very glad to see you,' he said as he kissed her."

In this way, wrote Phillips, she determined his life for four years. "He worked well at his profession. He read a great deal. He wrote fiction and essays in desultory fashion and got a few things printed in the magazines. He led a life that was a model of regularity. But he knew the truth—that Alice had ended his career."

Phillips knew better than to blame her. True, he thought that "entanglement shut him off from the men and women of his own kind who would have thrust opportunities upon him." But other judgments disturbed him. The fact was that he was still motiveless. Alice could give him no motive, but had he not found her—or she him—he would have continued to drift, waiting some tocsin within or without. He would have done as he did, "spasmodically tried to write stories for the magazines, contrived plots for novels and plays, written first chapters, first scenes of first acts." And what would have come of such efforts? The time was not yet ripe for Phillips, but it was nearly so, as journalists, civic workers, individualists of all sorts in business, politics, and on campuses drew themselves up for the concerted labors which produced Progressivism. Meanwhile, Alice filled a world lonely at best.

These were years of contentment. "Ambition had always been vague with him and now his habit of following the line of least resistance had drifted him into this mill-pond. Sometimes he would give himself up to bitter self-reproach, disgusted that he should be so satisfied, so non-resisting in a lot in every way the reverse of that which he had marked out for himself. If he had been chained he might, probably would, have broken away. But Alice never attempted to control him. His will was her law. She was especially shrewd about money matters, so often the source of dispute and estrangements."

Nevertheless, when she suggested an apartment, he made excuses. He regarded it as a degrading arrangement certain to end tragically. But then he found himself speculating about various apartments he saw as he walked the streets. At last he asked abruptly: "Where was that apartment you saw?" and she went on discussing it as though there had been no interval.

She took all the work upon herself. Detail for detail, Phillips tells how she did it, so that "he got a wholly false idea of the difficulties of setting up an establishment. And so, at twenty-six, he found himself a master of five attractive and comfortable rooms, his clothing, his books, all his belongings properly arranged. The door was opened for him by a clean looking colored maid, with a tiny white cap on her head.

"As he looked around and then at the beautiful face with the wistful, gold-brown eyes so anxiously following his wandering glance, he was very near to loving her. Indeed, he was like a husband who has left out that period of passionate love which extends into married life until it gives place to boredom, or to dislike, or to some such sympathetic affection as he felt for Alice."

Sometimes he felt qualms. It was deeply unfair to her, for he knew he would not change. And then again, it was he who proposed marriage, which she rejected with terror as a prelude to separation, declaring that she could not risk losing him. To keep him was to leave him free. She did not want his name, or his friends, or to be respectable. Only him.

Often she surprised him with such acute decisions. "Here," he said "I've been seeing you day after day all this time, have had a chance to know you better than I ever knew anyone in my life, have had you very near to me day and night. And just now as I look at you, I see the real you for the first time in two years."

" 'I have been wondering when you would look at me again,' said Alice with a small, sly smile.

" 'Why you are a woman grown. Where is the little girl I knew, the little girl who used to look up to me?'

" 'Oh, she's gone these two years. She proposed to you, and when you refused her, she—died.' "

On the whole, Phillips was glad to have been refused marriage. But he observed critically the "Anglo-Saxon" compulsions within his spirit which made him ashamed of "this, his real life," persuaded him to keep a room at his club, and conventionally conceal evidences of his relationship to Alice. And he retained with a bitterness which later made him a partisan of woman's rights the memory of "how many, many times, in their moments of demonstrativeness, she listened for those words which never came, listened and turned away to hide from him the disappointment in her eyes."

He was no longer spoken of as a "coming man." Phillips was one of the New York scene about whom "period" anecdotes would appear in such books as Thomas Beer's *The Mauve Decade* (1926). He was author of the legendary lost-little-boy "scoop" in the Catskill Mountains, esteemed as "literature" by the newspaper fraternity. He was the sensational captor of the great *Victoria* collision "beat" of later fame. That, and nothing more.

Park Row had no more to ask of Phillips. His creative work received few plaudits from it. The "coming man" bore different features from Phillips's. He became an editor or wrote books in the style of Richard Harding Davis. Phillips lost little, losing the attention of his associates. What troubled him was his inability to substitute anything for it.

"Vanity supplied him with many excuses and consolations. Was he not one of the best reporters in the profession? Where was there another, where indeed in any profession were there many of his age, making five thousand a year? Was he not always improving his mind? Was he not more and more careful in his personal habits? Was he not respected by all who knew him; looked upon as a successful man; regarded by those with whom he came in daily contact as a leader in his profession, a model for style, a marvel for facility and versatility and for the quantity of good 'copy' he could turn out in a brief time? . . .

" 'Why try to lie to myself?' he thought. 'It's never a question of what one has done but always of what one could have and should have done. I am thirty and I have been marking time for at least four years. Preparing by study and reading? Yes, but not preparing for anything.'

"On the last day of January—six weeks after his thirtieth birthday—he came home earlier than usual, as they were going to the theatre and were to dine at seven. He found Alice in bed and the doctor sitting beside her.

" 'You'll have to get someone else to go with you, I'm afraid,' she said with good humored resignation, a trifle over acted. 'My cold is worse and the doctor says I must stay in bed.'

" 'Nothing serious?' [he] asked anxiously, for her cheeks were flaming.

" 'Oh, no. Just the cold. And I am taking care of myself.' "

"A Little Candle Goes Out," Phillips entitled that chapter. The doctor told him that Alice was not long for the world. He answered dazedly, "Impossible," laughed strangely, and thought how just that morning he had thought he wanted to be free, and now he was to be free. He shouted "Impossible," again, struck the doctor in the face, then fainted. Phillips took her south, probably to Asheville, North Carolina, as he had to if she was to live even briefly. There Alice found her great happiness, for he loved her. Loved her because she was going, Alice "knew," delighting in every moment. Shortly after, she died.

"And then—the end came—like putting out the light."

Thus Doc Woodruff, a political manager in Phillips's first major publishing success, *The Plum Tree* (1905), some ten years after the event. The quiet death haunted him and affected many of his attitudes.

He returned to New York with only one plan: to "work, work with a purpose." A glance from the cab at the curtains of his home and he knew he could not go in. The maid was dispatched to close up his menage. He set up new rooms elsewhere.

"At the office all understood his mourning; but no one, not even Kittredge, knew him well enough to intrude beyond gentler looks and tones." So much for Phillips's independence, his efforts to hide his "real life," his Anglo-Saxon pride. He flung himself into work. Again, ambition!—but what could come of it? Phillips knew—his struggles with the *World* publisher Joseph Pulitzer underwrote the fact—that the price of success on a newspaper was bondage to it. Nonetheless, he tried.

"As it was, desperately though he fought to refrain from backward glances, he was now and again taken off his guard. A few of her pencil marks on the margin of a leaf of one of his books; a gesture, a little mannerism of some woman passing him in the street—and he would be ready to sink down with weariness and loneliness, like a tired traveler in a vast desert.

"He completely lost self-control only once. It was a cold, wet May night and everything had gone against him that day. He looked drearily round his rooms as he came in. How stiff, how forbidding, how desert they seemed! He threw himself into a big chair.

" 'No friends,' he thought, 'no one that cares a rap whether I live or die, suffer or am happy. Nothing to care for. Why do I go on? What's the use if one has not an object—a human object?'

"And their life came flooding back—her eyes, her kisses, her attentions, her passionate love for him, so pervasive yet so unobtrusive; the feeling of her smooth round arm about his neck; her way of pressing close up to him and locking her fingers in his; the music of her voice, singing her heart song to him, yet never putting it into words—

"He stumbled over to the divan and stretched himself out and buried his face in the cushions. 'Come back!' he sobbed. 'Come back to me, dear.' And then he cried as a man cries—without tears, with sobs choking up into his throat and issuing in moans.

" 'Curious,' he said aloud when the storm was over and he was sitting up, ashamed before himself for his weakness, 'who would have suspected me of this?' "

6

A Brilliant Failure

Phillips's journalistic talents were put to wide use. The specialization of later years was not so much as imagined in 1894, and Phillips does not seem to have anticipated individual regard, certainly for his creative ambitions. Such facts of life helped put his momentary pride in big headlines and infrequent by-line appreciation in chastening perspective. "It is not especially difficult," he later wrote with quiet irony, "to find a man who can write, well enough for newspaper purposes, the ordinary interview or descriptive article."[1] He continued to find some of his work, such as the keyhole type of reportorial assignment, unpleasant. There were compensations. His duties sent him continuously over the country, for example, to report on educational perspectives at various colleges and universities, and his acquaintanceship with the states became quite broad.

Back home in Indianapolis, Beveridge was doing well. It was Beveridge who helped Phillips think he was accomplishing little. Beveridge's career, legal and political, was leading him to Washington, while for Phillips there were only the shifting sands of daily news gathering. Phillips took pride in his friend's accomplishments and contributed his own time and mind to them as occasion suggested. He attended to bits of Beveridge's business which required New York information, admired the "great stuff" Beveridge wrote about a European trip, advised him not to accept an unspecified offer, and averred that he himself could write a whole book about Beveridge.[2]

Phillips's sister Carolyn, now separated from her husband, lived in New York. It is not clear just when she joined Graham as a companion.

Phillips exchanged ambitions with some of his co-workers in restaurants and over cocktails, and made it clear by repetition that he intended to stay in journalism only so long as it had something to teach him about life and writing, and no longer. There was never any doubt in his mind that his goal was to write fiction. Yet he had private feelings and facades outside of family and friends which some of his associates respected and others resented. "There was an earlier time [about 1894]," wrote W.J. Ghent, later a famous socialist, "when I knew him as a reporter on the *World,* and when he was brash, cocky, and excessively 'smart.' This Phillips I found intolerable. The later Phillips that I knew from about 1904 to the time of his death was a very different person."[3]

In December of 1894 Charles Edward Russell came to the *World* as City Editor and as Phillips's immediate chief. They renewed acquaintanceship. Unsavory assignments ended for Phillips. They became friends away from the office, often dining together and carrying on lengthy discussions on art and life. One arresting scrap of conversation between the two survives in which Phillips and Russell discussed realism. Phillips argued that no novel could be great which did not contain women as significant characters. Russell in opposition cited Robert Louis Stevenson's *Treasure Island* in evidence, whether he realized it or not giving his case away. But it was one thing for Phillips to prescribe for a literature which was in this respect slumbering, in a time when even so vital a semifiction as Edward Bellamy's *Looking Backward* contained female stereotypes. It was another thing for him to complete a persuasive fiction of his own containing dimensional women.

Russell and Phillips planned serious books as well as commercial books that would free them from journalism. But giving time to their fanciful enterprises proved impractical. Russell actually completed a volume of undisclosed content which Phillips tried unsuccessfully to get published. The subjects they turned over between them showed the bent of their minds. They were all about literature—literature, when there was a score of topics ready to hand which might have impressed editors. The Sherman Anti-Trust Act, for example, passed in 1890 and intended to preserve the freedom of citizens in commerce, demanded assessment in changing times of business consolidation and interdependent cities. Railroads then seemed the most ominous of monopolies, since they were literally the arteries of the nation. But in addition, oil . . . wheat . . . wool . . . steel—what concerned, literate citizen could fail to be interested in their status and condition?

Phillips might have tried a book on the Homestead Strike, which had electrified the country in 1892. The savage exchanges between workers and strikebreakers at the Carnegie mills in western Pennsylvania had chillingly suggested civil war. Phillips might have probed the record of labor unrest and radicalism in his time for light on new circumstances. Anarchism—anarchism not merely of theory, but of action—had come to Homestead; it was once an incredible idea in purportedly free America. There at Homestead the young anarchist Alexander Berkman had shot and stabbed Henry Frick, second in command to Carnegie. Berkman's social sympathies and good intentions could not hide the fact that his deed had harmed the strikers as had no calculated antilabor deed. Phillips believed in an honest day's work, but the problem of how to put individualism and group effort into one promising equation was not his alone.

In 1894 appeared a book, written with bitter wit and restraint, and drawn line for line from documents. *Wealth against Commonwealth*, by Henry Demarest Lloyd, created a sensation, and for good reason. Lloyd could in no way be termed a crank or socialist. He was a journalist, a lecturer on political economy, well-married, and independent of literary market standards. He respected law and order. It was this quality, in fact, which had impelled him to his work. His evidence seemed to prove that the great corporations habitually employed methods which made them a threat to free enterprise and indeed to community needs. In particular Lloyd cited the career of the Standard Oil Company. Such were the times that John D. Rockefeller was not once mentioned by name; reference was made to "the president" of the company, whose machinations were the principal reason for the existence of the trust.

Wealth against Commonwealth came unheralded, the first clear attack upon the new order, by one who dared believe the old still existed. There were other subjects which merited book-length probing, especially by journalists dissatisfied with daily information and sensations and dedicated to democratic principles. Poverty, boss rule in the cities, and the survival problems of workers and farmers demanded everyone's attention. Phillips's problem was to determine the role of imaginative fiction in such urgent issues of American life. His problem was also how to write for a general public rather than a cult, for a variety of Americans, male and female, well-to-do and poor.

There was less of a problem with overweening trusts, though they required special understanding of their own. Pulitizer's *World*, the leading Democratic paper in the country, conceived the idea of a series of articles on the trusts. Pulitzer chose Phillips for the work, one compliment of many which were to leave Pulitzer disappointed with a young man he considered a protégé of sorts, and who was supposed to grow along with Pulitzer and his assignments. Pulitzer

was not above ordering his editors and key writers to adopt a particular stance toward public men and issues, and then expressing fury
because "his" writers did not show that they had minds of their own.
His difficulty with Phillips was that part of Phillips's mind was elsewhere, even when he agreed with his employer.

In the present instance Phillips agreed thoroughly that trusts ought
to be dissolved, and he gave energy and care to a memorable series of
articles which accused President Grover Cleveland, and particularly
his Attorney-General Richard Olney, of violating platform pledges by
allowing trust leaders to stay out of jail. Phillips's articles cited the
Standard Oil Company and the Sugar Trust, among others, and their
known, even notorious misdeeds, calling the attention of Olney and the
World readers to the situation. Each article ended with the rather stiff,
formalistic words: "Such, Mr. Olney, are the facts, and here, sir, is the
law"; whereupon followed the same quotation from the Sherman Act:
"Every contract, combination in the form of trust or otherwise, or conspiracy, in restraint of trade or commerce among the several States, or
with foreign nations, is hereby declared to be illegal."[4]

More than ten years before he wrote his "The Treason of the
Senate" articles, then, Phillips sketched an indictment of national
leaders who subverted the laws; and he utilized a form which permitted a concentrated indictment to unfold itself in readers' minds. Only
a willful myopia has permitted a legend to live sluglike under cold
historical stone that Phillips was a hasty scribbler in the interests of a
latest master. His *World* series was in no wise comparable to "The
Treason of the Senate" articles in grasp, prose, or eloquence. The year
may come when Phillips's growth as a stylist out of journalistic soil
may be profitably traced. Meanwhile, it suffices that here as elsewhere
there was coherence and continuity in his social and cultural outlook.

In his newspaper work and private letters Phillips habitually followed the tenor of events. He expressed disappointment, sometimes
controversially, when he thought he saw flagrant flouting of the public interest. And he perceived no contradiction between a dedication
to society and a concern for self. He had yet to prepare a whole
philosophy that could ride through fair weather and foul. In the 1890s
he entertained cynical and despairing thoughts, but did not demean
them by identifying them with the public interest.

He followed politics intently, joining Pulitzer in his concern for
the Democratic Party. In 1896 Phillips argued unreasonably that William Jennings Bryan had won over William McKinley, presumably be-

cause of Mark Hanna's lavish expenditures in behalf of the Republicans, notably in Phillips's own Indiana. But if Americans had indeed been willing to sell their suffrage for modest fees at the polls, which appears to have been the case, it is difficult to see what Phillips's complaint was. No law then controlled, even formally, campaign expenses.

Bryan had presumed to speak to "a broader class of businessmen," including the man employed for wages, the attorney in a country town, the merchant at the crossroads store, the farmer, the miner, and others.[5] Were they too few for Bryan's cause? McKinley, claiming to "respect" both gold and silver, beat Bryan and his Silver Standard back into the bushes in 1896 and still further back in 1900. The public, Phillips was to declare, will forgive anything but a loose manipulation of principles, an epigram which failed to take into account the psychodynamics of social change. Bryan never moved an inch from his convictions, but he learned nothing beyond them. His diminished fame was a measure of the diminution of the midwestern philosophy to which Phillips still clung. It remained to be seen what might further come of it, and of him.

Pulitzer was now all but blind, and rendered perpetually anxious by the historic advent of William Randolph Hearst into New York journalism. Hearst was bolder and more unscrupulous than Pulitzer. He was also wealthier, and able to buy away choice writers and editors from the *World* staff. Traveling restlessly about the globe while in continuous telegraphic touch with *World* editors, Pulitzer sought constantly for companions who would satisfy his need for information, fetch-and-errand missions, and simple response. His decision to add Phillips to his entourage in 1896 was supposed to represent an advance for a still young man, and to be gratefully received.

Pulitzer liked Phillips's spirit, but, as always, Pulitzer was ambivalent in his feelings, yearning to be surrounded by creative as well as energetic personalities, all of whom he could wholly control. Phillips accepted the assignment, accompanying Pulitzer in his nervous and cerebral journeys, reading to him, writing in his behalf, discussing *World* policies and journalistic projects, and working along with others of Pulitzer's inner circle. All of this was supposed to prepare Phillips for higher editorial duties. Pulitzer noticed impatiently, however, that his protégé was developing his understanding of Pulitzer's goals and techniques at a much slower pace than his talents indicated he should. What Pulitzer could never accept or respect was that Phillips did not enjoy his role of attendant and was not content to move up the editorial ladder. "This part of the procession seems to be going backwards," he wrote Piercy, congratulating him on having had a story accepted by the *Atlantic.* And again: "It's hard to write well, isn't it? I'm in despair. The more I write, the farther I seem to be from the goal—and it's a modest goal, too."[6]

Pulitzer seems to have done his best to build up cordiality and understanding with "David Graham," despite his constant suspicions and anxieties. His recognition of Phillips's "imperious sensibility," as he termed it, involved a species of toleration and even affection. But it was evident that Phillips felt constrained on Pulitzer's yacht and in his company. Arthur Brisbane, soon to defect to Hearst, took cognizance of Phillips's dissatisfaction and shifted him back to New York and the editorial department of the *World.*

The great struggle for circulation between Hearst and Pulitzer merits a brief word for the grotesque comments it inspired cultural historians to record about Phillips. As one of the Pulitzer staff he was constrained to carry out its assignments and appears to have been dragged into the undistinguished efforts which Pulitzer ordered to compete with Hearst's lurid jingoism during the Cuban crisis of 1896–98.[7] But Phillips was, at most, a Pulitzer man, not a "Hearst man." And though he approved means for catching the attention of the masses of readers, he despised many of the notorious techniques Hearst employed which, for the moment, all but made newspapers unreadable. As he wrote:

> [He] wished to avoid an epidemic of that hysteria—the mad rush for sensation and novelty; the strife of opposing ambitions; the plotting and counter-plotting of rival heads of departments; the chaos out of which the craziest ideas often emerged triumphant, making the pages of the paper look like a series of disordered dreams.
>
> (*The Great God Success*, p. 169)

With his feel for epigram, which he would develop in succeeding years, Phillips phrased it that a newspaper should appeal "to intelligence, yes; to the intelligent, no. . . . We want people to read us because we're intelligent enough to know how to please them, not because they're intelligent enough to overcome the difficulties we put in their way."

Such was Phillips's dream. The reality was more complex. Phillips found imperialism wholly repulsive, yet found himself inculpated in Pulitzer's need to feed New York on tales of Spain's cruelty toward Cubans. He glowed with pride and affection when Beveridge fought off influential and wealthy opponents in Indiana to become the choice of its legislature for the United States Senate. "I know that your election [marks] an epoch," Phillips wrote his friend.[8] The new would-be latter-day Lincoln, however, hurried to the Philippines, where American troops were engaged in subduing Filipino guerrillas. Beveridge came home to Washington to utter a maiden speech which rang throughout the country and beyond:

> God has not been preparing the English-speaking and Teutonic peoples for a thousand years for nothing but vain and idle self-contemplation and self-admiration. No! He has made us the master organizers of the world to establish system where chaos reigns. . . . He has made us adepts in government among savages and senile people.[9]

If Beveridge asked Phillips's opinion of this speech, he apparently received no reply. Other friends of Beveridge such as the financier George W. Perkins were delighted by Beveridge's rhetoric and goals. Phillips later reviewed a manuscript of Beveridge's stressing the American right to intervene in Cuban affairs and complained that its argument was "specious" and not "consecutive." Ought it not to be called, Phillips asked, "Keeping Faith with Cuba?"[10] Since its basic intention was to direct American policy toward acquiring Cuba, it is obvious that the friends' minds moved in different directions.

In the next years, despite Beveridge's self-absorption and elite associations, he would value Phillips's sometimes sharp candor. In his turn, Beveridge helped by his life and decisions to qualify some of Phillips's all but pious faith "in the people," if only by underscoring for the novelist that life was not only a matter of principle, but of power and point of view. Phillips never entirely solved the Beveridge problem in his fiction, and his democratic hopes and asseverations are likely more a matter of literary history than of art, even though no one tried more than Phillips did to discover some essence of American experience which accounted for a Lincoln, a La Follette, and in due course an Al Smith. American authors tended to be more comfortable with a Huey P. Long, an enigma of Populism and corruption which somehow expressed American dilemmas.

Underneath Phillips's quasi-idealism was an intense concern less for "the people" than for people. It mixed pride in heritage with disillusioning experience, which Phillips felt compelled to relate. It was an inner drive which after the turn of the century drew Phillips out of journalism and into the career he had long planned.

7

Venture in a New Time

Despite the general air of satisfaction pervading the nation, as reflected in Our New Prosperity (1899), somewhat smugly portrayed by the soon-to-be-muckraking Ray Stannard Baker, Americans were heading for a crisis, not one of hunger and anxiety this time, but of philosophy. Phillips chose an appropriate time in which to discover once and for all what he had in mind. The disorders of the 1890s had left a residue for him as for others.

The Silver Question was dead, no longer able to divert attention from basic problems of government responsibility for trusts, labor-capital relations, the role of women in social decisions, and prospects for a middle class which held American ideals in custody and bulked largest in a population of 76 million citizens. The untidy scandals of the Grant Administration were far in the past, as were the "Boss" Tweeds of the now towering cities. Bribes and coercion were no longer blatantly thrust upon the public; they circulated quietly among organization men. Politicians were not corrupted; they were corrupt. Fixers in legislatures no longer practiced impudence. Their money bore all the indirect airiness of manna from heaven, in the form of gifts and loans and public recognition of services.

Erstwhile maurauders of business and politics were settling down, building castles in New York and Chicago and in the countryside, developing a genteel second generation. The American purchase of foreign titles through marriage became somewhat of a scandal, though it fascinated snobs and working girls and did indicate a search for standards and leadership in society. Thorstein Veblen exploited what he saw as barbarism among the rich in his Theory of the Leisure Classes (1899), but, masterpiece though his book was, there was still something to be added. The era lived with the incredible fact that John D. Rockefeller, Sr., was a billionaire; Phillips was to spell out its meaning not in muckraking but rather in a Saturday Evening Post article, "The Making of a Billionaire." But Rockefeller was also developing a new career as a major philanthropist and patron of the University of Chicago. Wealth was a responsibility as well as an accumulation of power. Here was a fact which shallow writers would in time forget, sometimes while enjoying the largesse of a "Rockefeller grant."

There was pull and strain within society, and also in its culture. Most exciting were the new, flourishing popular magazines, addressing themselves to the widest reading public in history. *McClure's, Everybody's, Cosmopolitan,* and *Collier's* were headlights into the new line. It was no accident that Phillips, as part of his new venture as an independent author, surveyed the field of editors and publications, with tact but not a little forthrightness ("Great Magazines and Their Editors").

William Dean Howells was the "dean" of American letters, but actually a nonentity among such new, restless talents as Phillips, who were asking esthetic questions in their prose which Howells could scarcely grasp. His friend Mark Twain, aging like himself, understood many things about human nature, but nothing about the complex nature of American social-political life. (He had provided the vitality, but none of the insight, such as it was, in his collaborative *The Gilded Age.*) American textbooks emphasized and would continue to emphasize the English heritage, especially in "English Departments" texts, which often ended with references to Walt Whitman's excesses and vanity, and perhaps a reprint of his formal verse tribute to Lincoln, "O Captain! My Captain!"

As early as 1885 Henry Harland, "Sidney Luska," as he called himself, startled literary circles with his novel *As It Was Written,* a tour de force about immigrant life he knew only from the outside and not well. The book was artistically worthless and the attention given it a tribute to its subject. Nevertheless, the very effort provided a precedent for future realists and naturalists not available in often better writings which clung to traditional American romanticism. Harland, at least, saw that there was a challenge mounting to established American cultural habits. Despite Populism, economic crisis, and the unearned prosperity of the Spanish-American War and the Alaska gold rush, many artists, notably in poetry, yearned to hold on to the dignity of the individual in ways which cities and the thunder of railroads seemed to negate. Poets and such authors as James Branch Cabell handcuffed themselves with verse forms which produced a few sensations, notably Edwin Markham's "The Man with the Hoe," but many more failures.[1]

Ernest Lacy (1862–1916) symbolized the dilemmas of literature.

A poet and playwright, and professor at the famous Central High School in Philadelphia, he staked his hopes for immortality—a concept which would be increasingly impugned by the harsh facts of transient life—on Shakespeare's iambic pentameter, though in his idealism Lacy avoided the Renaissance master's more rugged details of crime and passion. In his major effort Lacy sought to reach readers and audiences with the sorrows of the eighteenth-century boy-poet Thomas Chatterton as a martyr to genius. Lacy's one-act *Chatterton* (1893) was acted on stage by the well-loved Julia Marlowe. Lacy's full-length *The Bard of Mary Redcliffe* (1910), also detailing the Chatterton story, was promised production by Marlowe's actor-husband E.H. Sothern, but the promise was withdrawn.

Lacy felt with others of his sensibility that poetry was an outcast in America, overshadowed by materialism and subject to brutal masters. As he had Chatterton say, before his suicide:

> This yellow god [gold]
> Distributes favors with a curious hand.
> The kings of his creation are so low
> Of forehead that their crowns sit on their eyebrows.
> They have for motley fools, wise men—so called
> (Not wise enough to live within their age),
> Who feed upon the bones their masters throw
> Beneath the table.[2]

And he asked American audiences to respond to such stormy thoughts as Chatterton's:

> I shall not live
> To hold the candle nightly to the glass
> And watch my face grow old: to see the lines
> Deepen to ditches round the eyes and mouth
> When Time besieges Beauty; to make that fight,
> Which must be lost, against the first gray hairs—
> Plucking them out lest winged Love espy
> The ghostly vanguard of advancing years.
> Nor last, with taper held in palsied clutch,
> To view the muddy orbs, the lips caved in,
> The visage rutted, as if a thousand cares
> After long rains, had driven their heavy wains,
> With iron-bound wheels, across the features.—No!
> The spirit of my youth shall never peer
> Through Age's hideous mask.[3]

Lacy's sonnets were deeply felt, but differed from Emily Dickinson's verses, still then being released after her death. Where Dickinson questioned life, Lacy questioned rather life's frustrations. Although Lacy had a natural rhythm for his verse, it did not reflect life's cacophony with false rhymes, as did hers. Hers, too, was a supreme achievement of womanhood, which Lacy idealized out of relevance to changing social conditions. Lacy's sorrows were real enough, but their concern for the poet's mission, as distinguished from that of anybody else, was not concerted to reach beyond his era. His very title on patriotic feelings, for example, "Ad Patriam," though finely expressed, was calculated to put off later loose-rooted readers, even those such as Phillips, who loved Shelley and Keats, but who feared moodiness, at least as a literary topic, and who avoided foreign phrases almost on principle. Some of Lacy's thoughts, like those on Darwinism, were formidable enough in his generation, but suppressed during the Progressive era, settled for later generations, or simply superseded by other interests, as was the case with Lacy's sonnet "To an Ape":

> Hallo, ape! why dost thou grin at me
>   As though suppressing philosophic mirth?
>   Art thou so vain of thy illustrious birth,
> Thou hairy limb of my ancestral tree?
> That those were nobler times I must agree—
>   Those frolic days when monkeys manned the earth,
>   When nature's creamy brew gave bibbers girth,
> And bondless love begat posterity.
>
> I, too, with plaguing vermin do contend,
>   My itchy friend; I, too, have learned distrust,
> Yet on a pleasure-bounty must depend;
>   Into iron cages we have both been thrust,
> Where we can climb and chatter to the end;
>   We shall be one, proud ape, when we are dust.[4]

Phillips and other vanguard authors of the newer prose were in better condition to contribute to their times than Lacy. H.L. Mencken did not read Lacy, but he had some sense of what evasive poetry and prose were being regularly written and approved, and were being only feebly resisted in conventional journals, even in the elite *Atlantic* and *Century*. Mencken made relevant contrast between it and the new effort which the journalist-novelists were mounting:

> The [literary] revolt of the eighteen nineties in America, was an echo of the simultaneous English revolt, and it showed a good deal of warmed over feebleness. One turns back today to such things as "Songs [from] Vagabondia" [1894, by Bliss Carman and Richard

Hovey], and marvels that they ever fluttered the academic elms. The chief rebels, seen in retrospect, take on an almost ludicrous respectability. They fired their stinkpots at Richard Watson Gilder, James Whitcomb Riley, and Thomas Nelson Page, and began whopping for— James Lane Allen and Maurice Maeterlinck! . . .

I am old enough to remember the blast that *The Red Badge of Courage* made in 1895. . . . Who was this astonishing young man? A drunken newspaper reporter in New York! One of [Richard Harding] Davis's heroes. . . . [5]

Astonishing Crane was. But, reread three-quarters of a century later, how does one explain *The Red Badge of Courage*'s strange, continuing vitality, in contrast with the work of a Lacy, since, Crane's tale being of the Civil War, it might easily seem to be no more than fighting over old battles and personal dilemmas? Crane's genius was that he was able to take an old, worn theme and appear to be merely adding a new questioning of ancient heroics. In fact, he did what the poets seeking "universality" had failed to do: link the acceptable theme of the Civil War with ultimate questions of the meaning of life. For Crane's young coward-turned-hero of *The Red Badge of Courage* finds himself distinguished and admired merely as a result of an accidental wound. And he gains "courage" not by discovering patriotism or love of God, but the sweetness of social approbation. In effect, Crane said in double language that death was merely the absence of life, and this could be momentarily escaped only by clinging to such illusions of life as the value of being rated a "hero." Although his message was only vaguely realized and approved, it was sufficiently sensed to give Crane's tale a "classic" status.

Phillips later offered a somewhat similar thought in saying and repeating that this world, this body was all we had; but he intended the epigram as a spur to work for the common good. Crane was less bent on projects which dignified life. Life offended him with its futility. As such, he was a forerunner of what would later be designated as the "lost generation."

He was one of several authors drawn from journalism whom the shoddy aspects of life made aloof and indirect. It was a tribute to readers of the early 1900s that they bought romantic fictions of no value idealizing love, Lincoln, the American Revolution, and pioneer life, but that they also patronized a Crane. Their inquisitiveness into the irregular aspects of Crane's life—he preferred the demimonde to the genteel—infuriated the young man and caused him finally to leave America and live his last days abroad. Crane wrote journalese and juvenilia, but he was also an artist who chose such other artists as Joseph Conrad for company before his death at twenty-nine.[6]

There were others seeking a formula for the new time between romanticism and the grimier depths of naturalism, none more consciously than Frank Norris, who not only read Zola but directly imitated him, as in his early novel *Vandover and the Brute*, written in 1894–95, an almost laboratory dissection of his protagonist into idealist and animal. Norris's novel *Blix* (1899) was composed of the purest unqualified romanticism, and showed best the divisions of his mind when contrasted with *McTeague* (1899) and *The Octopus* (1901).[7] *McTeague* was Norris's naturalism under control. Norris described, with symbol and circumstance, the change in McTeague from blundering, good-humored dentist without professional certificate to crude sadist and murderer. *The Octopus*, on the other hand, owed little to Zola. It told with epic sweep the tale of California farmers and ranchers crushed by the awesome might of the railroads. It expressed seismographically the mood of an entire people wedded to ideals of individual achievement, but needing somehow to control the almost cosmic industrial power which threatened all individuals. Phillips's best fiction, when he achieved his style, was closer to Norris's than to Crane's.

Finally, the other Indianan, Dreiser, like Phillips, started later in fiction than either Crane or Norris, both of whom were dead by the time they got well under way. Dreiser was a less distinguished journalist than Phillips in 1900 when he published his first novel, *Sister Carrie*, but he was well established in journalistic and magazine circles and wrote hack articles in haste and great number for the publications. Norris, as a publisher's reader, encouraged publication of *Sister Carrie* and helped cut the unwieldy manuscript to readable size. Dreiser later encouraged a ghostly legend that his novel had gone all but unprinted, and that the publisher had restrained its circulation and ruined its market possibilities. In fact, the company had, though reluctantly, given *Sister Carrie* its chance among reviewers and the book-buying public. It had let Norris vent his enthusiasm for the book through circular material and his own endorsement, sent out 127 copies for review, and displayed this work by an unknown writer in its showroom. There was no conspiracy. The public had not chosen to buy.

Sister Carrie was, at very least, a landmark in American literature. Phillips's *The Great God Success* (1901) was a mere sketch, for all that it contained the tragic chapter of "Alice." But the circumstances behind the two works foreshadowed different literary careers for their authors. Dreiser was a slovenly and conscienceless journalist; he had lasted as a *World* journalist in 1894 only two months in an office where Phillips was a star. Dreiser had engaged in every sort of careless editing and scribbling at a time when Phillips labored to refine his political philosophy and social goals. Dreiser wrote *Sister Carrie* easily out of reminiscences of his demimonde sisters and their male associates, and out of their unrealistic fantasies of success, springing from sexual frustration and revolving around drives to power and its fulfillment in sex, all expressing the drift of their lives and their helpless amorality. Phillips took time from responsible journalistic duties, robbing himself of sleep to complete *The Great God Success.*

So far as style went, both Phillips and Dreiser reflected their newspaper training. What distinguished their work was purpose and point of view, as has been seen (pp. 25–26). What was remarkable was the drive toward a pessimistic view of life as being the one true view of life; this lay not only in Dreiser but in numerous associated intellectuals who, on the surface, honored their country and helped direct its affairs. For example, Dreiser's manuscript version of what became *Jennie Gerhardt* circulated for ten years—throughout the Progressive era—among such of his friends as H.L. Mencken, the journalist-critic James Huneker, and others in editorial and related work. Dreiser's original draft about a kept woman with an illegitimate child whose lover married elsewhere contained a happy ending, with the United States senator "becoming reconciled to the child and bringing wedded joy to Jennie."[8] Friends persuaded Dreiser that leaving Jennie forlorn and bereft to the end was more poignant— more in keeping with the dignity of the European social tragedy they admired—and so changed a novel which was like *Sister Carrie,* overwritten and brought down ultimately from some eight hundred pages to half that size. Dreiser's wife, whom he betrayed on every possible occasion before leaving her, did some of the cutting of pages. Other friends helped, including one who, doubtless thinking of *Anna Karenina,* fantastically called Dreiser "the American Tolstoi."

Dreiser himself worked disorderedly on three novels while considering what his chances were for advancement. As he wrote Mencken: "[I]f there is no money in the game I [am] going to run a weekly. I can write a book every six months I think so I won't be so long out of the editing game unless perchance I should make a living this way."[9]

It is popular to think that World War I released a current of cynicism and "disillusionment" because of the malfeasance of pretentious leaders like Woodrow Wilson. But Dreiser's were the views of influential American intellectuals long before the war helped them justify their personal disorder and cosmic bitterness. They had as clients a large potential audience which was tired of American traditions of hard work and just reward. It longed for euphoria and for relaxed morals, both concealed from public view or disguised in conventional trappings. Yet the public also dreamed of justice and meaning in life, and followed the events and personalities of the Progressive era with interest and emotion. It was to the latter which Phillips appealed when he turned from his journalistic past to become a writer of fiction.

For Phillips, doing so was his greatest adventure. As a *World* editor he was paid eight thousand dollars a year, worth vastly more than in the later part of the twentieth century. But Phillips not only demanded a high standard of living, proudly symbolized by the extreme clothing he fancied all his adult life. The salary was his freedom, his security against want and impositions, against social sanctions and hard conventions. Salary was an assured home, travel, and preferences. In leaving the safe harbor of salary and venturing out into article writing and novels, Phillips jeopardized his status in circles he had chosen or conquered.

Yet his sister Carolyn encouraged his venture, as she had others. Beveridge helped by introducing Phillips to the new young editor of the *Saturday Evening Post,* George Horace Lorimer, also a midwesterner, whose career was almost sensational in its persistent commonplaceness. The son of a distinguished minister, Lorimer had attended Yale and returned to Chicago to work for the packing-house magnate Philip D. Armour. Lorimer came to head the canning department and to travel half the year for the company. When he married in 1892 Armour generously granted him honeymoon time, adding, "You might call on the trade as long as you're traveling."[10]

Lorimer chose journalism as a new field, despite Armour's promise to make him a millionaire. He attended Colby College in Maine, where he read in English and history, and took a job with the Boston *Post,* then the *Herald.* In 1898, learning that the *Ladies' Home Journal*'s successful owner Cyrus H.K. Curtis had bought for a thousand dollars the name and goodwill—almost all it had—of the *Satur-*

day Evening Post, Lorimer wired the publisher asking for work and was given it. By then Lorimer had made firm his philosophy of editorship, one that was to raise the circulation of his magazine within two years from 10,000 to 250,000—only a beginning for what was to become the nation's premier periodical.

In the 1920s Lorimer was to have lunch with the young and arrogant F. Scott Fitzgerald and to listen to his rantings against American magazines which nurtured "mediocrities and nobodies." It was safe to say, Fitzgerald declared, that no one at their table had heard of the most important writer of the early 1900s, Frank Norris. Fitzgerald was confounded by Lorimer's good-humored recollection of having published in the *Post* both *The Pit* and *The Octopus* by Norris. He had also published a staggering array of other literary figures including Bret Harte, Stephen Crane, Joseph Conrad, Willa Cather, John Galsworthy, James Branch Cabell, and, in time, Sinclair Lewis, Ring Lardner, Stephen Vincent Benét, and Fitzgerald himself, among many, many others. What such critics as Fitzgerald did not understand was that Lorimer's choices were dictated by a central philosophy which enabled him to take as seriously as he did artists the work of numerous other authors of patently shabby yarns.

Moreover, Lorimer took his articles and editorials as seriously as he did his fiction, printing accounts or the work of outstanding politicians, opera and stage personalities, travelers at home and abroad, business people, women—anyone who might appeal to the largest possible audience. The results, rigidly supervised by Lorimer, were often shallow, often important, and not infrequently indispensable. Such a commentator as Will Rogers became precious to *Saturday Evening Post* readers, yet Lorimer did not hesitate to edit his star's *Letters of a Self-Made Diplomat* when they seemed to him to transgress interest or what he deemed good taste.

Lorimer himself was one of his own best-selling authors, capable of such bathos as his "Legend of the Child Who Is King," cloying in its genuflections to the Christmas tale.[11] His *Letters from a Self-Made Merchant to His Son* (1902) helped make the *Post* and sold some 300,000 copies in book form. It was also lavishly reprinted in parts by business firms as inspirational writing and was translated into twelve languages. These letters, worldly-wise, parochial, and bent on success, infuriated would-be radicals. Upton Sinclair was to relish the quote from his friend George Sterling's versified diatribe against "Lorimor," two lines of which read: "If the young folk build an altar to their vision of the New,/ Be sure the great dog Lorrimor shall lift a leg thereto."[12] What Sinclair could not perceive, in his bitter *Money Writes!* (1927), was that Sterling was himself a failure, and that his ideals were unable to break out of poetry-killing verse forms. Sinclair invidiously compared the vigor of the *Post* during Progressive years with its conservatism in the 1920s. He could not accept that it was the same *Post* in both eras, serving the larger American public in its trifling interests as in its liberal and conservative impulses.

Phillips and Lorimer took to each other, Lorimer with that calm reserve which enabled him to accept and reject, suggest and discourage stories and articles, no matter who the author might be. He seems to have begun with an interest in Phillips's editorial expertise and his almost crotchety distaste for excess: overeating, overspending, emulating the vices of the rich, and the like. Phillips went on to write for Lorimer articles on a wide spectrum of topics. His fiction also received some of Lorimer's patronage, in time at the expense of article writing. Lorimer was a major support for the first half of Phillips's literary career, though even then Phillips had to turn to other magazine outlets for full expression. Lorimer rejected much of Phillips's writings forthright. What kept them friends—kept Phillips visiting Lorimer in Philadelphia and even considering moving to the area— and kept Lorimer visiting Phillips in New York, was their agreement that life needed strong people and a positive, hopeful approach.

Phillips finished his first novel and in the fall of 1901 held in his hand *The Great God Success,* printed under the pseudonym, soon abandoned, of "John Graham." The reason was not, as careless academics were to imagine, that it dealt with Pulitzer, for it did not. It was because Phillips's *World* contract stipulated that he was not to write for publication other than in the *World.*

No illusions confused for the author the meaning of publication. As Phillips wrote: "At fifteen cents a copy, I have to sell ten thousand copies before I get enough to live on for four months" (*The Great God Success,* p. 13). Though less greedy than Dreiser, Phillips required substantial returns to support his way of life even modestly. Pulitzer's congratulations on the book could have no more encouraged him than Pulitzer's recommendation that he read Dostoevsky disheartened him. Public conjecture that the book, dealing with the moral downfall of a newspaper publisher, was aimed at Pulitzer was idiotic. If Phillips had anyone in mind, it would have been Dana, who had betrayed his early Brook Farm idealism. What was remarkable was that this absurd opinion should have wandered mindlessly far into the twentieth century, in writings by critics who had no idea about the era they were supposedly explicating. Interesting was the fact that the novel, a mere sketch, should have turned contemporary readers to thinking of real people. This was a talent of Phillips's which would ultimately lead to his death.

The novel was well-received—too well-received, though critics of the time were wise enough to enjoy its current flavor without taking it too seriously. The title was to persist among critics with compulsions to derogate Phillips, who saw nothing irrational in commenting upon it as though it was a major Phillips writing, while writing off Phillips's patently more complex works with vague generalizations. Not one substantial account of Phillips's later writings materialized, not even of *Susan Lenox*, though it was suffered to exist as a title in literary annals. *The Great God Success* is chiefly notable as marking the distance Phillips traversed in the years of life left him.

Not that an intelligent reader could fail to find evocative passages in the book other than the "Alice" episode. Phillips displayed his gift for epigram, as in his comment, poignant today, on a past New York:

> "Why everybody says we have the worst climate in the world."
> "Far be it from me to contradict everybody. But for me New York has the ideal climate. Isn't it the best of any great city in the world? You see, we have the air of the sea in our streets. And when the sun shines, which it does more days in the year than in any other great city, the effect is like champagne—or rather, like the effect champagne looks as if it ought to have."
>
> (*The Great God Success*, p. 100)

Such comments could be found on many pages. But for the most part the reader of 1901 had to fill in the novelistic gaps of character and circumstances with recollection of direct experiences of his or her own. Despite Phillips's wit and observations, the book is one for the intelligent literary historian. For readers interested in Phillips it expressed something of his hopes and fears, his moods and loneliness, his worry that he might be corrupted or lose direction. It gave almost nothing of the optimism and poise which a satisfying control over his affairs would release.

The relative success of the novel decided Phillips on a break with the past. Most of Phillips's associates were surprised by his courage or foolhardiness, and Phillips himself voiced tremors and uncertainties.[13] Yet in leaving journalism he far from cut his bridges. He held on to newspaper connections and explored the magazines for empathetic contacts. But he entered into his new regimen with the same total commitment that had characterized the old.

He began with a series of articles for the *Post*, "The Story of the City Daily," and told of its cost in money and men, of the race for circulation, of the new journalism. One of Phillips's tainted critics was to call the articles not particularly complimentary; a camp follower added "acidulous."[14] In fact, Phillips, leaving the field, remembered the best of it: its educational value, its "light bringing" qualities. He recognized that most papers were "organs" and many of their campaigns shallow. But the time for Upton Sinclair's *The Brass Check*, an exposé of venal journalism, was far off. Lines of editorial control were not tightly drawn, and Phillips took cordial note of the fact.

> It is an unnatural life [he explained], this of the tumultuous, eager, insistent, incessant "new journalism"—that is, it seems unnatural to the average early-to-bed and early to rise citizen. But it has an enormous fascination for those who live it. It makes other lines of endeavor, however arduous and exacting, seem slow and humdrum. The newspaper office, where the eyes and ears are filled with the very latest happenings in all parts of the world, gives an elsewhere unattainable sense of being in the midst of affairs in touch with the world's life. It is a pace that kills for those who direct, but they feel that, if they are dying more quickly, they are compensated by living more swiftly, living every second of every moment of their conscious hours.
>
> ("The Race for Circulation," p. 12)

Even in the burgeoning field of belles lettres, journalism, and magazines Phillips's name soon became noticeable. His work appeared in *Collier's* and in *Everybody's*. For a while, and reminiscent of his efforts in observation and social comment stretching back to his earliest days in Cincinnati journalism, Phillips ran a column in the *New York Times*. *McClure's* received and published his "Thursday at Three," a short story of no particular moment. *Munsey's* displayed a sketch called "That Person." *The Critic* of July 1903 was only being amiably surprised when it opined that "Mr. Phillips seems to be an industrious writer, for it is almost impossible to pick up a magazine or a weekly or even a daily newspaper in which there is not something from his pen."

In May of 1902 appeared Phillips's second novel, a short one: *Her*

Serene Highness, the theme almost certainly suggested by a publisher. It snatched the Graustark craze from the air, a craze reflecting the yearning of the reading public for romance in fiction as well as poetry, as a shield against the hard realities of urban and industrial life and the weighty implications of Darwinism.[15] *Her Serene Highness* was no more than a pot-boiler, a working effort. Phillips lacked—as did Stephen Crane, whose *The O'Ruddy* was a lengthy and absurd effort at a swashbuckling novel placed in an earlier era—the talent for depicting fantastic kingdoms which James Branch Cabell was soon, even in the Progressive era, to manifest.[16] As early as 1905 Cabell's *The Line of Love* was composed of short stories set in medieval times.

Yet, as Phillips had broken ground in *The Great God Success* with a story about a journalist, so he added a touch of novelty to the Graustark nonsense by inflicting upon it an American businessman who asserted American democratic principles in the midst of a benighted nobility. It was an inadequate performance, and one in which Phillips took no pride; he never included it among his works. Yet *Her Serene Highness* contained touches and gleams quite vivacious, and so quaint a page as the following:

> [Zweitenbourg] had once been almost a kingdom. It was now shrunk, through the bad political and matrimonial management of the reigning house, to less than two hundred and fifty square miles. But the Zweitenbourgians were proudly patriotic—they disdained mere size; they were all for quality, not quantity. Besides, they were as vague in general geography as the average human being; they thoroughly knew only the internal geography of Zweitenbourg. In their textbooks, the Grand Duchy posed as the central state of civilization. In their school histories, its grand dukes cut a great figure. For example, it was their Grand Duke Godfrey who, slightly assisted by a Prussian general Blucher, won the battle of Waterloo. Wellington comes in for a mere mention, as a sort of "among those present"—"a small force of English under Lord Wellington," so runs the account, "was defeated in the first day's engagement and almost caused the rout of the Grand Duke Godfrey and his allies; but on the second day, after the English had been beaten, and when they were about to run, the Grand Duke and Blucher came up with the main army and Napoleon was overthrown." In the Zweitenbourgian atlases the map of each country was printed on a separate plate, and all are apparently of the same size. And, finally, all Zweitenbourgians knew that their men were the bravest and their women the most beautiful in the world, and that all foreign nations were inhabited by peoples who were ignorant, foolish, and perfidious.
>
> (*Her Serene Highness*, pp. 26–28)

A Woman Ventures, issued in the fall, was better. It told of the plight of a young woman reared in luxury and left on the death of her father with nothing. So far nothing distinguished the plot except Phillips's unblinded explanation of her father's reputation for generosity, which had masked a cold, unthinking self-indulgence. But this was only page one, and what followed was once again new. For the young lady did not encounter romance. Her father's death meant shipwreck. It meant retiring from Washington to a small town in New England. It meant dry rot and stagnation. Several of Phillips's pages shine as clear today as yesterday, for all that some of the elements of choice for women in their search for a base of life may have changed in details if not in essentials:

> Year by year, with a patience as slow and persevering as that of a colony of coral insects, Stoughton developed a small number of youth of both sexes. Year by year the railroads robbed her of her best young men, leaving behind only such as were stupid or sluggard. Year by year the young women found themselves a twelvemonth nearer the fate of the leaves which the frost fails to cut off and disintegrate. For a few there was the alternative of marrying the blighted young men—a desperate adventure in the exchange of single for double or multiple burdens.
>
> Some of the young women rushed about New England, visiting its towns, and finding each town a reproduction of Stoughton. Some went to other cities a visiting, and returned home dazed and baffled. A few bettered themselves in their quest; but more only increased their discontent, or, marrying, regretted the ills they had fled. Those who married away from home about balanced those who were deprived of opportunities to marry, by the girl visitors from other towns, who caught with their new faces and new man-catching tricks the Stoughton eligible-ineligibles.
>
> At twenty a Stoughton girl began to be anxious. At twenty-five, the sickening doubt shot its anguish into her soul. At thirty came despair; and rarely indeed did despair leave. It was fluttered, sometimes, or pretended to be; but, after a few feeble flappings, it roosted again. In Stoughton "society" the old maids outnumbered the married women.
>
> Clearly, there was no chance to marry. Emily might have overcome the timidity of such young men as there were, and might have married almost anyone of them. But her end would have been more remote than ever. It was not marriage in itself that she sought, but release from Stoughton.
>
> (*A Woman Ventures*, pp. 11–12)

Others would tell the complete story of Stoughton, and steep the pen in gall for the work.[17] Phillips had other work to do. He took his Emily to New York and gave her a job on a newspaper. Here Phillips's writing became less sure, more experimental. For what would Emily do? She had to overcome her inbred repugnance for life in the worka-day world. Vanity would make it difficult for her to learn from bad-tasting experience. Men would complicate her plans. Dreiser's Carrie had little sense of life's choices and no cerebral talents for coping with them. Emily was endowed by Phillips with an acute set of stan-dards and concerns, still sketched rather than developed, but indicat-ing the tendencies of Phillips's narrative. Phillips's achievement here was clearly that of a pioneer rather than a fulfilled novelist; *The Price She Paid,* published after his death, would show the difference.

Aside from that, there were awkward and unpersuasive pages in *A Woman Ventures,* as in other of Phillips's work of a more distin-guished order. Moreover, Phillips's style was affected by the sharp differences in place and personnel, so that it ranged from shaky to fully controlled, even in *Susan Lenox,* as will be seen.

A striking example of a marred page in Phillips's *A Woman Ven-tures* involves his use of his Tennessee strike experience earlier noted (see pp. 34, 47), which he had originally reported by rigid journalistic standards. In *A Woman Ventures* he had Emily reporting the event. Phillips concocted a tragic episode as part of the bloody proceedings which was exquisitely sentimental and incredible. It was curious that although Phillips was to be accused of writing "mere journalism," not a few of his weaker fictional projections resulted from his efforts to separate his own style and substance from merely accurate descrip-tion. In time his most successful plots, pages, and books would result from a consummate union of his journalistic grasp and imagination.

Meanwhile something of the pressure of day-to-day journalism did lie on his writing as he labored to establish himself with publica-tions and publishers, as well as dig into his own resources for ideas and treatment. That pressure clipped his thoughts and overhastened his narrative. Though he worked over his fiction, building a backlog of unresolved manuscript, giving it four nights a week, revising and again revising, and although his work developed strength in steady progression, in his first phase of writing his articles overshadowed his fiction.

They took a novel tone, being intensely concerned for Americans and Americana and avoiding old "essay" formulas such as the *Atlan-tic* and *Century* still provided for their leisurely readers, and which Phillips recognized as unsuitable for a more democratic audience ("Great Magazines and Their Editors," p. 309). Sometimes Phillips emphasized the information he was supplying. On other occasions he called attention to an interesting event or institution. In analyzing as a working operation St. George's Church in New York's Stuyvesant Square—a church from which he was to be buried—and explaining its businesslike organization; in describing for *Post* readers "The Millionaires," offering detailed accounts of their expenses, their psychology, their retinues; in discussing such a typical political careerist as David B. Hill, a New York Stalwart, Phillips contributed to a trend of writing which others were also developing, but with less effort to limn what was in some respects a new society. That trend defined heavily what he could say and wished to say. He described the new type of emerging lawyer, whom he would depict in several of his novels, told how Roosevelt had become President, and interviewed Owen Wister, now famous as author of *The Virginian*.

Ida M. Tarbell saw Phillips from the prideful perspective of *McClure's Magazine*, which esteemed itself as committed to fact-finding, though in actuality it developed a middle position on social affairs as directed and contrived as any other. Thus in 1902 Upton Sinclair wrote Lincoln Steffens an "open letter" describing what he deemed "wrong" with the capitalist system which, as an opinion, was a fact like any fact, and which Lincoln Steffens on *McClure's* was eager to publish. However, he petitioned for the article in vain.[18]

Nevertheless, Tarbell's view of Phillips helps to define something of the Progressive effort to enlighten its readers even when persuading them:

> Mr. Phillips always put into his discussions an emotion and an imagination which we did not indulge ourselves much on *McClure's*. The basis of all our work were the documents in the case, and it was the rule of the office that these documents be used for their worth alone. It hampered our style considerably at times, but as a whole we stuck pretty close to the law. I am inclined to think this holding ourselves to the facts in the case as nearly as we could establish them by research, was the reason the public gave us the confidence and respect that it did.

And the following prim conclusion:

> Mr. Phillips was more a novelist than a journalist. He should be judged by the field in which he worked, not by that in which some other people work.[19]

Beveridge was delighted to see Phillips fairly launched, and their personal relations deepened. Beveridge now followed Phillips's writings, as well as Phillips his friend's. Phillips continued to mix praise with caution and even criticism of Bev's style as turgid or otherwise inappropriate to a democratic readership. Later he would more sharply criticize Bev's program. They met in New York and looked forward to further meetings. Beveridge "longed for the sight of [Phillips's] face"; Phillips wanted "a long talk with you (about yourself)." He thanked Beveridge for his "news" about *The Great God Success,* adding: "I admit the authorship now and am writing altogether under my own name—the other scheme was commercially unwise." He sent a Christmas telegram in 1902 to Bev with all good hopes for the coming year. During the following year he continued his watch on his friend's career, urging him to be "careful" about tariffs, Philippines, and trusts: his indirect way of deploring Beveridge's faith in the Republican dogma of Protection, imperialism, and big business.[20]

Late in 1903 Phillips went across to the Continent for a few weeks with his sister Carolyn, "and mighty glad I'll be to rest—if my devil of unrest will let me," Phillips wrote from the Manhattan Club, which he favored at this stage of his career. His living arrangements he now shared with Carolyn, wholly dedicated to his well-being, as she would be later to his memory. A vignette of her, and something of the tone of their conversation he would utilize in his *The Grain of Dust.* Beveridge, who was capable of spelling his friend's name "Grahame," asked Phillips to give his regards to "Miss Frevert."

Phillips lived a surprisingly normal life considering the legends of his unstinted labors which were woven about him. During the day he transacted business and stopped over to newspaper offices, always walking; he developed a fanaticism on the subject of walking, not only for health but in order to see people at eye level. In the evening he might enjoy a visit or a dinner engagement, or the theater, which he followed faithfully. He visited Ida Tarbell's home, and Lincoln Steffens's, among many others, enjoyed a talk with the now aged Carl Schurz, and wrote appreciative notes afterwards.

But whatever else he might have been about, the conclusion of the evening was likely to find him settled to writing chores. It soon got around that he wrote even on shipboard, when he went abroad. It was significant of the dark, disturbed world hidden in the womb of the open, optimistic Progressive era—one which would prefer a Dreiser to a Phillips—that Phillips's ardor and commitment to work made him less a target for admiration than for criticism and even contempt, once he became important enough to have enemies.

8

Success Story

On February 14, 1903 Phillips scored a furor with his *Post* article "The Real Boss of the United States." He named Senator Nelson W. Aldrich of Rhode Island. Reread, it is clear that what excited the readers was Phillips's concept, not his treatment. Phillips was not ready to discuss the subversion of power—Lorimer would not have used his article—only its existence. But what he had to say defied American democratic legends. Lorimer welcomed power, even one-man power; Phillips feared it. His reasons for fearing it would appear elsewhere.

Work like this, though not yet sensational, deepened the public sense of Phillips's presence. References to him appeared more frequently in literary gossip. He wrote a brief one-act play, "A Point of Law," for *Red Book Magazine*, later printed in 1908 along with his full-length play, *The Worth of a Woman*. "A Point of Law" merits a word of its own. It depicted a girl who had innocently become the wife in all except name of a cynical gentleman who loved her but did not care to marry. She traps him in the home of a southern gentleman with antebellum ideals, having learned that in that state a woman who signs a deed becomes the property owner's wife. Colonel Pickett is moved by her tale, shaped as having happened to another woman. He declares he would kill such a scoundrel if he were his own best friend. The "scoundrel" signs a contract along with his apparent wife, and when she then tries to tear up the paper, fearing to lose his love, he prevents her. "You win," he says. "So do I."

Phillips here commits himself not only to fine southern gentlemen "who know only two kinds of women—innocent ones and bad ones [and] two kinds of men—gentlemen and scoundrels." He commits himself also to a social code which needs to be circumvented, rather than broken down. In his lengthier play, *The Worth of a Woman*, he did better ideologically though not in human representation. The remarkable point was that he had an audience to deal with, one firm in the dramatic limitations it put on American playwrights.

It quarreled with but learned from George Bernard Shaw, whose plays were just then invading the American stage, and it learned even more about the sexual aspects of man-woman relations from French dramatists to whom it granted a curious tolerance: French women were not American women. Foolish critics who later noted the work of Shaw and others to implement their derogation of even Phillips's "pioneer" status failed to realize this vital distinction. In the Progressive era American prejudice hamstrung the American playwright and forced him to twist language and presentation to express points, if not art.

Phillips had problems with fictional art, many of which he resolved. His problem with drama was more fundamental. His plays were laboratory artifacts revealing his struggle with the conditions in life he wished to treat.[1]

Meanwhile Phillips's fourth book, which had been serialized in the *Post,* was on the market. Once again, *Golden Fleece* received more attention than it ultimately merited, for reasons which were wholly contemporary. Not only were international marriages and the buying of titles both fascinating Americans and making them uncomfortable, but a species of "Anglomania" was infecting society: "Pink coats and cricket pads. Broad a's and high teas. Canes and the trouser cuffs whose pioneer wearers were taunted with, 'Must be raining today in London!' "[2]

Phillips was to treat the phenomenon of Anglomania in ways which transcended the subject, in one of his most formidable novels. For *Golden Fleece,* which depicted an amiable English Lord coming over to marry money, he adopted a light tone. The novel had interesting facets. It enabled Phillips to send his good-natured Jason to the principal American cities, and so permit Phillips to display his own knowledge of them. It permitted Phillips to distinguish the anglicized American from the rough-hewn western millionaire. Indeed, several scenes in this novel foreshadowed strong scenes in *The Husband's Story* of later vintage. *Golden Fleece* was a success, even appearing in a popular edition, to Phillips's material benefit. It became so patently obsolete that a wise criticism would have concentrated on more modern equivalents, such as the shallowness of "jet set" leaders and their hangers-on, marriages with Greek shipowners, and those who followed their exploits in the press. The French *plus ça change, plus c'est la même chose* was quoted by sophisticates who in literary criticism could have better revealed their grasp of the continuities in history.

Later in the year appeared a Phillips novel of greater moment. *Golden Fleece* had mentioned one Galloway, a millionaire whose story Phillips now told.

> I cannot remember the time when I was not absolutely certain that I would be a millionaire. And I had not been a week in the big whole-sale dry-goods house in Worth Street in which I made my New York start, before I looked around and said to myself: "I shall be sole propri-etor here some day."
> Probably clerks dream the same thing every day in every establish-ment on earth—but I didn't dream; *I knew.*
>
> (*The Master Rogue*, p. 3)

So begins the story of *The Master Rogue*. With a rude, violent pencil—so different from what he had employed in his Lorimer-shackled *Golden Fleece*—Phillips etched out a portrait of a moneymaker. It made a compelling tale, but not because of any emphasis on violent events. Phillips underscored the violence inherent in the solitary lust of any man, and in the home life it created. The pages vibrate with the restless ambition of the financier. Galloway roams, an ignorant man with tremendous will, but with neither dignity nor health.

Beveridge, following his friend's career closely, noted that *The Master Rogue* was infinitely stronger than *Golden Fleece*, but mildly criticized Phillips for having chosen to "state the bitter side of the man of affairs. Yet I can see the excuse for that too. The book has such sincerity, such conviction, and, in short, it smells so thoroughly of the truth."[3] Phillips thanked his friend "for the opinion on Croe-sus. Perhaps I'll work around to great souls after a while. I do the best I can—and keep plugging away."[4] Faulty the book was, if not formless; in outward shape, it was obviously influenced by Lorimer's *Letters from a Self-Made Merchant to His Son*, giving the reverse side of Lorimer's friendly presentation of the magnate's views, a fact which none of Phillips's "radical" critics was acute enough to no-tice. As with *Golden Fleece*, the rude Galloways have passed into history along with the amiable earls. But if energy does not die and is transmuted into other forms of energy, then once again there can be some profit in finding modern equivalents for the prototypical tycoons. Rod Serling's *Patterns* (1957) depicted exhibitions of unfeel-ing power in the business world, which suggested that the impulse Phillips dealt with in *The Master Rogue* had not disappeared from American life.

The Master Rogue established Phillips with the most distinguished of the liberal editors of the time as the most promising of
younger writers since Hamlin Garland. B.O. Flower of the *Arena* foresaw trouble in society and sought a rallying point for Americans determined on evolutionary change. He published the first of his several
articles on Phillips, expressing his hopes for Phillips's progress in
what he deemed "radical" change:

> The early novels and stories of Hamlin Garland, some of the later
> fiction of William Dean Howells, the magnificent romances of the late
> Frank Norris, the thought compelling work of Jack London . . . the
> keen, analytical, faithful and fearless stories of David Graham Phillips,
> instinct with the rugged spirit of democracy, are among the evidences
> of the presence of a realization among our present day novelists, and
> especially of our younger writers, of the high demands which progress
> imposes upon the men of intellect and conscience. . . . [5]

Phillips, interviewed by Flower, was quoted in terms of his creative
intentions:

> I particularly abhor the novels, histories, poems and every work of
> art that attributes to things essentially revolting, as war, tyranny, class
> distinctions, etc., qualities of beauty and charm which they do not in
> themselves possess. I think that the artist should never lose sight of the
> truth that humanity is evolving—is on its way upward, that we must
> look in the past for the germs of the fine and the high which are
> budding in the present and will blossom in the future. In a word, I
> think the novel-writer is under the universal obligation to tell the
> truth, and he should strive to add as little as his human frailties will
> permit to the fog of lies which becloud the path. [6]

Phillips thus seemed to show possibilities of defining an area for
himself which would serve the middle-classes primarily, that which
was creating a socialist party of intelligent and articulate men and
women with roots in social organizations and even in elements of the
working classes. Before the era was over Phillips would be known to
many of them. His belief in well-earned success, however, and in the
rewards of such success separated him from later versions of similar
types who would profess "working class" sympathies which never
interfered with their own hungry search for maximum comfort.

1903 and 1904 were Phillips's great years for article publication.
Thereafter his magazine work dwindled in quantity, and he proved
more selective in subject matter than before. His energies sharpened
to refining his mastery of fiction. He was almost depressingly con-

scious of what he was about. "Perhaps in ten or fifteen years . . . ," he
wrote one of his sisters. "I am still an obscure apprentice who must
work very hard every day. . . . And sometimes I grow weary of having
to work twice as hard as some other people for everything I get."

Only one novel appeared in 1904. *The Cost* was not only a more
difficult book to write, but what became *The Mother Light* anonymously was perplexing him. Undoubtedly *The Plum Tree* was also
engaging his attention, in addition to *The Social Secretary*. Phillips
may have been amused by an editorial comment in *The Critic* which
spoke of him as having left journalism in order to enter the pleasant,
easy, and remunerative career of novel-writing.

The Cost narrated a tragedy attending an early marriage, but it
did more. Its first section leaned heavily on Phillips's recollections of
DePauw. Later incidents in the novel involved politics and stock market drama, and the vagaries of love. The book was not long, it involved many characters briefly, and the action could be but sketchy at
best, as appreciative and generally judicious reviews noted. None of
this interfered with the contemporary pleasure the book gave its numerous readers. At one point Bobbs-Merrill, the Indianapolis publisher, announced that it was meeting orders as fast as possible, but
still needed time to fill them all.[7]

The novel featured an evil genius, John Dumont, and his antago-
nist Hampton Scarborough, patently based on the essential character
of Beveridge as Phillips saw it. In time, Scarborough's awesome integrity could be justly questioned by critics as overdone and without
depth. The difficulty was that they could not see what friendly contemporary critics saw, that Scarborough was only a sketch of what
Phillips aspired to limn. Phillips was well aware that characters must
be credible, but also that mere realism would not serve to highlight
the basic qualities public service required. Later realistic fictional portraits of malfeasant public servants and even presidents failed because
they could not rise above the newspaper accounts on which they were
based. Phillips's Scarborough was inadequate, in *The Cost*, but not
because Phillips did not assess Beveridge adequately.

An incident in the book itself better explains Phillips's novelistic
point of view. Scarborough, a young man working his way through
Battle Field University, did so well as a subscription agent during a
summer's work that he was given the job of training a group of young
men, in this way making himself a sum of money.

He selected a hundred young men and twelve young women, the most intelligent of the five hundred self-supporting students at Battle Field. Pierson, having promised to behave himself, was permitted to attend the first lesson. The scholars for the Scarborough School for Book Agents filled his quarters and overflowed in swarms without the windows and the door. The weather was still cool; but all must hear, and the rooms could barely hold half the brigade.

"I assume that you've read the book," began Scarborough. He was standing at the table with the paraphernalia of a book agent spread upon it. "But you must read it again and again, until you know what's on every page, until you have by heart the passages I'll point out to you." He looked at Drexel—a freshman of twenty-two, with earnest, sleepless eyes and a lofty forehead; in the past winter he had become acquainted with hunger and with that cold which creeps into the room, crawls through the thin covers and closes in, icy as death about the heart. "What do you think of the book, Drexel?"

The young man—he is high in the national administration today—flushed and looked uneasy.

"Speak frankly. I want your candid opinion."

"Well, I must say, Mr. Scarborough, I think it's pretty bad."

"Thank you," said Scarborough; and he glanced around. "Does anybody disagree with Mr. Drexel?"

There was not a murmur. Pierson covered his face to hide a smile at this "jolt" for his friend. In the group round one of the windows a laugh started and spread everywhere except to seven of the twelve young women near Scarborough—they looked frightened.

"I expected Mr. Drexel's answer," began Scarborough. "Before you can sell *Peaks of Progress* each of you must be convinced that it's a book he himself would buy. And I see you've not even read it. You've at most glanced at it with unfriendly eyes. This book is not literature, gentlemen. It is a storehouse of facts. It is an educational work so simply written and so brilliantly. . . . "

Pierson was now no more inclined to smile than were the pupils.

(*The Cost,* pp. 141–43)

Scarborough, as a matter of fact, was in no mood for the enthusiasm he had himself engendered; and after the class was over:

When the two friends were alone, Pierson said, "Do you know, I'm beginning to get a glimpse of you. And I see there isn't anything beyond your reach. You'll get whatever you want."

Scarborough's reply was a sudden look of dejection, an impatient shrug. Then he straightened himself, shook back the obstinate lock of hair from his forehead. . . . "Yes," he said, "because I'm determined to want whatever I get. Good fortune and bad—everything shall be grist for this mill."

(*The Cost,* p. 145)

But there is a more illuminating aspect to the matter, beyond the story. On September 8, 1900 an article by a Robert Shackleton appeared in the *Post* on Beveridge, and Phillips, as his old roommate, was interviewed:

> "I was his roomate [sic] for a year [Phillips said], and probably had better chances of knowing him than most men had. In the first place, his determination to succeed was inflexible. All his wonderful energies were bent to that end. . . .
>
> "One summer vacation towards the end of his course, he became a subscription book canvasser. He did so well that the publishers offered him the agency of the State of Iowa for the next summer. Beveridge began his work characteristically. . . . [He selected his corps and trained it.] First he went through the role of an agent—went through it with exhaustive detail. Then he made his pupils act the same parts while he took the dual role of critic and possible book buyer. He drilled them in classes and privately. *I used to think it was the funniest performance I ever saw* [italics added]. *It was so serious, so deadly serious.*"

The boy Phillips, intellectual and aloof, could afford to see the absurdity in the show. But he had learned that life in crises did not have much dignity; and in novelizing the incident, he conceded to reality what he hoped was its essence. Humor is a sense of proportion, justified or not justified by the value of our actions. Phillips, who had not yet approximated mastery over his pen and purposes, over his thoughts and experiences, had still a way to go before he could imaginatively control his.

1905 was Phillips's year of public triumph. It placed him securely with the reading public and made him all but a best seller. It carried to its crest muckraking, sustained by others, *not* Phillips. Charles Edward Russell, also a fugitive from journalism, set aside his notions about verse and exposed the Beef Trust for *Everybody's*. Samuel Hopkins Adams made his landmark investigation of the patent medicine field for *Collier's*. Thomas W. Lawson, Boston financier, wrote *Frenzied Finance*, a series of articles which shook the financial structure of business and opened it to inquiry. Elsewhere exposures in popular magazines showed heretofore unrealized relations between the law courts, Congress, politics, and above all commerce.

Upton Sinclair, a would-be poet turned socialist, went to Chicago and was overwhelmed by the conditions he observed in the packing plants, the plants Lorimer had festooned with good humor and approval. It was significant of that era that Sinclair did not respond with rhetoric or displays of data, but with fiction. Sick, shocked, he wrote as he was able to write only two or three times in his long life, with the agony of a man who had been hurt. Phillips came upon Sinclair's *The Jungle* running in newspaper form and dashed off a note to the younger man:

> I never expected to read a serial. I am reading "The Jungle" and I should be afraid to tell you how it affects me. It is a great work. I have a feeling that you yourself will be dazed some day by the excitement about it. It is impossible that such power should not be felt. It is so simple, so true, so tragic and so human. It is so eloquent, and yet so exact. I must restrain myself or you may misunderstand.

This was written, Sinclair commented, "while the story was appearing serially in the [socialist] 'Appeal to Reason' and it turned out to be a prophecy."[8]

He never forgot Phillips's generous gesture, one unappreciated by those who imagined him to be sour and unsympathetic, or who knew of his spontaneous good will but found it confusing to their assessment of his work. Phillips himself feared his own tendency toward open-handedness, and, as with Beveridge, took pains to seem as critical and objective as possible.

In February Phillips began serialization in the *Post* of "The Social Secretary," an idea of Lorimer's first proposed to the essayist Charles Macomb Flandrau. That month too was published Phillips's *The Mother Light*, furnishing an extraordinary contrast. "The Social Secretary" was run in magazine form anonymously, probably to pique readers with this purported "diary" of a secretary to a Washington senator's wife. Though technically sounder in form than *The Master Rogue*, it was far less ambitious: "the most lamentable volume of [Phillips's] amazing career," Flandrau thought.[9] Reviewers of the time were less rigid in their estimates, and when the tale appeared in book form with authorship acknowledged, enjoyed the political gossip interspersed with a light love story.

The Mother Light was also issued anonymously, but for other reasons. Here Phillips attempted to express some of his views on the religious searches of his time, with a particular eye on Christian Science. The puzzle in his mind was whether belief affected spirituality, independently of the materialism to which he adhered as necessary to rational living. The results were pallid. Phillips gave little sense of the public passion aroused by religious hopes, or of the character of his major figures. Yet he had labored over his manuscript. And he had somehow persuaded himself that Lorimer—Lorimer!—might be interested in his book, or at least advise him. Possibly the fact that Lorimer's father had been a famous minister influenced his fantastic hopes.

From Paris he wrote Lorimer that he had rewritten "The Light," as he called it, almost entirely. He would not say it was better, but it was different. He regretted that he had not talked to Lorimer about the book before going abroad, for he was sure Lorimer could have offered some "valuable criticism." Lorimer seems to have hastened to propose that the book be issued anonymously—he may have meant, if at all, one of Lorimer's numerous ways for hinting that it was not for the *Post*. Phillips got the hint and himself suggested that it was not.[10]

Aside from such considerations, there seems little to say of the book in this era, since it struck no vein of experience or character portrayal in Phillips. The F.A. Stokes Company, which had published his first books, may have been uncomfortable with the theme. *The Mother Light* was published by D. Appleton and Company. So began Phillips's association with its editor Joseph H. Sears, though Phillips was to have a mutually profitable season with the Bobbs-Merrill people of Indianapolis before he settled down as an Appleton author. A curious detail in *The Mother Light* was the name he gave his chief character, Maida Clafin. He was probably thinking of Victoria Woodhull, a female demagogue who began life in Ohio as Victoria Claflin and had a career of fraud as a "spiritualist" before engaging in profitable "suffragist" and other ventures exploiting the women's cause.

The Mother Light contrasts with Sinclair Lewis's distinguished *Elmer Gantry* (1927), which also probed the activities of religious adventurers, but with a grasp of public psychology and of its dominant figures such as Phillips could not match. Lewis and Phillips had much in common, and the fact that both were concerned for similar artistic goals helps to put the hectic decades between them into perspective. Both were midwesterners. Both created towns, Lewis Gopher Prairie, Phillips St. Christopher (St. X), to symbolize their region's major tendencies. Both were disturbed by changes in social relations which blighted old ways of living without providing satisfactory new ways. It was a sign of the wreckage of American social and psychological continuity that Lewis's *Main Street* (1920) and *Dodsworth* (1929) in particular reminded no one of Phillips's directly comparable novels, *The Hungry Heart* and *The Husband's Story*.[11]

Phillips's most vital articles of the year appeared not in the *Post*—Lorimer may have thought they were "unpleasant"—but in *Cosmopolitan*, and showed an increasing cohesiveness in his thought and expression. "The Delusion of the Race Track," "The Empire of Rothschild," and "The Assassination of a Governor," though disparate subjects, posited a sound social base for human activities, whether serving economic masters or people in the street and at the races. Phillips more than "exposed" the demoralizing nature of horse racing. He explained the calculated roles of its several components: the bookies, the wealthy sports, the bettors. "No one learns save by experience," he wrote; he himself had lost money on horses in his younger and less established New York years.

His history of the House of Rothschild continued his studies of society's tycoons, which included Morgan, Rockefeller, and Morgan's second in command, Beveridge's friend George W. Perkins—pillars of society whom only the flightiest of idealists could afford not to know. It is not quite clear why Phillips could not have placed this article with Lorimer.

Phillips's account of the murder in Kentucky of Governor William Goebel was elaborate. It showed the tragedy as a product of complex social tendencies and personalities. It is as evocative today as it was when published in April of 1905. It seems in its indirect plea for understanding of the American character only a step away from consideration of the meaning of Huey P. Long's assassination in Baton Rouge, Louisiana, on September 8, 1935, and even such other events as the attempted assassination of Governor George C. Wallace in 1972.

In March Bobbs-Merrill published *The Plum Tree*, and with that novel Phillips's public standing was assured. The book was a sensation. It did not sell quite so well as then-current best sellers; but with thousands of copies circulating and receiving comment and serious consideration from the conspicuous men of the land, Phillips's place among them was, for better or worse, established. Bobbs-Merrill advertised the book widely. It solicited comments from members of Congress, mayors, men of affairs. Many of them responded with enthusiasm, including Vice-President Charles W. Fairbanks, the governors of Iowa and Minnesota, Robert M. La Follette, Tom Watson of Georgia, and the famous mayor of Cleveland, Tom Johnson. Beveridge, of course, endorsed the book fulsomely. Senator Chauncey Depew thought *The Plum Tree* "well written and dramatic," with no premonition that Phillips's later writings would link him ignominiously with its theme.

Lengthy reviews of *The Plum Tree* poured in from all over the land. The *New York Times* opined that the book was "sure to raise Mr. Phillips to a very high place among novelists." The sayings of Phillips's main protagonist, Harvey Saylor, were excerpted from the book and circulated to reviewers for reproduction, as revelatory of the thinking of practical politicians. With orders for the book keeping pace with publicity, the publisher had constructed a small artificial tree, with plum-shaped objects bearing dollar signs hanging from branches, and sent it out to booksellers requesting it.[12]

There were a few plaintive responses. Tom Platt of New York, whose hapless thought it had been to bury Theodore Roosevelt in the vice-presidency, now thought that "the book does not give a very accurate portrayal of political conditions, as I have found them." Roosevelt himself turned the pages of the book, but felt inclined only to report privately on it to his friend Owen Wister:

> David Graham Phillips has written a book called *The Plum Tree*. I have only read the first half. In it he portrays all politics as sordid, base and corrupt. Sinclair, the Socialist, has written a book called "The Jungle" about the labor world in Chicago. He portrays the results of the capitalist system in Chicago as on one uniform level of hideous horror. Now there is very much which needs merciless attack both in our politics and in our individual and social life. There is much need for reform; but I do not think the two books in question, though they have been very widely read and are very popular and have produced a great effect, have really produced a healthy effect, simply because, while they set forth many facts which are true, they convey an entirely false impression when they imply that these are the only facts that are true and that the whole life is such as they represent it.[13]

Roosevelt's point was well expressed, but it did not take into account the fact that excessive circumstances required excessive response. Roosevelt himself was being upbraided by old friends of "Goo Goo" days for being excessive, though, as President, he was resisting the tide of change at least as much as he was riding and encouraging it. In addition, Roosevelt did not take into account that he was dealing with fiction. A later commentator, of little cultural quality except as a weathervane, looked back at Roosevelt and Phillips and summed up one general phase of the matter, though as a climax of a doubtful argument:

> Drop Phillips from the history of political fiction, and an element is permanently gone. Although he and [the American Winston] Churchill are alike in their belief in "honest" men . . . Phillips . . . attempted in *The Plum Tree* a far more grandiose theme than the corruption of a single New England state. The Harvey Saylor who shakes the plum tree . . . is a president-maker, nothing less—the brains and power of the majority party. It is as if Phillips wished to expose the entire system at one swoop. . . . Phillips is, of course, far less circumstantial than Churchill, for all his reportorial training and ability.[14]

Chamberlain, unfortunately, could not hold on to the difference between pamphleteering and esthetics, and his comparisons lacked depth. Churchill's *Mr. Crewe's Career* (1908) and such other "political fiction" as Gertrude Atherton's *Senator North* (1900) did little more than capture a sense of grievance from the air and build castles based on traditional novelistic forms. They achieved the fate of mere imitation. Phillips, on the other hand, did more than set a fictional pattern for political analysis based on the whole life of an American—a pattern which would indirectly affect several of the works inspired by the disturbing career of Huey P. Long. Phillips achieved his first successful focus. Without repeating the unanalytical praise bestowed upon *The Plum Tree* by Frank Harris, it can be safely said that if any of Phillips's works of his first period merits reading, it would be *The Plum Tree*.

Phillips was first of all a novelist, a premise upon which critics correctly built their judgments of his work. Unfortunately, they built their "cases" against him on the wrong works. It is as though Henry Miller was judged by his adoration of the works of Marie Corelli.[15]

Phillips was much interested in Harvey Saylor, his idealist turned practical politician, as a personality he had first infused with his own youthful Indiana feelings. His empathy gave a warmth and philosophical tempo to his book which had been lacking in earlier experimental works. *The Plum Tree* was a short novel, when set beside his later works, but it had a soundness of texture which left his earlier writings far behind. It was this fact which gave the book its curious novelette quality, since the happenings described existed only as they molded Saylor's thoughts and saddened his days. His tragedy was that he had a well-founded character, with none of the "mortal sickness of a mind," as Phillips put it with an arresting duplication of A. E. Housman's phrase, such as made Saylor's pawn, President Burbank, ultimately insignificant.

Something should be said for the sophistication of Phillips's contemporaries:

> A good many people are amusing themselves [*Bookman* reported], trying to identify originals of *The Plum Tree*. On dit: President Burbank is McKinley; Senator Hanna is Senator Saylor; Scarborough is Bryan or Beveridge. The author . . . disclaimed all intention of singling out individuals of national fame for praise or pillory, maintaining that his characters are composites.[16]

The story assumed the first person as *The Master Rogue* had done, and *The Social Secretary*, trifling as it was, was doing. Saylor told the story of his rise from nonentity to kingmaker, his "fall" from moral and intelligent young man to Machiavellian. Now could Saylor—or anyone—put such drastic alterations into perspective? And yet there were thousands, perhaps tens of thousands of Americans who, for example, professed themselves "socialists" in their youth and even adulthood, who in later years wholly engaged in the combative economic struggle which could be termed capitalist. Phillips's was a parable which reached far beyond the limits of party politics.

"Harvey Saylor, Swineherd," Phillips called the still astonishing chapter in which the Boss cracked his whip over the party creatures he controlled. Phillips had a political wisdom which reflected dangerous aspects of the political world better than it did novelistic exigencies, a fact which in a better integrated society would have demeaned neither his political ideals nor his creative ambitions. In a society which listened respectfully to both committed ward politicians and devout utopians, his effort to equate the two caused no more than a passing sensation and the establishment in quasi-literary annals of a phrase, "the plum tree." It was just as well.[17]

Flower, reviewing Phillips's books of this period as they appeared, looked forward to something "epic" in the manner of Frank Norris. He was, however, pleased by the appearance of *The Reign of Gilt* in September of that watershed year. Phillips had collected eighteen of his articles, written more or less according to plan, and assembled them into a volume of discourses on democracy and its hazards. Seen together, they inadequately stated his intentions. Their major positive quality was their expression of faith in the American destiny, their demand for justice not generosity, their definition of education as a system breeding citizens who could think for themselves, their hatred of idle women—idle men were incredible in that era, unless they were criminals—and their eagerness to promote equality between the sexes:

The new employment of men in this country includes laundry work, cooking, general house work, nursing, keeping boarding-houses, teaching primary and kindergarten pupils, dressmaking, millinery. . . . Wherever we find a woman plastering, or keeping books, or driving a street car, or managing a store or corporation . . . [it is because she could find nothing more remunerative to do]. And this modern principle wholly ignores sex and looks only at the work to be done and the comparative fitness of the male and female applicants for it.

(The Reign of Gilt, pp. 268–69)

Phillips was thus as modern in his ideal as realistic keeping up with the news and social developments could make him. But his expression of faith took into account too little the actual tempo of events affecting males and females, putting his words closer to piety than to prophecy. Phillips saw the sweatshop controversially, for instance; he saw it as offensive to the American tradition, produced by Old World slave labor conditions, and doomed under American circumstances. The coming decades would in fact wipe out many of the most hideous areas of sweatshop oppression, and even raise debates among intellectuals about the best uses of leisure time for workers and means for reducing their boredom on assembly lines, debates which would have dazed labor leaders of the Progressive era. Nevertheless Phillips's high optimism failed to perceive the hells of industrial warfare which would have to be crossed before such states of society would materialize.

Most interesting was Phillips's quarrel with Thorstein Veblen as author of *The Theory of Business Enterprise* (1904).[18] Phillips evidently did not know Veblen as author of his first book and only masterpiece, the enigmatic *Theory of the Leisure Class* (1899), which mixed satire with compulsive opinions stemming from Veblen's long march as an unemployed intellectual. Phillips made an ironic comment on Veblen's "passionate professional predilection for polysyllables." H.L. Mencken's equally myopic view of Veblen, expressed in his *Prejudices* (1919), was as a pompous ass.

Phillips himself had preceded his passage of arms with Veblen with a number of essays condemning the money crazed, charity ("pauper-making"), and caste; and he had described "plutocracy at home," utilizing such stiff abstract figures as Mr. Multi-Millionaire in his case against plutocracy. But Phillips believed in work and in utilizing machines for work. He had no insight into Veblen's insecure position at the University of Chicago, where his eccentric cerebration at an assistant professor's level and his philanderings were about to

set him adrift as an uncommitted quasi-academic personage and social speculator, admired on general principles by liberals and radicals.

Phillips, reading Veblen on businessmen and business management, saw him as "the courageous spokesman of the majority of the
classes who write and speak; he is putting into scientific formula the
sneer of every snob who professes contempt of business and, indeed,
of all other forms of modern democratic activity" (*The Reign of Gilt*,
p. 163).

Phillips's defense of business, then, proceeded from his belief
that a working capitalism would cleanse itself of its autocratic and
"plutocratic" elements and serve the masses of workers it led. In time
Veblen, who was far from a foe of leaders or the machine, would
conjecture about the viability of a "soviet of engineers" for dominating industrial life—a concept not far from Phillips's, though phrased
in terms outlandish in Phillips's lifetime. Phillips could hope for par-
ity with Veblen in public esteem only if the capitalism he espoused
should find equally modern means for articulating its ideals.

Wrote Phillips in summing up his positive vision of democratic
hopes:

> Through the ages this Common Man has been building like the
> coral insect—silently, secretly, steadily, strongly. History has little to
> say about him or his work, and that little misleading. . . . But the real
> story of the past of the human race as an interpreter and prophet of the
> future is the story of the building of the coral continent founded
> broadly and deeply upon freedom and justice, upon Intelligence and
> Democracy. . . .
>
> Let us read the past aright. Its departed civilizations are not a
> gloomy warning, but a bright promise. If limited intelligence in a
> small class produced such gleams of glory in the black sky of history,
> what a day must be now dawning!
>
> (*The Reign of Gilt*, pp. 294–95)

In October appeared in book form *The Social Secretary*, and yet,
incredibly, another novel, *The Deluge*.[19]

Thomas W. Lawson's series on *Frenzied Finance*, beginning in
July of 1904, was still running in *Everybody's Magazine*. Readers of
Phillips's book would not miss it as in part a commentary on this
vivid, colorful businessman who was making public some of his own
secrets and those of his highly placed financial colleagues. Lawson's
series is a matter of history, and Phillips's novel takes its place in his

own developing career as having characteristics which are barely dependent for interest on the circumstances from which it took off.

Of his lesser books, *The Deluge* was Phillips's last to employ the first person. The elements which composed it were similar to those of *The Cost*, except that *The Deluge* scarcely touched on politics and gave less of an impression of being a potpourri. *The Deluge* lacked something of the relative depth provided by Harvey Saylor's musings in *The Plum Tree*, but in its place substituted a new element, one which critics noticed as they passed the book in review—a sense of time and movement, of flash and clamor as from the very streets of New York. Phillips evidently wrote the tale rapidly out of his feeling for the character of Lawson, named "Blacklock" in his tale. It was a rough, powerful slag of words and symbols, any page of which serves to illustrate Phillips's free sweep of expression:

> Some one has written: "It was a great day for fools when modesty was made a virtue." I heartily subscribe to that. Life means action; action means self-assertion; self-assertion rouses all the small, colorless people to the only sort of action of which they are capable—to sneering at the doer as egotistical, vain, conceited, bumptious, and the like. So be it! I have an individuality, aggressive, restless, and, like all such individualities, necessarily in the lime-light; I have from the beginning lost no opportunity to impress that individuality upon my time. Let those who have nothing to advertise, and those less courageous and less successful than I at advertisement, jeer and spit. I ignore them. I make no apologies for egotism. I think, when my readers have finished, they will demand none. They will see that I had work to do, and that I did it in the only way an intelligent man ever tries to do his work—his own way, the way natural to him!
>
> (*The Deluge*, pp. 2–3)

It was such writing as this which often made, and no doubt can still make readers resentful of Phillips, and to some extent properly. He challenged them, rather than solicit their patronage. Fearful of failure in himself, hating it in general, he adopted the tactic of scorn rather than compassion. In a society of gamblers, such as the stock market world represented in his time, the approach made sense to a degree: readers were well warned to be in fighting trim in order to survive. But as society became more interdependent, and so subject to conditions they could scarcely understand, let alone control, the policy of exhortation became less relevant and effective.

To be sure, Phillips was portraying the Lawson type, rather than endorsing it; and, for that matter, Lawson was himself to be forgotten in time, despite his genuine services to a changing society. What made *The Deluge* a lesser work, despite its high readability and astounding prediction of the Panic of 1907, was the imbalance created by the figure of Blacklock made tall at the expense of the circles and personalities among whom he moved. Blacklock lectures the reader overmuch at the expense of the events which are determining his career and the careers of all about him. As he inveighs against the sharks of Wall Street who are manipulating the finances of hundreds of thousands of little people, we cannot but recall that he himself has made his millions where others have lost their hundreds, and that in fighting for himself as he insists all must, he has necessarily ignored the rights and the will of others. His scorn of thieves and betrayers, therefore, loses much if not all of its capacity to move us. It impugns his vision of himself as an active man in society, as distinguished from parasites of the leisure class, among whom is a woman whose love he seeks. And it reduces interest in his love affair—something to which, presumably, he solicited our attention. Phillips had a keen grasp of the stock market and its tempests, but the deep flaws in character assessment, taken seriously rather than as adjuncts to a tale of finance, drained them of ultimate vitality.

An interesting review in Albert Shaw's antiseptic *Review of Reviews* brought up a point more relevant to Phillips's later *The Fashionable Adventures of Joshua Craig,* but it helps to indicate the human vibrations which were operating in the midst of social and political sensations. Edith Wharton's *The House of Mirth* was a novelistic sensation of 1905. It told of a gently raised woman who, thanks to her character and conditions, is unmarried and subject to the merciless assessment of high society. The marriage aspect of *The Deluge* was but half the novel, but Shaw's reviewer, who probably knew little of finance, was moved by *The Deluge* to a terse comment:

> *The Deluge* as containing a situation analogous to that of Lily Bart and one of her prospective husbands [sic]. . . . The palpable coarseness, the repellent obtrusion, of a blatant, unscrupulous upstart, Mrs. Wharton paints in their real aspect, Mr. Phillips, on the other hand, attempting to produce a picture of great moral strength with these same colors. No wonder he fails![20]

How much assertive boors deserved of society, time would tell. Phillips's view of a working society was another matter. Frank Harris, as an admirer of a Phillips he did not know personally, seized on a helpful point in arguing that Phillips was at his best in working with mundane scenes of middle class living and aspiration. In such scenes, which increasingly succeeded earlier scenes of financial and political crisis—indeed, they all but disappear in his matured writings—he could concentrate on the drama of interrelationship rather than that of clashes in the market place.[21] Phillips had such intimations himself in this novel of financial ruin and resurrection. As he has Blacklord say: "Take a cross-section of life anywhere, and you have a tangled interweaving of the action and reaction of men upon men, of women upon women, and of men and women upon one another" (*The Deluge*, p. 3).

Later he has a policeman respond to Blacklock's query about "this business of living":

> "I'll tell you, Mr. Blacklock. . . . I used to fuss and fret a good deal about it. But I don't any more. I've got a house up in the Bronx, and a bit of land round it. And there's Mrs. Mulholland and four little Mulhollands and me—that's my country and my party and my religion. The rest is off my beat, and I don't give a damn for it. I don't care which fakir gets to be president, or which swindler gets to be rich. Everything works out somehow, and the best any man can do is to mind his own business.
>
> (*The Deluge*, p. 465)

Blacklock, in personal misery, feels like laughing aloud that he should envy a policeman his potato patch and his fat wife and four brats, but at the novel's end he recommends Mulholland's philosophy to the reader. It was not Phillips's last word on the subject, but he was hard at work on others.

9

Fiction and the Senate Blast

Phillips's astounding coup of 1906 is now so well established in history as a classic as to need here less attention paid to the often irrational comment which passed for judgment upon him, not only by patent conservatives resentful of his radicalism, but by such presumed Progressive associates as Mark Sullivan of *Collier's*, and later by the forthright communist Granville Hicks. No fewer than three book printings of "The Treason of the Senate" attested to its durable qualities, though it was buried half a century following publication. The last such printing included a full historical analysis of attendant circumstances and results. The present author has treated the series twice in historical contexts. It remains here only to be seen in association with Phillips's literary career and personal growth.

Phillips did not seek the assignment; it sought him until he agreed to accept it on his own terms, terms he largely, though not entirely, was able to maintain. Charles Edward Russell claimed credit for the original idea of attacking in a popular magazine the Senate as composed of stipendiaries of major corporations, though the idea itself had been much in the radical air. Russell seems to have spelled out the project not only to John O'Hara Cosgrave of *Everybody's,* made great by Tom Lawson's *Frenzied Finance* series—*Everybody's* turned it down as too risky—but also to Bailey Millard, discoverer of Edwin Markham's "The Man with the Hoe," and now brought East from California by Hearst to edit his newly acquired *Cosmopolitan Magazine.* Russell was to have done the series himself, but he was commissioned by *Everybody's* to go around the world seeking solutions to America's social ills, and another had to be found for the work.

Millard had not yet met Phillips, but he had read and admired and written in praise of *The Cost* and *The Plum Tree,* and he now approached Phillips with his invitation to do the series.

"But I am up to my neck in fiction," Phillips objected. "I don't intend to write any more articles. I don't want to be known as an article writer, anyway—what I want the public to know me for is a novelist. Why don't you get William Allen White or some of those fellows to do it for you?"[1]

White refused, but what he could have done with the theme is not beyond conjecture, in view of his many writings of the time and after. White had a David Harum touch of wisdom, a homely wit, and a sincere hatred of patent cruelty and greed. All this hid during the Progressive era his lack of insight into the processes which were forming Progressive measures while at the same time disintegrating them for the coming generation. White's "Treason of the Senate," had it been done, would have been made up of tales of individual senators selling their authority to special interests for fees or political support, cases involving insurance, oil, meat processing, and other fields showing the laxness of government and the connivance of senators. But to have treated the senators *themselves* as agents of malfeasance in office required an approach which would distinguish the author from a Sinclair or a Tarbell.

White lacked the wherewithal to concentrate on the conditions of affluence and authority which had permitted the Senate to become not merely conservative, which it had always been and had been intended to be, but subservient to industrial interests which had congealed power without attendant responsibility. Earlier Senates had wielded power aligned with programs affecting banking, territorial administration, regulations of other fields of government, and relations with the British, the Mexicans, and the Canadians. Such duties had fashioned senators of the stature of Henry Clay, Andrew Johnson, and George F. Hoar, guardians of the public weal, or at least its will. The state of the Senate in 1905 could be measured by the contempt it as a body accorded its new member, Robert M. La Follette of Wisconsin, whose Progressive crusade for attention and laws within that body became legendary.

That the Senate required a new structure, a new relationship to the people it was supposed to represent, was all but a public scandal. The problem was to find some approach which could tear it away from its routine habits and expectations and implant it in modern social soil.

White could have provided moral indignation and invective without difficulty. What he did not know how to do was to draw portraits of the senatorial products of the system wherein state assemblies, subject to all the intrigue of state political machines, nominated and voted on favored candidates and so foisted them on the nation as a whole. What White could not do was persuade a national audience of readers that by its very undemocratic nature the system was inadequate for its mission: to provide the leeway, the popular force to mold senators not bound to local leaders and promises, or at least to divide their allegiance with others outside their tight political combines.

White saw the senators as good or bad, or as sometimes good and bad, or, again, as wholly bad. The steady examination of backgrounds, personal development, individual and social influences over which Phillips brooded was beyond White's talents. His own novels were successful enough to make him appear a fit contemporary to Phillips; and, in fact, those novels responded to a perishable aspect of Phillips's outlook, as will appear in the discussion of Phillips's *The Second Generation*. White's perspective included a broad streak of sentimentality which exploited cynical actions only as a foil to unmotivated evidence that God ruled after all, and that justice compelled men even after they had succumbed to weakness. Although Phillips rarely descended, even at his worst, to White's bathos—White was capable of supernatural visions for his "good" people—and never used irrelevant wit as did White to cover weak spaces in his story terrain, Phillips's faith in hard work and its inevitable triumph did appear to put him in a camp with the hearty Kansan.

White's circumstantiality even made such a novel as his *A Certain Rich Man* (1909) seem more full-bodied than, for example, Phillips's *The Cost*.[2] The key to such a comparison lies in the fact that *The Cost*, with all its weaknesses, had a texture and purpose such as White could not esthetically fathom, and that Phillips could not in that apprentice work consummate. As earlier indicated, *The Cost* was no more than a sketch, momentarily successful beyond its deserts, which full-blown would have added up to a tale with premises of social goals and women's roles which White could not psychically comprehend. Phillips aspired to portray women with bodies and independent desires; White was satisfied, and satisfied his ephemeral legions of readers, with female angels and other stereotypes. Phillips sought to penetrate social conditions and social evils he saw some industrialists and politicians as actively abetting. White saw their misdeeds as no more than deviations from the eternal verities of life. Phillips, in *The Cost*, attempted unsuccessfully to utilize symbols of righteousness and evil as literary devices, as Norris in *The Octopus* and *The Pit*; it is likely he had these in mind as he experimentally wrote. White had no inkling of the meaning of symbols in fictional contours. He had his Kansas memories and he had his convictions. These made him a good companion to others like himself, including Phillips. They did not make White the equal of Phillips in the task he was asked to assume.

Millard appealed to Phillips's social conscience and he, "up to my neck" in fiction, reluctantly promised to consider the proposition: "As to the Senate series I don't know what to say. I'm so tied up for the next few months that I don't see how I can do it. The subject is a good one and would attract attention. But the work would be exclusive of all my other work and would require a great deal of toiling terribly."

Phillips named a "high price" intended to discourage Millard, but to Phillips's dismay Millard accepted and he was committed. Phillips was provided with assistants, his own brother Harrison, then a Denver newspaperman, and the socialist grubber Gustavus Myers. Phillips himself went to Washington to hunt up senators and otherwise develop his program and materials. Many rumors circulated respecting his work in those agitated months, one being that Beveridge had provided him with some of his most telling points. The likelihood is that Beveridge helped little, since he was partisan to his fellow senators and found the basic idea of a "treason" distasteful. However, some of Phillips's more novel revelations were said to have been suggested by senators eager to throw off the "yoke" which limited their services.

Phillips's first paper, on the New York senator Chauncey Depew, was his usual "curious manuscript": typewritten, then practically rewritten in pencil. There was more scribbled matter in the painstakingly altered passages than was typewritten. Phillips urged Millard not to read it till it was set up. Involved in the reading too was Hearst himself. Mrs. Fremont Older, wife of the crusading journalist, in her partisan study of Hearst portrayed him as judicious in editorial comment, on the information of George von d'Utassy of *Cosmopolitan*, and as much admired by Phillips. It was on such meager gossip and allegation that Mark Sullivan, for example, felt free to maliciously describe Phillips as "a Hearst man."

But Phillips seems to have written as he pleased, and to have fought the editorial blue pencil consistently:

> Phillips, as I knew only too well [Gustavus Myers recalled] did not fully have a free hand. The facts that I turned in, he, in all honesty, used—in his own way, of course,—sparing no Senator who deserved condemnation. But he found himself on several occasions called upon to conform to the instructions of Hearst or his business management. Hearst, then deeply and personally in Washington politics, had his predilections or aims, pro and con. I was so indignant at one flagrant suppression that I took it upon myself to expose it at the time. Phillips had not done so, and I considered that the public had a right to know. Perhaps I was overzealous in doing this over Phillips' head, but somehow I have never regretted it.[3]

But it was Millard, working between Phillips and Hearst, who bore the brunt of the former's displeasure over the pressures he felt:

> David Graham had no great admiration for Hearst, though he did admire his money of which he received a considerable sum first and last. . . . When Hearst insisted on cutting out what his lawyer said was libelous matter, Phillips was furious. No, he didn't have any great love for W.R.H. If he had, he never expressed it in my presence.[4]

Phillips was no "Hearst man." Yet it is always worthwhile to recall that there were many Hearsts, whose combinations of "radical" and grossly reactionary thought reflected the potential of the great American public. The Hearst who interested Phillips was the one who permitted his work to pass or who stymied its publication. It is interesting that Phillips manifested an assertiveness in this venture which appears nowhere in his correspondence with Lorimer. Phillips understood that Lorimer operated on the level of sensibility, which had to be accepted or rejected. Phillips had written his Aldrich essay for Lorimer under wraps. The Phillips Hearst saw was the inheritor of Populist wrath and demands who took seriously the democratic avowals which studded the Hearst papers. Phillips protested the cuts made in his work. He upbraided Millard for them and threatened to withdraw from the whole arrangement. "Maybe I am intemperate," he said. "But it's enough to make anybody intemperate when he considers what is being done by those fellows in the Senate."

The sensation which Phillips's first article, published in March of 1906, created—an article which exposed Chauncey Depew as a calculated, long-term contriver, though he was normally pictured as a good-natured and felicitous after-dinner speaker—has been many times noted. It differed from routine and often useful exposure in drawing a memorable portrait of talent gone astray; it was *The Master Rogue* made real. Readers responded to the portraiture, and to the machinery by which the Senate was controlled, which Phillips proceeded to describe. He once again urged Millard not to attempt to read his second article until it had been set up. He also explained why he had run over his allotted space:

> I had to choose between a weak article and a long one. Aldrich is the boss of the Senate, and to show him and his system took space. I am worried because the article is longer than you wanted, but I don't see how so important a thing as the central mechanism of the treason can be dealt with piece-meal or slightingly. I think, too, that most of my points are new or new statements of familiar but little understood matters.

"The treason" had become close and real to Phillips, and his careful fitting of pieces made a vivid impression on readers across the country which was to affect the movement which in 1913 added the Seventeenth Amendment to the Constitution, providing for the direct election of senators. The strategic achievement of Phillips was to plot the workings of senators through personalities. On one side was Aldrich, operating through his majority party and committee heads. On the other was Arthur Pue Gorman, Democrat, "the left arm" of Senate leadership, and as dedicated as Aldrich to the will of the corporations. Phillips coined the term "the Interests" to describe the true constituency of the Senate, a term destined to endure.

Month after month the articles appeared, exciting increased interest and concern, the flood of letters from readers warming to the editor's heart. Each article was headed by the same solemn quotation from the Constitution (Article III, section 3): "Treason against the United States shall consist only in levying war against them, or in *adhering to their enemies, giving them aid and comfort.*" *Cosmopolitan*'s circulation boomed in response to the series; in the April issue it was announced that 450,000 copies of the magazine had been sold, and reprints of Phillips's articles carried his message much further. Endorsements of it poured into the magazine's offices from all parts of the country. At that moment in time Phillips stood as clearly in the public view as a personality and as a creed as he ever would in life. The sentiments he voiced as he passed key senators in review were those which had haunted the public since the power of railroads and monopolies had become manifest.

The Senate, Phillips had asserted in his opening blast,

> is the eager, resourceful, indefatigable agent of interests as hostile to
> the American people as any invading army could be, and vastly more
> dangerous: interests that manipulate the prosperity produced by all, so
> that it heaps up riches for the few; interests whose growth and power
> can only mean the degradation of the people, of the educated into
> sycophants, of the masses toward serfdom.
>
> ("The Treason of the Senate," p. 6)

If such did not occur it was not because of some libertarian element
within the Senate or its commercial peers, but because of the labors,
partly self-interested, partly idealistic, of such protagonists as Phillips
and their empathetic readers. They did not express their will in a
benign setting. Phillips received threats of assassination, which he
learned tragically to ignore; he was censured in the conservative publications; and his name was brought up for abuse on the floor of the
Senate itself.[5] Beveridge was unhappy about the series and published
an article defending the Senate which Phillips took personally. "I
have read your scream on the Senate," he wrote, "and I'll try to
answer it in two or three months. You and [Benjamin R.] Tillman and
LaFollette [sic] might at least refrain from defending the indefensible.
But after all, that is your business, not mine."[6]

In time he answered the question in the back of many minds.
Would he spare Beveridge in his examination? His account of the
"Beveridge" meat-inspection bill—product of the great pure-food
fight of that period—was thorough. It did not impugn Beveridge's
intentions. It did by indirection criticize him for submitting to compromise solutions which did not solve the problem of security in
meat production. Retrospectively, Beveridge was at least as right as
Phillips. The public did not want domination of the meat industry. It
was satisfied with regulation. And a regulation which would have
totally enforced purity in meat or any other business was beyond the
free enterprise tenets of the Progressive and later generations.

Phillips was happier with Beveridge's fight for a child labor law:

> I cannot tell you how delighted I am about that bill. It is making, I
> think, the impression it deserves to make, and I sincerely hope that
> you will push it for all there is in it every way. I wish you could make
> a big speech on it before anybody else gets a chance. That's the kind of
> thing I like to see your name associated with. It is the best thing you
> have done since you have been in the senate, and I do not say this
> because of my personal interest in reforms of various kinds, but from
> the standpoint of real practical politics.[7]

Phillips's judgments were far from infallible—for example, there was to be no child-labor law in that generation—and in the context of a reform wave it was possible for him to set expectations higher than human nature could normally bear. What was strategic was his will to betterment in civic life and his desire to contribute to such a goal. As he wrote Beveridge, who seems to have been concerned that Phillips might be betrayed by the mercurial Hearst:

> The only possibility of trouble would come from the other side over which I have no control. I don't mind telling you that I would even make sacrifices in order to carry the thing to some sort of a decent finish. However, I don't think sacrifices will be necessary, as Mr. Hearst has shown every disposition to leave me entirely alone.[8]

It is not clear how smoothly this situation progressed. Roosevelt had long since given his "muckrake" speech, which conservatives under pressure from reformers had hailed as a turning point in what they saw as an assault by irresponsible writers on all law and public order. Phillips had been deeply offended by the Roosevelt declaration, which by general agreement was seen as aimed directly at himself, and as making more difficult the task of reforming the Senate. He was unmoved by Beveridge's belief that the speech was an "emphatic endorsement of everything that you people are writing."[9] And when Roosevelt, who sought consistently to propitiate anybody who was anybody, sent emissaries to Phillips asking that he visit the White House, Phillips refused. Roosevelt finally sent Samuel Blythe, a favorite *Post* writer and Phillips's friend, to urge him to come. Phillips agreed, and made a better impression on Roosevelt as a personality than he had as a writer.

Such was the high point of Phillips's public career as commentator and activist. He had maintained the role as a duty, and it had inadvertently blurred to some extent his purposes and ambitions as a chronicler of American life and habits. His novelist's imagination had contributed to public service, but it was with the novel itself he hoped to reach his core reader. "The Treason of the Senate" marked a dividing line between the Phillips who had toiled six years to discover his best themes for self-expression and the means he might employ for portraying the lives and relations of people as he had known them and as they had interested him. In contemporary terms, Phillips was a full success: somewhat quarrelsome and hard to please, critical of the going establishment in life and politics, and exuding restlessness rather than the inner peace and optimism in the well-regarded writings of such an author as the American Winston Churchill.

What Phillips planned to do was to turn from the figures of state and to examine the individual not as politician, businessman, or journalist, but as man, as woman. In a sense, that was what Dreiser had undertaken to do from his own beginnings in 1900. Phillips had come to the same point after having worked his way through the experiences attending his making a place in the world. His men and women would be of different capacities from those fancied by Dreiser, not drifters plagued by lusts and feeble goals, but, for better or worse, people of affairs with whom others had to cope, whether they would or not.

With so much done, and so much in preparation, it is all but shocking to pick up Phillips's novelette *The Fortune Hunter*, published in May of 1906 while "The Treason of the Senate" was in full swing. It was a dashed-off thing Phillips evidently could do nothing more with and gave to Bobbs-Merrill in order to rid his desk of it, and possibly in order to have his fiction before readers who were bemused by his expository prose.[10]

And yet Phillips's impulse, in *The Fortune Hunter*, had been generous, to salute the people who lived on Avenue A in New York as constituting part of "the real New York—the three and a half million who work and play hard and live plainly and without pretense." The book was vivid and informed, and gave Phillips a chance to use the odds and ends of the German language and lore from his days as a journalist and from his travels abroad. It was nevertheless an inconsequential performance, as Phillips knew; as with *Her Serene Highness*, he did not list it among his works, when they came to be listed in later volumes.

It was not that the subject of simple people and their honest girl, briefly befuddled by a pretentious "ham" actor and a cheat, did not inspire Phillips. He sincerely respected and was even enthusiastic about the "common people" who, he believed, produced everything of art, industry, and politics which was important. And he was, if anything, fixed on the subject of hard work and the contemptible nature of social parasites. *The Fortune Hunter* failed because the theme aroused the fictional rhetoric in him and caused him to substi-

tute class clichés for individual motivations. The middle class living
its simple, healthy, and, yes, humdrum lives gave him no focus for his
novelistic work. His Hildas and Feuersteins and Ottos were people in
their own right, no doubt, but they had no story for him to tell.

Phillips needed to touch American life at critical points, its point
of manipulation, as with Harvey Saylor, of aspiration, as with Scarborough. Even these had given him no deep eloquence. He needed to let
himself loose on what most interested him: the private lives of the
conspicuous characters on the American scene, those who got into the
news, of whom readers dreamed, and dreamed of emulating.

There is no need to seek a happy phrase or paragraph in *The
Fortune Hunter*: the book is safely consigned to oblivion. More interesting was the friendly comment in *Bookman*, in October of 1906, by
Harry Thurston Peck, himself a cultural meteor and tragic figure of
the era:

> Phillips tantalizes us with the richness of his material and pro-
> vokes us by the comparatively meagre use that he has made of it. Here
> is the real essence of a genuinely New York novel. To what marvelous
> ends Balzac would have employed it all! For that matter, what a de-
> lightful and satisfying performance Mr. Phillips could have achieved
> had he cared to do it! However, let us not grumble. *The Fortune Seeker*
> [sic] is good, very good.[11]

In January of 1907 appeared another of Phillips's novels, marking the
true dividing line between his past as a novelist and his future. It
requires a distinct judgment consigning it to Phillips's past as part of
his experimental and apprentice period, because it seems, on the face
of it, to be a mature work, because it sold well and was well received,
and because it was maintained by Phillips's new publisher, D. Appleton and Company, in popular editions even after his death.

It was also a book Phillips had looked forward with some emotion
to writing, as he fashioned plots and implemented them with characters and events. As he had written one of his sisters, several years
before: "I'm going to write a story and put father in it within the next
two years. I have cast about many times for some way of presenting
my view of him and his life, and I've about decided that the best way
is through a fiction story."[12]

Phillips was always conscious of the technical aspects of his craft
even while he worded his projects as unpretentiously as possible.
Novel writing, he said, was a matter of trying to think of things to
write about and getting them down in the best form possible. He read

often in the lengthy eighteenth-century novel-in-letters *Pamela,* by Samuel Richardson, saying it contained an endless number of ideas for stories and situations. Phillips followed the careers of his books and, for example, showed appreciation of Bobbs-Merrill's good management of his early work it published.

As a result, he seized on a variety of themes as widely separated as *The Fortune Hunter* and this dream of a novel idealizing his father, all of which forced him to juxtapose people and circumstances in his mind for good esthetic results or ill. All Phillips's early fiction, even some which, like *Her Serene Highness,* did not suit his talents at all, provided passages and pages illustrating his successful fictional statements and others which fell into traps of bathos or absurdity. *The Second Generation* was a particular challenge to him, for he felt compelled to pay his debt to his midwestern upbringing, despite all the shockingly different scenes he had witnessed on his road to becoming a New Yorker. He was unable, therefore, to think of the novel in any but personal terms, which suffused his memories and family loves. The result was paradoxical: a commercial and popular-critical success, a severe artistic failure.

Phillips's intention was to portray Hiram Ranger as an ideal workman, a master cooper and miller who, with another young midwesterner, Charles Whitney, had grown rich in a business employing 700 workers. But Whitney became the financier of the two, operating out of Chicago, adept at exploiting businesses and men; Hiram remained a worker among his Indiana employees, dispensing justice and filling the hours with honest labor. Their wives comported with their characters, one shallow, the other generous and maternal. Their children—each family equally endowed with a young man and young woman—seemed equally, at the book's beginnings, "spoiled" by eastern snobberies and temptations.

One cannot ask a novelist why he did not write Booth Tarkington's *The Magnificent Ambersons* (1918) which, for all its fundamental faults, reflected some semblance of actual Indiana life and social contrasts, and did not entirely shame the Pulitzer Prize it was awarded. Phillips was somehow unable to write of his father's actual life as banker and citizen; perhaps his intense sense of privacy, as well as his remoteness from youthful scenes and impulses, deflected his imagination from the realities he had witnessed and led him to set up a morality play intended to distinguish virtue from vice. *The Second Generation* gives a measure of the compulsions he was fulfilling through his manuscript, forcing him to revive earlier feelings separated from their material circumstances. The novel was not a portrait of the midwest, and scholarship was right, as in Herron's *The Small Town in American Literature,* to pass it by.

The Second Generation surveyed the distance Phillips had traveled from his roots. The space between him and his protagonists was chasm-wide. Phillips built a setting of mill and home almost Edenlike in its serenity. He brought back Hiram Ranger's son Arthur from Harvard in a dude's clothing, smoking cigarettes in public and sporting horses in tandem; he described his daughter Adelaide with a pet monkey, and the two youths engaged to marry the Whitney children, the cynic Ross and the spiritual hypocrite Janet.

It is unnecessary to go on with the narrative, and more profitable to examine its elements, which affect every part of the story. A dying Hiram Ranger disinherits his children in order to stop their descent from democratic ways. The Whitneys jilt them. They make new alliances, Adelaide with the splendid young workman Dory Hargrave, Arthur with the fine young daughter of the crotchety Dr. Schulze. It is incredible, but apparently true that Phillips did not notice that much which he praised in the novel he did not himself in life endorse. The same was true of much which he scorned. Harvard was explicitly condemned as dominated by snobs and as the maker of snobs. But Princeton, which Phillips loved, was probably as capable of encouraging class distinctions as Harvard or any of the other elite institutions.[13]

Hiram wears work clothes and disapproves of his son's stylish garments, but no one was more fastidious about clothing than Phillips himself. No one smoked more cigarettes than he did, who made cigarettes a symbol of effeteness in Arthur. Phillips implanted distinctions throughout his book intended to reveal snobberies and insincerities in clothing, deportment, ambitions, and human relations. But if the ideals he had derived from his parents and his early environment were to be modernized and made fit for use in 1907, Phillips said little here—he said much in succeeding novels—to enable an inquiring reader to perceive differences between substance and tinsel.

A typical chapter depicting everything Phillips rationally opposed, but to which he emotionally succumbed, was "Man and Gentleman." It contrasted Lorry Tague, a master workman in the mills, with Arden Wilmot, a worthless drunkard from a decayed aristocratic family whose sister Estelle had "disgraced" it by becoming an independent milliner, and who loved Lorry. Arden, as a "gentleman," feels it necessary to kill "the fellow" for insulting his sister by loving her in return. The murder lets loose a whirlwind of public indignation, hazily described, which leads to his lynching. Phillips's reborn Adelaide rouses the blood lust of the mob with her denunciations of the degenerate Arden. She then tries to quell its fury with her cry: "Let him alone! Don't touch the creature! He'll only foul your hands"—a strangely indirect compliment to the mob. But it has its way, as Phillips intellectually would have preferred that it did not. There are exquisitely sentimental touches respecting the "beauty" of the honest, dead workman and of his distraught love which would daunt the most undiscriminating admirer of Phillips.

The Second Generation contained numerous shrewd observations throughout, and such passages as that respecting Simeon, Adelaide's monkey, which transcend the book's infirmities. Unfortunately, there was enough miasmic regard for old myths in the reading public of the Progressive era and after to draw approval to the book and so muddle critics of a later generation. Phillips's own generation was less peremptory in its judgment of his development, but its superficial accuracy suffered from a lack of depth. One reviewer spoke for many in good-naturedly affirming that "the story 'works out' well, and though it is made to sustain the theory of the writer it does so in a very natural and stimulating manner."[14]

For Phillips's maturing craft, *The Second Generation* did little. A rejuvenated Arthur Ranger, turned into a true successor to his dead father, makes the mills a utopia of fulfilled workers contributing to society's wants. His father's money, diverted from him and his sister, builds a great local university. It has on its campus a colossal statue of Hiram Ranger. For the woman's equality theme which so unflaggingly troubled Phillips and haunted the manuscript pages and ideas of "Susan Lenox" on which he continuously worked, *The Second Generation* did little. Phillips praises the art of homemaking. He approves women preparing for serious roles in the world as tradespeople, as doctors, as architects. What he did not probe here to any degree were the enigmas of sex as he was doing in his bolder and intrinsically more committed fiction. For *The Second Generation,* the solution to sex was marriage. Later novels would be complicated by divorce, secret liaisons, the mysteries of affinity, and prostitution.

Technically, the novel rationalized some of the problems of Phillips's earlier books. It provided his largest canvas to date and entwined plots and personalities in greater complexity than before. It said a final word on some of Phillips's sketched characters, notably Scarborough. It created St. X, his midwestern city, in which he would set most scenes of his fiction other than New York. Janet, who married a title, was a sketch of what became Edna Loring in *The Husband's Story*. Phillips permitted Dr. Schulze to orate against the weak and wandering human race, abusing it for its own good: a spiritual equivalent of one facet of Phillips's own personality. Phillips hastened on to new works and to new enterprises; and his reader was wise to move on with him.

Symbolic of change was Phillips's leaving Bobbs-Merrill as publisher, a link with Indiana. Their relations had been cordial and mutually satisfying. The success of *The Plum Tree* was a kind of reprimand to Phillips's fears for the book. It should sell, he thought, if Bobbs-Merrill could induce the men to read it. "There is little hope of winning the women to it." The men at least had. By 1908 he was ready to make final arrangements with Bobbs-Merrill giving him full rights, "the money value of the books [being] about exhausted."[15] Appleton, when it began to issue Phillips's books in uniform binding and format, drew another line between Phillips's past and present.

10

Harvest

For the March 1907 issue of *Book News Monthly* Phillips wrote a sardonic article, "The Novelist—Theoretically Speaking," in which he observed: "As all the world knows, every laborer is worthy of his hire but the literary laborer." His irony, like so much else that he did, would be wasted on a later generation made up of a vastly larger percentage of college graduates and presumed readers than his, who identified literary labor with other forms of labor, and who had no need for Phillips's appeal that it be respected in its democratic expression. There was, to be sure, a question of equality incorporated in his assertion, and here Phillips's scorn of fancy writing and sentimental readers betrayed him. The dross of his generation would be superseded by other dross. But the lack of a responsible critical establishment, one able to relate the past to the present and so to assess rationally the literary accomplishments of the Progressive era, would leave them at the mercy of changing times and of critics partial to other à la mode cultural ideals.

In the latter part of the year Phillips issued *Light Fingered Gentry*, and Beveridge, having read it, wrote: "David Graham Phillips is the master novelist of America today." He accurately felt the swelling power and control which the book exuded, and knew that his tireless and restless friend had finally achieved his goal and could now do what he had always hoped to do: paint freely his native and preferred scenes. The life insurance frauds which the book treated were not its motif, as empty readers of later years would imagine. Phillips had not "seized" upon a sense of grievance in the air and "exploited" it, any more than Stendhal had "exploited" the Napoleonic Wars, or Mark Twain the riverboats on the Mississippi.

Problems of life insurance had tugged at the lower levels of public consciousness for many years. The revelations of the great Armstrong Investigation of 1905 in Albany, resulting in a sweeping battery of laws aimed at protecting the general public, had sunk deep into its consciousness. Phillips was not in any sense "muckraking" insurance. He was using it for the occasion to unfold the effects of public skulduggery on the private lives of people.

Insurance in Phillips's generation was modernized and made as subject to public supervision and actuarial controls as the specious promises of insurance agents and the vain hopes of their clients at every level would allow. But the problem of the misuse of funds collected and disbursed for allegedly philanthropic purposes was as real in 1978 as in 1906. In the later decades of the twentieth century there would be horrendous frauds revealed in welfare, in agencies supposedly set up to service children as well as the needy aged. These frauds would stir less outrage than a sensitive public, presumably superior in sophistication to the Progressives, should have felt. It was a public which needed to review its attitudes toward the needy: to its own degraded relatives, for example, in Veterans Hospitals as well as in "homes" for the aged. There were studies published about such circumstances, but fiction about them was rare, and even more rarely memorable.[1]

Phillips's story was about people: about Neva, and Horace Armstrong, and the Sicilian-born Boris Raphael, an artist, among others. Beveridge felt the presence of such a gallery of characters as creative writers seek, including the strong subordinate types which can round out a reader's feeling that he has entered into a world of individuals and ideas. Here was New York as Phillips had not before attempted to paint it. A firm line of his pencil delineated Battle Field, Indiana—long ago introduced in *The Cost*—in which subordinate western scenes were laid. Phillips here stabilized his views of a Midwest he had mishandled in *The Second Generation*. He had a New York protagonist still taking the old hometown paper: "It's like a visit at home. I walk the streets and shake hands with the people. I'm glad I came from there— but I'm glad I came [here]" (*Light Fingered Gentry*, p. 155).

He now noted poetically the "canyons" of Wall Street and the "snow-draped sky scrapers, plumed like volcanoes and lifting grandly in the sparkling air." It was no accident that Phillips for the first time highlighted art and architecture in his fiction, featuring Alois and Narcisse Sierdorf. Their work for and with the rich enabled Phillips to discuss the quality of life in New York and to link it to human motivations of beauty, as well as of conspicuous consumption. Phillips knew some artists and was overgenerous in estimates of those he deemed "American." He does not seem to have known the "Ash-Can" school of rebels in art, including such painters of the common scene as John Sloan, and he died too soon to estimate the great Armory Show of 1913 which opened psychological floodgates to new artistic experiments. But in much later decades, which poured honor and largesse on an Andy Warhol, Phillips's commonsense approach to art has something to offer to the future, reflecting as it did the explorations of a Thomas Eakins, a Winslow Homer, a Whistler, a Mary Cassatt, and the architecture of a Stanford White, a Louis Sullivan, and a Henry H. Richardson.

It was possible to read *Light Fingered Gentry* for the story, to skip pages of discussion of motives and character, and description of businesses and businessmen. But, as Phillips here said:

> To understand a human being at all in any of his or her aspects, however far removed from the apparently material, it is necessary to understand how that man or woman comes by the necessities of life— food, clothing, shelter. To study human nature either in the broad or in detail, leaving those matters out of account, is as if an anatomist were to try to understand the human body, having first taken out the vital organs and the arteries and the veins. It is the method of the man's income that determines the man; and his paradings and posings, his loves, hatreds, generosities, meannesses, all are either unimportant or are but the surface signs of the deep, the real emotions that constitute the vital nucleus of the real man. In the material relations of a man or a woman, in the material relations of a husband and wife, of parents and children, lie the ultimate, the true explanations of human conduct. This has always been so, in all ages and classes; and it will be so until the chief concern of the human animal, and therefore its chief compelling motive, ceases to be the pursuit of the necessities and luxuries that enable it to live from day to day and that safeguard it in old age. The filling and emptying and filling again of the purse performs toward the mental and moral life a function as vital as the filling and emptying and refilling again of heart or lungs performs in the life of the body.
>
> (*Light Fingered Gentry*, pp. 436–37)

With such an approach, clarified by his years of experiment, Phillips moved ahead. *Light Fingered Gentry* did away with the compulsive strain noted in *The Second Generation*. The spirit of home and of father no longer haunted him. Phillips was now dealing forthrightly with his familiar terrain in growing and triumphant New York. He studied objectively his major character Fosdick, exploiter of common people's insurance needs, evil in his unprovoked plots to limit and sacrifice those under him, though often generous, Phillips observed, and even noble in some of his attitudes. Such other fatal figures in insurance as Atwater and Trafford were individualized, the one passionately fond of music, the other having been a New Jersey school teacher, and with a wife of equally humble origins whose business uptown with fashions and the fashionable affected his life downtown with finance.

The theme of the novel was stronger than that of *The Second Generation* in that it interwove lives in a radically more complex pattern. No simple mandate brought them together or divided them as Hiram Ranger's last will and testament had done. *Light Fingered Gentry* told of Horace Armstrong; Phillips borrowed the last name of the Albany legislator who immortalized himself by heading the committee which shook insurance loose from its past. Armstrong on his way to power cast off his wife, whom he had married without love to give his career an upward impulse. They meet again in New York, where Neva has gone to study painting—and to seek him or someone else— and where a noted painter brings out her personality, frozen by a puritanical upbringing and imperceptive husband.

Those who would agree with Frank Harris's notion that Phillips was most akin to Frans Hals in his predilection for "ordinary" people would find a challenge in the personality of Boris Raphael. Phillips in time painted other creative individuals: George Brent, the dramatist, who moves in the pages of *Susan Lenox*; the novelist Hartley; the painter Wade. But among these, Boris was least an extension of Phillips's own ideas about his work and creative self. Phillips gave Raphael feminine sensitivity and subtlety, as well as sexuality and financial intelligence.

The strength of Phillips's theme lay in this: that Neva, seeking a new life, and Armstrong, seeking work and philosophy in the world of high finance, both complicated their lives and reached decisions while pondering their human feelings for one another. They sought love, but love not in the traditional ideal sense, nor yet love as the cynics saw it, or as Dreiser did, as a simple sexual compulsion, but as something which was bent or changed according to the individual personalities. Phillips clearly believed, or his characters did, that love was a hunger mixed with other hungers in human lives.

The book was a landmark in Phillips's career. It gave him his first extended opportunity to work intensively the man-woman theme which had dominated his thought from the beginning. *Light Fingered Gentry* was first of all about love, not insurance: about the meaning of

love to two people who had been emptily married and divorced, between Neva and the experienced artist Boris; about love between Amy
Fosdick and the architect Alois Sierdorf, and their marriage and its
effect on the love of Alois and his sister Narcisse, who had to re-
nounce him to Amy. Here were permutations of love over which Phillips pored, utilizing feelings and actions, and which were to receive
no attention of any kind from his various commentators, who perceived only "muckraking" in nebulous lights. Yet to Phillips love was
the spur, the occasion, the meaning of everything that happened. Not
to talk about love was not to talk about life.

Amy's love of Alois destroys his career as an architect. Armstrong's reawakened desire for Neva raises almost insupportable questions of his role in business. Raphael needs love, but, Neva thinks, he
has squandered his psychological resources among too many women,
and his dedication to beauty makes him a matchless friend, although
no one she can live with and grow with. Phillips in his generation
saw marriage as the proper fulfillment to love, but he saw the man-
woman dialogue as necessary in leading to or from that goal.

Accordingly, *Light Fingered Gentry* included numerous passages
of discussion on love in an era which also produced the last rays of
Henrik Ibsen's career and August Strindberg's, as well as the expand-
ing career of George Bernard Shaw. Theirs was a time which needed
to consider intellectually as well as emotionally what society could
ask of its men and women without vitiating them, and Phillips
through fiction entered into the crucial discussion. It was only two
years earlier that Shaw's *Mrs Warren's Profession*, concerned with
brothels, had shaken New York; its spokemen had agreed with the
Herald critic that "Shaw's play is morally rotten, but a morbidly curious audience packed the theatre to suffocation and doubtless will
continue to do so so long as the play is permitted to be given."[2]

Esthetically, Phillips came to terms with his views of feminine
beauty, which had long disturbed him. He had paid his tribute in *The
Plum Tree* to his mother's beauty in old age as incomparably more
appealing than "the shallow beauty which the shallow dote on." But
it had bewildered his apprentice pen while he marked the lines of
character in female as well as male faces. Beauty, undefined and un-
described, had helped thin the pages of *The Second Generation*. In
Light Fingered Gentry Phillips wrote with greater confidence of the
qualities of beauty in women, aside from their natural endowments of
clear or muddy skin, strong or sensuous mouth, and other attributes.

He portrayed Neva, for example, as at first somewhat unusual in body and face, though not strikingly so. She emerges as amazing in her delineation by reason of her divorce and renewed ambitions to be a creative person. Amy Fosdick Phillips sees as lovely rather than beautiful, with tendencies toward fat and—he hints at connections—inconsequence. And so others whom Phillips ponders in assessing the mystery of the physical in the life of the spirit.

Neva knew nothing of business. It had not been business which had wrecked her marriage; it had been Armstrong's will to succeed at the expense of his other human needs. But if he had degraded love as secondary to worldly power, he was also unwilling to be broken into harness by New York's "downtown" financial giants.

Neva's way was not Armstrong's but Boris's, and yet artistic beauty did not suffice for her needs. Though a "new" woman in critical respects, she was also a woman who wanted an Armstrong, but a less imperious, less asocial Armstrong, one who took into account her responses and outlook. Armstrong did not at first understand. "If these notions were to prevail among the women," he said, "about all the strongest men in the country would lose their wives."

But that was not the question for Neva.

> "I'm only trying to make you acquainted with me. . . . I see I didn't express myself well. I'm not trying to make conditions. I've simply shown you what kind of woman you were asking to marry you—and that you don't want her—that you want only that part of me that for the moment appeals to your senses. If I had married you without telling you what was in my mind and heart would it have been fair to you?"
>
> Armstrong could see that. He had come seeking a mistress. "Whether I want her as a wife, I don't know. Whether she wants me as a husband—I don't know."
>
> (*Light Fingered Gentry*, p. 404)

Armstrong, when he chose not to submit to the exigencies of finance, did not do it "for her," but because he had been driven into such a corner as to have had to choose between being a person or a pawn. As Phillips observed, in a passage relating to himself as well as his character:

> Everyone belongs to some section or class; he may quarrel with individuals in another class, he may quarrel with individuals in that class, or with the whole of another class; but he may not break with

the whole of his own class. Be he cracksman or financier or preacher or carpenter or lawyer or what not, he must be careful not to get his own class against him. If he does, he will find himself alone, defenseless, doomed. Armstrong belonged to the class financier. He stood for the idea financier in the minds of financiers, in his own mind, in the public mind. His battles with his fellow-financiers, being within the class-lines, had strengthened him, had given him clear title to recognition, as a power in finance; he had been like the politician who fights his way through and over his fellow-politicians to a nomination or a boss-ship, like the preacher who bears off the bishopric from his rivals, the doctor who absorbs the patronage of the rich, the lawyer who succeeds in the competition among lawyers.

But this new policy of Armstrong's was a policy of war on his own class.

(Light Fingered Gentry, pp. 407–8)

Here begins the last, the "unreal" section of the novel. Critics who had reproved Phillips for cynical portraits untrue to the lives of financiers would be succeeded by critics who protested against his new conclusion. No one in actual life did what Armstrong attempted. A flesh and blood Armstrong could not have withstood organized finance and forced it into honest ways. . . . Times change; and it could be that a new cultural consensus, recalling Teapot Dome, the Insull Empire, and Watergate, would agree that "happy endings" do not necessarily transgress a reader's sense of reality. The very insurance trials of 1905 which superficially gave Phillips his "documentation"—actually there was no documentation, as Dreiser's *The Financier* (1912) depended on his researches into Charles T. Yerkes's career—was evidence that Armstrong's conversion could occur. Phillips himself had called the roll of corrupting agencies in "The Treason of the Senate" and not been destroyed.

That the "Augean stables of finance" had been cleaned through muckraking and new laws was widely believed in Progressive times. Phillips himself was less sure that this was the case. Armstrong won his momentary fight. He won Neva. So the novel ended on a note of hope for others.

Light Fingered Gentry is by no means so austere as is here indicated. There was in it discussion of painting and of architecture. A chapter discusses the idea and the building of "Overlook Lodge." There is the tale of Joe and Letty Morris: Joe, a brilliant lawyer wedded to the interests but with capacities for making something of himself within the financial structure; Phillips may have been turning over in his mind Charles Evans Hughes's capacities as lawyer for the

Armstrong Committee. Phillips knit his characters together and did not fail to remind his more attentive readers of old Galloway of *The Master Rogue,* now dead, but no less part of the legend of the American business of his time.

There were flaws—there would almost always be flaws in this single, solitary author laboring to fashion signs and symbols for Americans prone to fall apart not because of famine and disease but because of unearned affluence and lack of care for details of their civilization. (One such flaw was the coincidence of Neva's feelings about finance being wrung by an elevator boy whose father had just died, and whose family had been cheated by an insurance agent, *Light Fingered Gentry,* p. 344.) John Steinbeck would later be dimly perceived by supposedly informed academicians as having been the author of but "one" fine novel, the rest being flawed or inconsequential, though the least thoughtful survey of his writings would have shown at least three or five works of superior creativity and control.

Phillips had reason to feel pleased with this latest novel, yet even within it he wrote in minor cadence:

> For the free workman there is always the joy of the work itself— the mingling of the pain which is happiness and the happiness which is pain, that resembles nothing so much as what a woman experiences in becoming a mother. But with the mother, birth is a climax; with the artist, an anti-climax. The mother always sees that her creation is good; her critical faculty is the docile echo of her love. With the artist the critical faculty must be never so mercilessly just as when he is judging the offspring of his own soul; he looks upon the finished work, only to see its imperfections; how woefully it falls short of what he strove and hoped. The joy of life is the joy of work—the prize withers in its winner's hand.
>
> (*Light Fingered Gentry,* p. 310)

Legend has it that *Old Wives for New* marked a new period in Phillips's work: that he "gave up" muckraking and devoted himself to writing on the "woman question." The point has dovetailed with another, that this "coincided" with the decline of muckraking and showed Phillips's "sensitivity" to change in public taste.

The fable would be amusing, considering the gyrations of the critics involved, from communism to anticommunism, to individualism, to lack of interest in fiction, did it not reflect grotesque views of American experience. Muckraking did not "end" at the time rudely indicated, and the "woman question" had been strong and vigorous before Phillips. What was at issue was Phillips's integrity of purpose, and the role of fiction in then contemporary matters. The most casual glance at Phillips's books—at his titles, even—shows the congruity of his intentions. The first novel, *The Great God Success*, in its most meaningful section dealt with an unconventional attachment. *A Woman Ventures* had described an unorthodox marriage and contained the record of one divorce and all but a second. *Golden Fleece* had discussed marriage as a moneymaking proposition. For that matter, Phillips was far from done with business and politics in his "new" phase; several of his later books were to deal substantially with these topics.

It was not subject which differentiated *Old Wives from New* from Phillips's earlier novels; it was quality. His earlier novels had merely erected scaffolds for his purposes. Now, human relations could entirely absorb him and give him a focus for the story he wished to tell. If public opinion set *Old Wives for New* apart from Phillips's earlier work, it was because it involved the combustible subject of divorce as it had not been treated before.

It marked an era in fiction. Dreiser was revealing at the same time the nether world of material hunger and lust. Phillips chose to cope with the problems of those who had to live with the world on its own terms. It was a world in process of being shocked by its own divorce rate: one marriage in twenty was being dissolved, an unprecedented figure which Phillips among others read in the news and had to assimilate.

It was this that sold *Old Wives for New*, and shocked its readers, and crystallized resentment against Phillips's methods and concerns. It was also this that "dates" the book, the first American novel to treat divorce in fictional detail. Attention later shifted from divorce to the amplitudes of sex, and it passed from recollection that literate society had once been more concerned for divorce than with sex. In the end, the one viable issue was the reality of the characters, and these are as recognizable as though more than half a century did not stand between.

Phillips suited his technique to his theme. He had felt compelled to choose a disastrous "western" approach in *The Second Generation*. *Light Fingered Gentry* had a businesslike conciseness and format suitable to a big-city narrative. *Old Wives for New* was the obverse of Dreiser's *Sister Carrie*. The latter concentrated on the impulses of its two main characters. Phillips moved his major protagonists through situations involving the demimonde, marriage customs, and dependence and independence in women. For a tale interweaving unrelated and disparate individuals caught in changing mores, Phillips erased all expression from his style, though it leaned toward naturalism. *Old Wives for New* was written with the coldest pen then present on the cultural scene.

Phillips's protagonist was Charles Murdock, a financier of the new type following in the steps of the rough industrial barons. Murdock, we are told, had not allowed scruples to stand in his way; this is impressive when we read the book's prologue depicting Murdock as a boy, filled with dreams and ardor (see pp. 18–19). Yet if the details of his financial rise were known, we would likely find such moral uncertainty in his career as Armstrong of *Light Fingered Gentry*, and others of Phillips's gallery, had experienced.

Murdock had worked for economic freedom, and now, in his middle years, his children grown, he was free—his business sold, his fortune secure, and he substantially retired. Here the story begins, for Murdock has little of a vital nature to do with his era. He seems uninterested in politics, in reform, in travel. This is perhaps because he has a problem larger than any other, that he is married to a slattern, no more recognizably the healthy and simple bride of his early years than he is the infatuated youth who married her. They have not been man and wife for years, but so slowly has their relationship changed that the personal crises, unconsciously shelved for years, have accumulated. The open break finds Sophy Murdock sullen and refusing to face the fact that her husband looks years younger than she, that he is offended by her unwashed hair, layers of fat, her headaches and complaints. He wants companionship. Her shiftlessness and lack of intellect are driving him to a conscious recognition that his "duty" to her is intolerable.

Sophy has made few friends in the course of life. She does not know how to use the money Murdock has amassed. Despite her vague defenses, she has not made a satisfying home. She has no incentive for living and deems it scandalous for her husband to look young.

She visits Dr. Schulze, Phillips's old favorite, as biting and epigrammatic as in his earlier appearance in *The Second Generation*. He becomes all but a crucial character in the tale, with his insistence on health as fundamental to normal life and his lack of interest in psychological justifications for the loss of love and the failures of married life. Sophy can expect no sympathy from him.

"The genuine tragedies of life are three" [Ludwig Lewisohn quoted Phillips as saying], "poverty, disease, and bereavement. All others are simply vanities of bloated self-exaggeration." Of course that is a very partial truth. But it was a truth that so needed to be sounded and to be embodied in American fiction. And Phillips proceeded to embody it by stripping of their self-importance and self-deception and unclean parasitic pretences especially the married women of the middle-classes.[3]

Phillips was broader in vision than Lewisohn's endorsement perceived. *Old Wives for New* weighed the meaning of love not only in Sophy's sad deterioration, but even in the new love that entered Murdock's mind. Juliet Raeburn, with whom he is finally to be united following lengthy difficulties and misunderstandings, is clearly superior to Sophy in all respects, as woman and as successful business woman. Yet Phillips underscores in a dozen scenes that Murdock might have made a life with Sophy had she found means for reestablishing health, attractiveness, and usefulness to Murdock. She would then have become another person, and Murdock would have found interests other than the passion that engrossed him. Phillips held that love could be worked for and attained. He saw no particular destiny in the consummations individuals sought and found.

And yet he was less bound by dogma than Lewisohn imagined. Generally the critic errs in taking the creative writer too literally. Phillips was less harsh than he often thought it necessary to seem, and even his writings, to say nothing of his private letters, show his essential pity for weakness and ignorance. He struck out repeatedly at "artistic" temperament. Yet he respected achievement when it came out of lives which conflicted with his own. What, for instance, could have been weaker than the brief career of Ernest Dowson, the English decadent poet of the 1890s? Yet Phillips wrote appreciatively of the author of the poem "Cynara." Phillips referred to Oscar Wilde as "that very great mind" at a time when Wilde's name was the equivalent of obscenity. But Phillips was determined to have his say, and in *Old Wives for New* he did.

Sophy did not exercise and made no effort to modernize her ways or try to understand the needs of her long-indulgent and distinguished husband. She read the Bible stubbornly, while Murdock felt apologetic for his interest in life, his will to enjoy it. Unlike his friend and former partner, Tom Berkeley, he was sober and serious, with no impulses toward sybarite diversions.

Berkeley was the scientific roué, as finely drawn and individual as any of Phillips's characters, with a well-cared for body and a perfect constitution. He was getting on in years and finding it necessary to parcel out his pleasures so as not to overtax his powers. His pleasures were so many cigars per day, so much liquor, sexual adventure, comfort. In his own view he was a good citizen, and firm on the sanctity of the home. As he explained to Murdock:

> "As a free American citizen, I've got my constitutional rights—to life, liberty, and the pursuit of happiness."
> "And *her* rights?"
> "Of course," Berkeley waved his hand generously. "Don't she assert them—all the rights she's got? When a woman and a man marry, the man agrees to support her and their offspring, and in exchange for that she agrees to—behave herself. A woman's virtue is all there is to her, so far as marriage is concerned. . . . Do I ever bother about married women? No, indeed, I pay for what I get; I despise a man who takes what another man's paying for. And a woman that cheats ain't fit to live. That's good business man's honor, isn't it?"
>
> (*Old Wives for New*, pp. 126–27)

Berkeley, Murdock observed, was riding hard for a nasty scandal; but Berkeley was not afraid. He was paying, he was rich, and he had the whip in hand. Nothing could unhorse him.

Everything came to a head for Murdock. Self-discoveries precipitated action for a divorce. Sophy proceeded to make life difficult for Murdock, despite his gallant efforts to be considerate and to leave her an independent fortune. Phillips left little for the devout among his readers to seize on who sought reasons for demeaning Murdock or his creator. But money at this stage signified little to Sophy, who had always had more than enough, and had neither the knowledge nor the will to use it.

At this point the derailing of Murdock's private car attached to a passenger train cut the story in two. It was this chapter, and chapters like it, which raised the critics of his time in a body about Phillips, and made it evident that new goals separated him from the older Populists and the more sentimental of the Progressives. Phillips spared no details of the tragedy: the shrieking victims, the burning cars piled one on the other, Murdock's private car, "[a]top the heap of splintered, riddled coaches for ordinary people . . . of triply-braced steel, upside down but almost uninjured" (*Old Wives for New*, p. 213). Phillips recorded "the groans, the screams, the yells" about Murdock, "and not quite so piercingly horrible sounds from far beneath, from the passengers buried, trapped, impaled in the ruins of the other cars, and there burning to death." As blood-chilling was the selfishness of the doctors who hurried from agonized patients to attend the wealthy Murdock. One reader of the novel commented:

> While I was reading [*Old Wives for New*] I stopped one night just after the train wreck. It was so vivid that as I took up the morning paper, the next day, I glanced at the headlines for news of Murdock's condition, and to find whether the scandal had come out.[4]

Now this was surely the height of journalism! The logic of antipathetic critics, in Phillips's time and among later ones, went as follows: Phillips moved his readers only as the frightful tragedies of every day touched readers vicariously, as potentially recording their own anguish in like circumstances. Phillips reached the reader with journalism, not art.

It has already been seen that Phillips's background of newspaper work made up a bulwark of experience from which he drew evocative insights. Dreiser had actually witnessed a train wreck and given a faithful and memorable account of its details, from his hopeless and despairing standpoint.[5] Phillips, in his account, suggested that the train wreck had occurred because it had been raining heavily throughout the region, "and the overworked track walkers had been unable to do their duty." In both cases tragedy had furnished occasion for individual development, the one in autobiography, the other in fiction. There was nothing in Phillips's account to suggest that he had not himself faced the mental crisis of horrid and unnatural accident with the same courage he asked of his readers, and in time manifested in his own life tragedy. Nor did he anywhere imply that such realism was all there was to literature; only that it was necessary to his art. No puppets died or were injured in that wreck, but men and women whom Phillips had looked at steadily, and whose fate affected his philosophy. Murdock all but died in it—Murdock, whom Phillips had worked so hard to realize.

Murdock did not die. He lived to divorce his wife in sensations of scandal for which he paid with his reputation—a bloody sacrifice by modern standards, but not more so than any other sacrifice any year's tawdry sensations can show. For Phillips's own era, his control of complex circumstances in conventional society, its interplay of light women and shady men was outstanding. Murdock briefly joined Berkeley in a round of forgetfulness with Viola Hastings. Here Phillips discussed in a single passage an experience to which Dreiser had committed his entire *Sister Carrie*: Viola had originated in a dull New Jersey town from which she had been tempted by a "drummer" to a career of promiscuity. Berkeley's death at the hands of another of her set, made jealous through having been abandoned by Berkeley, is a high point of Phillips's resourceful novel.

Equally impressive, however, is the resurrection of Sophy, which was to irritate Dreiser and no doubt others who shared his philosophy, to whom such an "optimistic" turn of events seemed unnatural. It is not clear why, especially in America, where so much was made of outward appearances and so many opportunities provided for improving them. In addition to which, Sophy does not accomplish the miracle of renovation by herself. She is aided by Murdock's secretary Melville Blagdon, come down from a wealthy family and ambitious to marry the divorced and wealthy Sophy. She takes hold of herself, gains much from an inspiring trip to New York's fashion marts, is helped by corsets, clothing, and cosmetic features. Striking pages of the novel describe the efforts of Sophy's female contemporaries to rejuvenate themselves, even through surgery, long before such techniques became fashionable in the 1920s (*Old Wives for New*, pp. 288 ff).

Sophy learns to spend money. She has the careless gold fillings removed from her mouth and porcelain pieces fitted. The "Agnes-Fleury Corset" chapter commemorates and explains this article, as "falsies" and the bra-less effect can help memorialize our own era. Indeed, the agonies Sophy endures in fitting the corset do much to decide her in favor of divorce, and thus move the novel as much as do more profound issues; this seems to be what Phillips is grimly suggesting.

Sophy changes—an impossible event in the Dreiser gallery. True, she becomes even more commonplace than before in her new marriage, but the task of the novel is to serve verities, not to make propaganda for despair. Certainly, the memorable Sophy is the useless, physically degenerate Sophy, envious of her husband's youth. Phillips, however, worked carefully over this "new" woman, with an interest in her rejuvenation Dreiser could not have begun to feel. Sophy, in his hands, would have gone the way of Eleanor Cowperwood of Dreiser's *The Titan*: taken to drink, perhaps, or to some ill-nourishing cycle of religion, which Sophy was investigating before being shaken awake.

This, then, was *Old Wives for New*, which shocked readers and critics early in 1908. It stamped Phillips in fiction as "The Treason of the Senate" had in public affairs. In his time and after he was accused of lacking a sense of humor, though conscious and unconscious displays of humor suffuse his pages. It here illuminated the character of Murdock's son, for example, pompously and ineptly trying to be the "man" in his family, having seen his father's fall from grace. Humor plays about Blagdon, disloyal to Murdock and endlessly rationalizing his hunger for an alliance with Sophy. It even affects Murdock in his awkward search for ways to ease his private needs.

Phillips was aware of this charge of humorlessness. There were always, he said, writers who possessed what was called a sense of humor, but which was no more than complacency. He was ready to risk his chance of preserving a sense of proportion.

11

Legends

It may still be some time before a consistent record of Phillips's days and ways may be called for and supplied. Half a century of derogation and pseudo-criticism have taken their toll of his tragedy and the visible aspects of his reputation, either of which have at least called for period pieces such as were arranged for Stephen Crane, C.D. Gibson, Stanford White, and Richard Harding Davis. They have also taken their toll of the materials which might have helped reconstruct the era of which he was part. Fugitive materials survive (see Bibliographical Note), and caches of letters might yet turn up, thanks to the spectacular nature of his death or because of one or another family tradition. But some may have been handed down to casual heirs, anxious to strip their apartments of old rubbish. Undoubtedly, too, some letters or other documents Phillips or his close associates deliberately destroyed for confidential reasons.

Phillips himself was a curious combination of strict regard for privacy and an almost passionate desire to know and be known. So his scraps of correspondence which fluttered into one or another haven surviving the ruin of years veer between firm and forthright business notes, and a personal and social graciousness which was all too outgoing. Progressives of his time, hardened by long service under weighted clouds of Darwinism, and persuaded that the stars were indifferent to their ramblings and rationalizations, were in many cases practical to the point of insensitivity. As a result they left relatively few traces of their odysseys on earth, and could hardly complain if their children lived in immediate terms as they had.

Phillips was more forward looking and concerned about the meaning of his times than were many of his fellows, but he despised the self-centered gestures of contemporary authors who soulfully posed in studios, hoarded their letters for posterity, and wore out words like "immmortal" and "great." Phillips himself dashed off notes to friends, editors, and hostesses, some of which they must have had difficulty in deciphering, and many of which they may have nodded at and tossed into wastepaper baskets. Phillips himself does not seem to have kept his own correspondence, and he avoided the kind of fixation on literary contacts which made so many of Hamlin Garland's memoirs a dull array of exchanged compliments, inscribed first editions, and other trivia.

By 1907 Phillips had entered into what was to prove a last full era of achievement and personal satisfaction, though to the end harassed by "the crazy thing inside of me [which] won't let me stop."[1] To Beveridge he wrote more wistfully, confiding that he still had his "intellectual belly ache although the severity of it has somewhat abated—I shall always [prefer] it to realities—I grasp at the moon like a child." His mood in that letter swiftly changed, as he added:

> "I have just thrown a mass of shit! into the wastebasket—a story on which I have spent many dreary hours—I have read over my work—It has found a grave in the wastebasket. I shall hatch again—I am suspicious—like a deluded hen that I am sitting on a china egg. But like her I shall continue to sit—I have nothing else to do—why not?"[2]

Phillips was now in entire control of his days and purposes. There were those who saw him as writing, writing, always writing, and who could make of this not a life of dedication but an empty exercise in scribbling. In fact, though he was indeed unswervingly committed to his art, his life had a tang and variety which few could claim, even those who were avoiding research or consistent labors for lack of quality or purpose. Phillips lived high over Nineteenth Street in New York in towers overlooking Gramercy Park, from which he could view the then exquisite, high-gated preserve, or look over it to the old Stanford White house, which had become the Princeton Club. His sister Carolyn attended to the care of their ample apartment, and sometimes accompanied him to a Broadway show or other engagement. After he had worked through the night, she was as likely as not to have a late "breakfast" with him, friends sometimes joining them. The usual empty-headed rumor raised its eyebrows from time to time at this brother-and-sister arrangement, even conjecturing incest. But most of Phillips's associates had too much sense or knowledge of his life—and of their class's subterranean connections—to waste time on such surmise. Better established were Phillips's nocturnal habits, and the assurance given by a glance up at his windows, where his lights gleamed, that Graham was there as usual, "pounding away at his old black pulpit."

His very desk enjoyed a measure of fame, and he himself described it in his own fiction, adding too the fact that it accompanied him on his numerous trips abroad, on ship as well as in residence, notably in Paris, which he loved.[3] None of this made any impression on critics determined to see careless composition whether in defiance of reality or not. Phillips wrote and rewrote, pondering stories and ideas which went back as far as his early 1890s *Harper's Weekly* sketches. He estimated that he rewrote as often as nine times before giving his work to the editors.

Phillips learned not only from his own experiences with manuscript, but from his editors. To one at Harper's he expressed appreciation for its handling of *Her Serene Highness:* "I can't tell you how delighted I was with the way the book looked—it is most artistic—If I'd dreamed my little picture was to have such a fine frame I fear I'd have [rewritten?] it altogether, trying to make it better."[4]

Phillips had gone on to offer Harper's *A Woman Ventures*, which it had rejected, and Phillips expressed gratitude for the attention it had been given: "Perhaps I owe you an even deeper debt for your refusal of the other story—As a result I'm rewriting it throughout— And if you'll take the trouble to read it next fall when Stokes puts it out, I think you'll see why I'm 'obleeged.' "[5]

With some editors Phillips developed closer relations and as with Lorimer, held them to be his friends. He met with them singly or in groups. Thus there were meetings not only with Beveridge, but with Beveridge and Joseph Hamblen Sears, of D. Appleton, his publisher, who accounted himself a friend of Phillips and was at his funeral, but who rated Beveridge higher as a "genius."[6] Meaningful too to Phillips was such a personality as John O'Hara Cosgrave of *Everybody's*, with whom he discussed writings and also expressed more personal feelings, in response to sentiments of some sort from Cosgrave:

> You are not quite just to me, I think—You see, there is so much in one's life that one may not show to anybody and that's sure to make the causes of conflict—I don't think it's fair to judge—and so far as you are concerned, I had for you feelings of the most cordial friendship from the very first—I liked your mind and your way of looking at things and your way of doing—and it was a matter of sincere regret that I did not see more of you—and had my hours not been so peculiar and certain affairs which I cant [sic] speak of so exasperatingly absorbing, I'm sure you'd have had as [illegible] a chance as ever man had to get sick and tired of me.[7]

Phillips had full days during which he walked—his favorite and almost only form of recreation—to newspaper and editorial offices to see friends and discuss projects. As his great decade wore on, however, and thanks to his increasing fame and notoriety, his associations took a firmer form. Phillips held himself to the end more concerned for people with brains than for socialites, and esteemed such a center—there were others—as the X Club, named for an English counterpart which had included the scientists Huxley, Wallace, and Tyndall. The New York club valued free discussion and broad membership:

> [It] continued [reminisced Hamilton Holt, editor of the *Independent*] for many years under the secretaryship of W.J. Ghent who kept it together. I can't remember all the members but I recall John Martin, Raymond V. Ingersoll, Robert E. Ely, [Cleveland] Moffett, editor of Collier's Norman Hapgood, Professor Franklin H. Giddings. . . . It was a very brilliant group and entertained such celebrities as H.G. Wells when they came to town.[8]

Such contacts, which further included Upton Sinclair, John Spargo, and Phillips's old friend Charles Edward Russell, kept Phillips close to the seething socialist milieu of the time and enabled him to assert in one of his *Cosmopolitan* articles (December 1904) that socialism was the only force for popular education of that time. Phillips attended a dinner held April 10, 1906 to welcome Maxim Gorky to America and to collect funds for the then-admired Russian revolutionists, defeated and dispersed following their abortive uprising of the year before. It was a visit made catastrophic because the great author was not formally married to Madame Gorky, the reason being the austere Gorky's opposition to Greek Orthodox Church policy.[9]

W.J. Ghent perceived that the core of Phillips's associations was elsewhere: "[As] a rule he seemed to prefer the society of well provided, well-dressed and good-mannered persons."[11] Not, of course, that Ghent and his associates were not also so endowed. They had, however, a doctrinaire character which limited intimacy, so far as Phillips was concerned. He preferred an Alfred Henry Lewis, who had been a cowboy, had written enduring fiction about his past, and who was now a Hearst writer. Such friends gave him entrée to others of uncertain and even outcast status, information about whom he sought, especially for his lengthening *Susan Lenox* manuscript:

> Accompanied by Alfred Henry Lewis, Lieut. Frank Peabody, of New York's Central Office [,] Detective Burway . . . and myself [Arthur Little recalled] Phillips would go night after night studying the under-

world life of New York. Then other nights with Lewis and Val
O'Farrell, the private detective, and Dick Butler, the President of the
Longshoreman's Union and a great local political leader of his day, Bat
Masterson, the famous Sheriff of [Lewis's] "Wolfville Days" and the
boy hero of "The Battle of the Adobe Walls," Judge Joseph E. Corrigan,
at that time a City Magistrate, Kid McCoy, the great prize-fighter—and
dozens of others of every rank and every field of activity, trotted out
for him by Alfred Henry Lewis—he would study the life of the sporting world and the municipal political world.[11]

Such persons and experiences impressed Phillips as much as did any.
But he did not continuously seek copy for his books. A reminiscence
by William Allen White suggests a touch of the spontaneous and
purposeless which have given color and joy to all generations, whatever their bottom impulses:

> Thirty years ago and more, [Phillips and I] were walking down
> Seventh Avenue from the park, two young bloods in our thirties, with
> those four cocktails in our blood, not in our belly, that give every
> youth exuberance and joy. We were both relatively poor; the magnifi-
> cence of this Babylonian civilization on the island, even thirty years
> ago, made our eyes bug, and we fell to talking in hyperbole about our
> revolution. We passed a grim and forbidding warehouse that looked
> like a fortress, and we decided that when our mob came charging up
> from the shambles we would have made of lower New York, we would
> drop out and take our loot from this gorgeous old storehouse. We
> elaborated on the idea with much persiflage and ribald bawdy delight.
> I can see his eyes now dancing and hear his clear strong baritone
> hooting and honking in syncopation to the rococo pattern of our
> thoughts.[12]

This was another Phillips from the one who attended society functions, and did that with discrimination. He was disgusted that William Howard Taft's first official appointment as president should have
been J.P. Morgan's son-in-law Herbert Satterlee, "that impossible
ass. . . . We sure are getting a ruling class in name as well as in fact—
Well, why not?" He rejected a Beveridge invitation to visit the Van-
derbilts. "Don't like him—Have written things about his family that
are too true to be pleasant reading for any of them."[13] Even Ghent
noted that Phillips doubtless accepted some of the company of affluent people in order to find materials for his books, on one occasion
accompanying Richard Harding Davis, whom he superficially resem-
bled in some ways. Indeed, many of the editors and writers, John
O'Hara Cosgrave observed, were sought out by the rich for gatherings,
for stimulation, and even for sons-in-law. Phillips was not only clear

in his mind about the virtues and necessity of what he saw as "the great middle class," but of the need to avoid "silly charivaris"; and he warned Beveridge: "I hear you hurry from dance to supper—you're getting quite a reputation as a social celebrity and old reliable dinner man—and are building up quite a nice little social position."[14]

Nevertheless, one of his or, more probably, Carolyn's close friends was Robert W. Chambers, whose novels of the era enabled him to make of his ancestral home at Broadalbin, New York, humble in the eighteenth century, a grand estate. Chambers was in time to be made an unread symbol of shabby fiction writing, and to be equated by mindless critics with none other than Phillips. It was Sears and the bereft Carolyn's incredible decision to have Chambers write a personal impression of Phillips as an introduction to *Susan Lenox*: one of the numerous decisions, probably inevitable, which would contribute to the critical darkness which gathered about Phillips's life and work.

Chambers himself appears to have been unpretentious in his work, an aristocrat supporting himself in democratic circumstances, as did J.P. Marquand later on. Chambers described himself as an "entertainer" and sincerely admired Phillips as a seeker of "truth." In time, perhaps, a scholar of Popular Culture might decide to read some of Chambers's actual prose and perceive what it was which gave him his army of purchasers, who read and passed on. The simple fact was that they had much to learn from Chambers. His moral structure was simplistic. His ability to skirt serious problems of his time was resourceful, hinting at sex, liquor, and cheating in business and personal relations without detail and with abstract distinctions of good and evil guiding his swift narrative. One light mention Phillips made of his friend, in *Susan Lenox*, when he has the young girl Susan "reading about the wonderful *him*—and she had spent full fifteen minutes of blissful reverie over the accompanying [Harrison] Fisher illustration" (*Susan Lenox*, I, 13)—in Chambers's latest story.

But, to repeat, readers of the Chambers novels had much to learn that they wished to know about their social betters, as their progeny would later hunger for details and conjectures about "Jackie" and "Liz" and "Barbra." Chambers had begun life as an artist, had studied in Paris, knew the history of his own people extending into colonial times, and, in his rounds as a successful artist and tale spinner knew intimately the gestures, the dress, the homes, the routines, the sentimental goals which suffused the lives of the rich and to which those of lesser economic status aspired. Chambers knew their entertainments in detail and could describe as a participant and observer butterfly hunts, shootings, fishing, games, dances, clubs, and the relations of old and young, servants and masters, and mistresses. Chambers did so uncritically, and with no sense of any sort of the dynamics which ruled society and turned its protagonists and conditions around. But the identification of Chambers with Phillips was a worm in criticism which insured that, ultimately, the author of "The Treason of the Senate" and of *Susan Lenox* would have the last word over the babblers.

At his own home, at the Princeton and Manhattan clubs, and elsewhere, Phillips met treasured friends. Some were wealthy, like Arthur W. Little, heir to the fortune of one of the most successful of American printers, and himself editor of *Pearson's*, one of the lesser magazines of reform, or at least reformers, who serialized *Light Fingered Gentry*, but later chided Phillips for being too hard to reach and for not patronizing *Pearson's* sufficiently. Wrote Phillips:

> Dear Arthur:
>   You are mistaken in one respect. If you should fail you would discover that I would not be a great deal more willing to be seen with you, but that I'd hunt you up and insist on being seen with you. For, then you'd need me, while now you don't. So, if you want to see more of me and make use of me, etc., why all you've got to do is to lose your reputation and your money, etc. *Now*, will you be good?
>   Graham[15]

Little was one of those with whom Phillips felt exceedingly free, and with whom he could discuss his personal feelings and attitudes. As one of the most marriageable of New Yorkers, Phillips appears to have attracted women, daughters of the various families with whom business and social gatherings brought him contact, who cast nets in his and others' direction or who took advantage of their superior positions to initiate or consummate affairs.[16] Phillips evidently had his share of the less ultimate sexual commitments available to him. It seems fair to judge that his absorption in his work made them less urgent to him than to others in his circumstances. It is quite likely that he had left some part of his capacity for easy infatuation in a North Carolina grave some fifteen years earlier. Phillips hid a deep strain of sentimentality and longing for a home beneath his apparent harshness, and shared with some of his fictional protagonists their faith in love. His delight in Beveridge's second marriage and subsequent child was unqualified: "I'm delighted about the baby—it's the best thing I've heard in years—I envy you, Bev—it's honestly the regret of my life—You get everything—Don't you?"[17]

It seems likely that Phillips harbored a protracted guilty conscience with respect to "Alice," and his later cerebrations on women veered between ideals of love and a conviction that marriage ought to be approached with the same reasonableness that one accorded the buying of food in a market. This he was to repeat in several of his novels. At the same time, he could not resist the dream of love, and, as he said: "What is the difference between friendship and love? I had thought—and said—that love was friendship in bloom. But . . . [now] I knew the full truth. Love is friendship set on fire" (*The Husband's Story*, p. 467; compare *Old Wives for New*, pp. 76–77).

The fact that he was a bachelor was noticed widely by the realists or the nosey of his generation, and his general response appears to have been to attempt to assess the depths of his likes and dislikes. One rumor which came down to modern times, for which there was no evidence, was that he might have been seriously interested in one of the Duer sisters, Alice or Caroline, descendants of a distinguished New York family, who wrote verse and stories; Alice Duer Miller wrote the best-selling *The White Cliffs* (1941), a poem praising the defense of England against Hitler. Phillips insisted he was a dedicated bachelor, wedded to his art. On the other hand—a thought repeated in his fiction—he held that a man who could not go on without someone he "needed," but who was inaccessible to him, was no man at all. What these ruminations said of his own needs cannot be known. Nor can it be known whether or not he would have made an alliance which would have dispossessed Carolyn Frevert, had he lived.

In any case, there was life to be lived, and Phillips found it as much a problem as a pleasure to control his relations with women. To Arthur Little he complained that they wanted him to f— them all the time; and Little learned to know, he said, that when Phillips suddenly took off for Europe, usually with Carolyn, he was avoiding a particularly determined campaign by one of his woman friends. Such importunities were scarcely the worst for a man to endure, and Phillips enjoyed some of the signs of success. Little recalled accompanying Phillips to a drama agent's office and asking the telephone operator to announce him to her employer. "Not *the* Mr. Phillips," she exclaimed, "—David Graham Phillips?" "Phillips's face broke into the most delighted smile of boyish personal satisfaction, as he answered, 'The same.' "[18] And when the girl left to carry the message personally to her employer, Phillips turned to his friend and said, "Aren't you proud to know me?"

On the subject of health Phillips was patently a crank. Much of what he believed made sense: the constant walking, the shaven face, the repugnance to overeating, and for endurance, as he so preferred, hot showers immediately followed by ice-cold showers. But his concern for the health of friends had him crossing their individual lines of preference and lecturing them on avoiding motor cars on grounds that they would not only lose health but their democratic feel for humanity. He himself showered inordinately and was surely impertinent in urging Beveridge to "kiss the babies for me," but adding, "being careful to make yourself thoroughly antiseptic—thoroughly disinfected." On another occasion he warned Beveridge on no tangible evidence not to "eat so much of that fried stuff. It is making your handwriting very shaky. Don't be deceived by a thick coat of tan. It is probably largely liver."[19]

Yet he himself in 1908 was sick enough to require an operation at Mount Sinai Hospital, enough to turn his thoughts to "the one lesson life is teaching me[:] the lesson of love and tolerance—not *weakness.* . . . And I am becoming more and more tenacious of the few friends I have—and more eager for their friendship." One of his letters ended with the tremulous "God keep us all."[20]

Phillips greeted 1909 with *The Fashionable Adventures of Joshua Craig*, which had first appeared in Lorimer's *Post* as a serial. In the novel appeared a tone which helped define Phillips's years of fulfillment: a certain lightness of touch, a confidence that he was setting down and communicating what he had in mind. The striking contrast is, again, with the pieties of *The Second Generation,* which had treated the West as sacrosanct. Joshua Craig was a westerner, intended to suggest an unspoiled quality in the land, but the differences between Craig and the paragons of *The Second Generation* are basic. Craig is ambitious. He is a blusterer, suspicious of good manners, fearful of being put down by the smooth and insincere of Washington society, proud of his zest and masculinity. There is a contrast, too, between Margaret Severance of Phillips's novel and Lily Bart of Edith Wharton's *The House of Mirth* (1905). Both women have been too long unmarried, too long dependent on the sufferance of others. Lily's misfortunes are subtle and sensitive, Margaret's derive plainly from her overcritical assessment of available male catches of wealth and position.

Phillips was at his old game of exposing snobbery and its distortions of human values, but he offers subtleties of his own. The blundering Josh begins by believing in the refinement and ethereal qualities of the desperate young woman, though her very cynicism and intellectual boldness have created her predicament. Phillips portrays Craig too as distinctly egotistical, with no great sense of humor. Craig rages against the conventionalities of Washington society. He insults his genteel friend Arkwright who is of it, for fear of being inhibited by what he cannot clearly control. Craig, in an effort to assert his maleness and personality, makes himself obnoxious to Margaret, who has decided that he has a career ahead of him and must marry. He even challenges Madam Bowker, Margaret's grandmother and Washington's "mumbo-jumbo," to whom all defer and whom Margaret fears as her source of money and future.

Once again the puzzle of changing times rears itself to readers. Of what use are accounts of fashionable adventures, in a city as battered now as Washington, where there is no fashion? And yet the question of quality in government, and in the individuals who must administer it, remains. At the very least, Josh becomes symbolic of any young man who faces the dual task of making his place in government, and of avoiding the threat of being reduced to inconsequence by form and temptations.

Madam Bowker is of an older generation of dowagers, an arbiter of decor and status. Yet she has been born Lard, of "poor white trash," and is thus herself a product of the democratic fight for consequence. Phillips had no admiration for what smelled of the grave, but as always, he insisted on regard for strength and shrewdness. So he painted a picture, part repulsive, part admirable, of Madam Bowker, which can be readily transmuted into modern terms. Craig defeats her and takes her Margaret away; Phillips would have deemed it a tragedy for him to have been humbled and harnessed, even by Margaret. And would that have made a truer portrait of what life is, and can be? . . . Margaret wins too: a husband of genuine if stormy promise. So the upper classes are still capable of producing women worth a man's time. Or so Phillips thinks.

The novel excited bitter criticism. Wrote one outstanding critic of the time, Dr. Frederic Taber Cooper:

If Mr. Phillips's aim in writing *The Fashionable Adventures of Joshua Craig* was to present a new and particularly objectionable type of all around cad, the book must be regarded as an unqualified success. . . . By insisting on certain qualities of energy, eloquence and perseverance, Mr. Phillips brings his creature to Washington as assistant to the Attorney-General. There the animal is let loose to snort and bellow and glorify his own vulgarity and trample people's feelings to his own infinite satisfaction. What Mr. Phillips in his grim humor of creating the character seems at times to forget [continues Dr. Cooper, with an unconscious tribute to Phillips's skill in creating an individual open to a variety of interpretations] is that Craig is always and forever a sniveling snob and turf-hunter, at heart regarding any approach to breeding and good manners with venomous, envious hatred.[21]

Phillips himself disagreed. He thought it amusing that aristocrats should be bearded and embarrassed by a man with neither money nor power, who lived to tell the tale. Josh's escape from Washington, and with Margaret, was intended to give heart to those with a consciousness of worth and sound ideas of public service. What is striking, however, is how Dr. Cooper's view of Josh—as conventional in his time as approval of the Marquis de Sade would be half a century later—agreed with that of the least admirable people in the book. Hear, for example, Madam Bowker seeking to draw out John Branch, the Secretary of the Treasury, on Craig and his prospects:

"Branch," said the old lady, with an emphatic wave of the ebony staff, "I want that Craig man sent away from Washington."

"Josh, the joke?" said Branch, with a slow, sneering smile that had an acidity in it interesting to one so even as he.

"That's the man. I want you to get rid of him. He has been paying attention to Margaret, and she is encouraging him."

"Impossible!" declared Branch. "Margaret is a sensible girl and Josh has nothing—never will have anything". . . .

"What do they think of him among the public men?" inquired she.

"He's laughed at there as everywhere."

Her vigilance was rewarded; as Branch said that, malignance hissed, ever so softly, in his suave voice, and the snake peered furtively from his calm, cold eyes. Old Madam Bowker had not lived at Washington's great green tables for the gamblers of ambition all those years without learning the significance of eyes and tone. . . . "Can it be possible," thought the old lady, "that this Craig is about to be a somebody?" Aloud she said: "He is a preposterous creature. The vilest manners I've seen in three generations of Washington life. And what vanity, what assumptions! The first time I met him he lectured me as if I were a school girl—lectured me about the idle, worthless life he said

I lead. I decided not to recognize him the next time I saw him. Up he came, and without noticing that I did not speak he poured out such insults that I was answering him before I realized it."

"He certainly is a most exasperating person."

"So Western! The very worst the West has ever sent us. I don't understand how he happened to get among decent people. Oh, I remember, it was Grant Arkwright who did it. Grant picked him up on one of his shooting trips."

(*The Fashionable Adventures of Joshua Craig*, pp. 194–97)

Phillips was upset by the criticism. Sometimes, he told Bailey Millard, he despaired of ever being understood:

Josh, it seems clear to me, is a worthy fellow, and yet they call him a boor, a bounder, a disgusting creature. Now Josh is no boor. I know him thoroughly. The ungentle way he acted with Margaret was simply to impress her with his personality, his masculinity, and from the very first, he did impress her. He saw it and he kept it up. I tried to make his position plain to the reader, but perhaps I failed. It has been my lot to be misunderstood both as a writer and as a man. I have even been accused of being aristocratic—me the soul of democracy.[22]

An odd development was that Beveridge became convinced that Craig was intended for himself. Phillips diplomatically agreed that "possibly he does resemble you more than some," and he thanked Beveridge for suggestions he could no longer use, suggestions which were supposed to bring out how hard Beveridge had worked for his success, how he had overcome "simply unprecedented obstacles." Beveridge even concocted a scheme to advertise the book as depicting his own character and career, creating confusion in Phillips's and Sears's minds as to how this could be done without relating Margaret Severance to his own wife. In one of the odd remarks his lack of humor sometimes created, Beveridge wrote: "If I were not married, I would pay you money to [advertise what he saw as the facts]."[23]

In the usual course of advertising, the publishers revealed that they had received letters protesting the publication of *The Fashionable Adventures of Joshua Craig* as a reflection on the affairs of a certain family. This was taken to indicate the power and reality of Phillips's work, since he had had no one in particular in mind. The matter was noted and suitably forgotten.

12

Art and Social Change

Phillips's next volume in his amazing series, *The Hungry Heart*, was the work nearest his heart, and yet one which seemed most likely to appear obsolete, if only because its intensity demanded an emotional response succeeding generations of readers were unwilling or unable to give it. Had Phillips's novel appeared twenty years earlier, it would have had a historical significance enchanting to academics, and to their classes and graduate students. Appearing as it did, several years before Dreiser's *Jennie Gerhardt*, its moral structure and feminism seemed untrue to the life of shackled females, on one side, and to the propaganda of "emancipated" females—and males—on the other.

It sold well during the several remaining years of Phillips's life, and to women who could directly recognize their dreams or selves in Phillips's fictional creations. But such women had to assume their limited social options, had to hold to their need for personal values within those options, and had to consider how their children would gain or suffer by their personal decisions. Questions of love, of joy, of self-expression could more easily be projected through the docile, unintellectual, fatalistic women of Dreiser's gallery, and the abandoned and irresponsible women of F. Scott Fitzgerald's and Ernest Hemingway's imagination.[1]

That left the question of dependence and independence as important in male-female relations and needing Phillips's explication. Actually, the question did not cover even Phillips himself. He had said that any man who could not live and create because he was deprived of the woman he loved had no excuse for losing courage and deteriorating. But why did he need to be deprived? Was there not divorce? Was there not separation? What conventions were so vital as to give no leeway to people who cherished freedom and self-expression, especially if they were well to do, as Phillips was? The question of independence explained too little. Stanford White died because a gross pervert and wealthy wastrel, a person of no quality, Harry K. Thaw, was shielded by 1906 conventions about the sanctity of marriage and so could deny White's yearning for Thaw's silly actress-wife. Edith Wharton had an interlude of passion in her loveless marriage which remained hidden for decades following her death.[2] None of this helped Phillips's tale of a married woman, hamstrung by social conventions and love of her child. The permissiveness of the World War I period and after diluted its impact and usefulness to readers.

Main Street (1920) by Sinclair Lewis, one of the major profiteers of the new spirit, was given a kind of classic status, being issued in textbook editions with questions stimulating to students and the like. Nothing of the sort happened to Phillips's treasured work. As earlier indicated, Lewis was the patent successor to Phillips (see page 85); and yet such was the response to their similar messages that no literary comparison was projected, either by scholars or well-read critics.[3] At the present moment in time it must be assumed that only a high imaginativeness can give some reality to Phillips's tale, and that its base would have to be, not economic dependency, which the welfare state and other conditions have modified, but just what Phillips posited: the hungers of the heart.

A time later than Phillips's, later than Lewis's, would endorse hedonism as being as good as any other goal for ephemeral human beings. It would endorse Norman Mailer's *An American Dream* (1965) as containing in its accounts of murder and sexual excess valid metaphors for life's completions. But few would have given Mailer an official cultural priority, any more than they would have elected him mayor of New York. Gadflies were not administrators. If Phillips's protagonist in *The Hungry Heart*, Courtney Vaughan, was outmoded by 1920, it would help to understand why. Her chemist-husband Richard saw her as a sexual toy and insisted on her being one. Carol Kendicott's doctor-husband Will in *Main Street* had no higher view of his wife. Where was the difference?

Remarkable was the fact that Phillips's fiction was vastly more "daring" than Lewis's. The latter was concerned for no more than the pettiness of small town life. Phillips more fundamentally justified the adultery of his frustrated and spiritually insulted Courtney. What was it which enabled Middle America of 1920 to prefer the milder fiction of Lewis at the expense of Phillips's bolder equalitarian demands?

The crucial fact was that neither Courtney nor Carol was actually so confined by circumstances as they felt themselves to be, and persuaded their readers twenty years apart that they were. In Courtney's time as in Carol's, there were hordes of women as emancipated as any the twentieth century could display. If these women did not choose to experiment with drugs, with sex, with deliberate uprootedness as desperately as did some of their successors, it was not because they could not have done so. It was because their fulfillment was as entire as they could imagine or enjoy in the careers of a Jane Addams, an Emma Goldman, a Margaret Sanger, a Maria Montessori, an Ida M. Tarbell, an Edna St. Vincent Millay, an Anna Howard Shaw, whose lives ranged from virginity to sexual excess. Neither Courtney nor Carol was sufficiently trained or situated to aspire so far. They wanted husbands and children as well as, or more than, careers. They were drawn from main streams—not to mention Main Streets—and longed to contribute to their work and reality. The inability of these women to do so left them deprived and hungry.

It was therefore no accident that Sinclair Lewis, though a great name of the literary 1920s, should not have been so to the younger generation which was to carry the banner of change beyond that era. John Dos Passos, the successful young author of *Three Soldiers* (1921) and one of the ideologues of youth, did not care for *Main Street*, which he did not finish, or for *Babbitt* (1922). Lewis's books impressed him as "journalistic": one of the key charges against Phillips, though Lewis had no more than a trifling career as journalist.[4]

It was not, then, the younger generation which turned from Phillips, to say nothing of *The Hungry Heart*; it was those of Middle America who had once known of Phillips, who had read him with resentment, and who found it easier and more fruitful to cope with Lewis's Carol than with the dead author's Courtney.

One key difference between the two authors' novels was their structure which, in one case, concentrated almost entirely on the troubled lives of the several people involved. As Dr. Cooper, who liked the book in a myopic way, said:

> The entire action takes place within the house and grounds of the husband's ancestral home; the cast of characters is limited to just four people—two men and two women; we hardly get even a passing glimpse of any outsiders, friends or relatives, or even servants. And yet within this little world of four people we get a sense of universality of theme and interest, an impression not of learning the secrets of a few isolated lives, but of learning much that is big and vital about men and women.[5]

Phillips offered, then, a scene Ibsenesque in form, contrasting with Sinclair Lewis's larger social milieu replete with local types, streets, and activities, including peeking behind curtains, bigotry, and indifference to culture and the larger world. All this gave Lewis's readers more to think about and to compare with their own circumstances, wherever located.

And yet a question remains: is Phillips's book condemned to eternal disregard? It has already been seen that the mite of academic criticism Phillips received mashed together his writings and commented easily and triumphantly on his apprentice work, evading direct looks at his more complex, more matured conceptions. Yet if those readers whom his fictions should have touched found them expendable, that fact to a degree justified scholarly neglect. The problem, then, is to consider whether *The Hungry Heart* says anything to a world which has revolutionized man-woman relations and no longer confines women, even women with children, to the mercies of husbands and lovers.

Dr. Cooper, for all his cordiality, did not grasp what Phillips was saying:

> What gives the book its value is not the episode of the wife's frailty, but the wise, far-sighted understanding of the way in which two people, physically, mentally and morally well equipped to make each other happy, gradually drift apart through stubborn adherence to foolish prejudices, mistaken reticence, petty misunderstandings, and a hundred and one trivialities, *no one of which by itself is worth a second thought.*[6]

Cooper moved in heavy waters through much of his reading of the book, but his basic misunderstanding of Phillips is clear. There were no trivialities. Courtney, far from being reticent, shouted unheard by her husband, absorbed in his chemistry projects, content to treat her as a sex incident in his life and to keep the house as he had inherited it from his grandfather. What Cooper seems to have envisioned was a kind of frank discussion in which wife and husband aired their viewpoints and then reached a "compromise" preserving their separate roles, as Cooper imagined them, of male and female, husband and wife, father and mother, with the "trivia" of temperament subordinated to the greater goals.

Phillips saw the matter as involving what would later be derogated as "male dominance," a posture of superiority denying the woman her impulses and needs. This should have made the novel the flag of the future Phillips intended. Unfortunately for his expectations, the literary future was not with men and women who sought legitimate results through arduous effort and exhibitions of courage. It was with a viewpoint which saw human endeavor at the mercy of drift and accident, impulse, and subconscious motivations.

Courtney does not take a lover in revenge for Richard's obtuseness; she takes him because she thinks he understands her, is gallant and admirable and bound to her by love as she is to him. Her viewpoint is revealed early in the book in a shocking interview which shows her she has been living with a stranger, and one unmindful of her personality. She has understood that she, as mistress of their home, would be making changes transforming it to their desires:

> "What devil keeps nagging at you?" he demanded, pausing in his angry stride to face her. "It must be some woman's having a bad influence on you. I'll not have it. I'll not have my home upset and my wife spoiled. Who is it, Courtney?"
>
> She was silent.
>
> "Answer me."
>
> "It's myself," replied she, in a quiet, dumb way.
>
> "It's not yourself. *You* are womanly."
>
> "I've got to have something to do—something worthwhile—or I can't live."
>
> "Attend to your house and your baby, like all true women."
>
> "It isn't enough," replied she in the same, monotonous stupified way. "It isn't enough for me, any more than it'd be for you."
>
> "Nonsense," said he, with a man's feeling that he had thereby answered her.
>
> She said dazedly: "You didn't mean it. No, you didn't mean it."
>
> "Mean what?"
>
> "All my plans—my year's work—and such a beautiful house and place I'll make." She started up, clasped her hands about his arm. "O Dick—don't be narrow—and so distrustful of me. I *know* I can do it. Let me show you my plans—my sketches."
>
> He took her hands, and said with gentle, firm earnestness, for he was ashamed of having lost his temper with a woman: "Courtney, I cannot have it. I will not let you disturb the place my grandfather gave his best thought to."
>
> "But you don't like it, dear," she pleaded.
>
> "I respect my grandfather's memory."
>
> "But on our wedding trip you said—"
>
> "Now, don't argue with me!"
>
> "It's because you think I couldn't do it?"
>
> "I *know* you couldn't—if you must have the truth."

"Let me show you my sketches and paintings," she pleaded in a queer kind of quiet hysteria. "Let me explain my plans. I'm sure you'll—"

"Now Courtney! I've told you my decision. I want to hear no more about it."

She looked up into his face searchingly. He was just like the portrait of his unbending grandfather that made the library uncomfortable. Her arms fell to her sides. She went to the balcony rail, gazed out into the black masses of foliage. Taken completely by surprise, she could not at once realize any part, much less all, of what those words of his involved; but she felt in her heart the chill of a great fear—the fear of what she would think, of what she would know, when she did realize.

His voice interrupted. "While you're on the unpleasant subject of those notions of yours," he said with an attempt at lightness in his embarrassed tone, "we might as well finish it—get it out of the way forever. I want you to stop thinking about the laboratory."

She turned, swift as a swallow.

"I admit I've been at fault—encouraging you to imagine I'd consent. But I thought you'd forgotten about it. Apparently you haven't."

A long silence.

"I repeat, I'm sorry I misled you. It seemed to me a trifling deception."

She did not speak, did not move.

"When you think it over, you'll see that I'm right—that we're much happier as we are."

After a long silence, which somehow alarmed him, though he told himself such a feeling was absurd, she crossed the balcony to the window. As she paused there, not looking toward him, the profile of those sweet, irregular features of hers stood out clearly. That expression, though it was quiet, increased his absurd alarm. "It's getting late," she said, and her tone was gentle, apologetic. "I think I'll go in."

"Are you angry, Courtney?"

"No," she replied, "I don't think so."

"Why are you silent?"

"I don't know," she said slowly. "I seem to have stopped inside."

He went and put his arm around her. She was passive as a doll. "Why, you're quite cold, child!"

"I must go in. Good night."

"I'll join you in a few minutes."

She shivered. "No," she said. "Good night."

He was somewhat disconcerted. Then he reflected that she could hardly be expected to give up her whims without a little struggling. "It shows how sweet and good she is," thought he, "that she took it so quietly." And he went to bed in the room across the hall—the room he had been occupying most of the time since three months before Winchie came. As he fell asleep he felt that he had laid the "ghost"

and had settled all his domestic affairs upon the proper basis. He slept,
but she lay awake the whole night, watching tearless beside her dead.
(*The Hungry Heart*, pp. 44–47)

Phillips had begun his novel, he said, where most novels ended, with
the lovers married and happy. His Courtney differed from such heroines in that she needed love, could play no woman game with a
husband who was not a husband, and knew no other game. She was
rejected by her mother, whose primitive obedience was to the will of
God. Courtney could not join the "female rotters" of her locale, the
time-wasters, the intriguers. Here was a human condition, it would
have seemed, worth the attention not only of Phillips's contemporary
commentators, but of those following.

Nevertheless it was possible for sensitive people to pick out of the
air impressions which related Phillips with the thoughtless among
fiction writers; as, for example, young F. Scott Fitzgerald, a fiction
reader at Princeton University:

> Amory read "Dombey and Son," because he thought he really
> should read better stuff; Robert Chambers, David Graham Phillips, and
> E. Phillips Oppenheim complete, and a scattering of Tennyson and
> Kipling.[7]

A few years later Thomas Wolfe remembered his boyish impressions
of the rich who visited Asheville, North Carolina, where Phillips had
probably buried his love:

> He gazed for hours into the entrances of the fashionable hotels, staring
> at the ladies' legs upon the verandas, watching the great ones of the
> land at their recreations, thinking with a pang of wonder, that here
> were the people of Chambers, of Phillips, of all the society novelists,
> leading their god-like lives in flesh, recording their fiction. He was
> deeply reverential before the grand manner of these books.[8]

It is interesting that these authors missed the true difference between
themselves and Phillips: that they believed themselves first and above
all "artists," whereas Phillips thought that only moral purpose gave
dignity to fiction. In his own time he was at odds with critics in their
definition of moral purpose. Thus he would have rejected Cooper's
characterization of Courtney's affair with Basil Gallatin as an exhibi-
tion of "frailty." For Phillips gave Courtney no impulses toward common liaisons. Her saddest illusions derived from her feelings that
Basil was a fine man, a partner in love and understanding, everything

she had lacked. Phillips was to puzzle elsewhere how one could look up to a lover while also looking down. But in *The Hungry Heart* his final judgment of Gallatin was that he was small. Not cowardly, not dishonorable, not ingenuous—just small.

The action involves mounting tempests and furtive meetings in the shadow of an oblivious and even blindly encouraging Richard, as well as of servants who have carried over from the regime antedating Courtney's arrival. It is complicated by the advent of another woman, Helen, Richard's cousin. Richard wants to marry her off to his "friend" Basil. It moves on to the scene in which, pursuing the idea, he suggests Helen help Basil in the laboratory. Poignantly, he brings up the skeleton of what had helped destroy his own married life:

> "Really, I'd like it," said Helen, a good deal of nervousness in her enthusiasm.
> "She could try it anyhow," urged Richard. "We need someone— don't we Basil?"
> "Yes," said Basil. "You remember, I suggested you ought to ask Mrs. Courtney to take a hand."
> "Courtney!" Vaughan laughed gayly. "She has no fancy for anything serious. Now Helen is masculine minded."
> "Not a bit of it," declared Helen, much agitated by such an accusation, in presence of an eligible young man. "I'm so much a woman, that I'm what is called a woman's woman."
> "Helen prefers to stay here," said Courtney. "So I think *I'll* try."
> Richard stared and frowned.
> She smiled at Basil. "Richard is getting broad minded," she went on slowly, selecting her words. "A short time ago the idea of a woman in that laboratory of his would have upset him quite. I remember, when we were first married, I made the most desperate efforts to get him to let me help. He was finally quite rude about it." She spoke with no suggestion of resentment; and indeed, that time seemed so remote, so like a part of another life or another person's life that she felt no resentment.
> "I'm sure—we'll—both—be glad to have you," stammered Basil. He was confused before the instinct-born thought that those few apparently simple words of hers, so quietly and so good-humoredly spoken, were in fact the story of the matrimonial ruin he had found when he came—and was profiting by.
>
> (*The Hungry Heart*, pp. 282–83)

So Courtney came to chemistry at last, and having a real interest— which Basil did not—learned rapidly and well, and became a valuable assistant. The laboratory work was, in fact, the true solace of her hectic days.

The denouement develops through a long, slow fall of the story, following Richard's stunned discovery of the affair. His murderous instincts are baffled by circumstances. And Phillips defies, at least, the romantic conventions of his day. He has Richard close his laboratory and go away to think through this thing that has destroyed his life plan. Courtney reorganizes, too. Basil loves her, no doubt; but suppose his love should fail? She negotiates with her old college friend, Narcisse Sierdorf, about the landscape architecture and interior design in which she has trained herself. . . . And then Richard returns—but a new Richard, relaxed and aired by his vacation, and with a new viewpoint.

There must be a divorce, yes. But, meanwhile, he needs an assistant; and his reconstructed outlook allows him to realize that Courtney has been useful, after all, in his laboratory. Basil returns from a trip to find his paramour absorbed in laboratory work. She rejects his outraged romantic feelings. An emotional crisis is precipitated and overcome, but not before Basil has revealed himself as no more concerned for Courtney's life and future than Richard had been.

Upton Sinclair teased Phillips for writing novels which all came out the same length; he wished his own fiction would be as predictable. Phillips, he said, seemed inordinately concerned about this observation.[9] Actually, it was not true. Phillips's novels expanded in size and dimensions. Thus *The Hungry Heart* was longer than *Light Fingered Gentry*, even though the latter had a much larger cast of characters and a series of plots which required integration. Nevertheless it was also true that Phillips's technique raised esthetic questions, some of which he answered more satisfactorily than others.

For example, in *The Hungry Heart* he created a child, Winchie, who was in some ways central to Courtney's dilemmas. He was all the child Phillips ever had, and he could not resist fussing over him in old-bachelor ways, to the discontent of at least one reader, who thinks him a little prig. More serious is the validity of Phillips's concluding section, and not its "happy ending" which, as has been seen, related to Phillips's general outlook. It is, rather, Phillips's *tempo* which is here in question, and the implications of sequence with which he handles it. The Richard-Courtney reconciliation is developed with some restraint, and seems valid in view of their proved mutual interests, though it might have seemed more valid—Phillips toyed with the idea—to have had Courtney experiment with a New York career, with the novel's conclusion being drawn from it.

The dismissal of Basil is another matter. His vanity, his reluctance to admit that Courtney could repudiate him after their lengthy carnal relationship, explains his crude challenge to Richard which all but destroys them. But can the reader believe that only a few pages later Basil is able to turn to the bland Helen and exchange avowals of love with her? Phillips's logic in human relations holds up; Basil has esteemed Helen as a "good" woman—presumably better than Courtney. But the *tempo* of these developments is humanly flawed. Dreiser by virtue of his very philosophy of aimlessness and accident in the affairs of people was incapable of such neat cutting of fictional margins.

This quality of moving with overabundant swiftness and overneat efficiency was not peculiar to Phillips alone, and may have been related to his American tempo of efficiency and quick results. O. Henry was also to be criticized by academics and the younger generation of artists for having been too "mechanical" in his story form, too dedicated to the "O. Henry" ending. His readership was sustained in some measure by the fact that his tales could be quickly perused and digested, and also because they could be readily anthologized. Phillips's protracted and intense tales required a different amount of interest and involvement, which his flaws did not help create.

"A man needs a woman, and a woman needs a man. They call it loving. They might as well call eating loving" (*Susan Lenox*, I, 232). So says a cynical woman to the young Susan Lenox. *The Hungry Heart* was based on other premises, which subordinated sexual hunger to human dignity. The book required an empathy mixed with intelligence, which may have consigned it to cultural oblivion, along with so much else in American life.

"It is true, as you say, that I have declined of late to write of anything but love," Phillips wrote Arthur Little, curiously approximating D.H. Lawrence's words of several years ahead.[10] Yet one can see how, following *The Hungry Heart*, to say nothing of Lawrence's own explorations in love, Phillips's *White Magic*, issued in March 1910, could seem a mere contemporary confection, not worthy of notice. It spoke of love, to be sure, and between an older man, an artist, and a young heiress. And it had her throwing herself at his head, another Phillips novelty at the time. It had her father seeking to rid himself of what he saw as a mere adventurer, at best of no social consequence, and the artist seeing himself as infringed upon, impugned, and challenged to defend his way of life.

Phillips himself liked the book and the title, "a nice poetical name for love that turns and overturns—makes a snobbish girl romantic and an ambitious artist a lover, not to speak of the changes in papa and mamma. . . . "[11] It does not help much, no doubt, to realize that Phillips was in this novel half-satirically pointing to himself. His artist Roger Wade paints standing up. He too has extreme life-and-death ideas on life and love. He too thinks eccentricity a stupid caricature of originality. He too walks, always, no matter what the weather. "Show me a rich artist and I'll show you a poor one," says Wade. But on the other hand, he does not despise money. "Money is a kind of food. I want—and I try to get—all of it I need. My appetite is larger than some, smaller than others. I take—or try to take—in proportion to my appetite" (*White Magic*, p. 105). Love, he thinks, is a worrisome thing, marriage baneful: "An artist who marries is a fool—and worse. If he's happily married imagination is smothered to death. If he's unhappily married it's stabbed to death" (*White Magic*, p. 41).

And such a colored pinwheel of opinion as:

> "Love is all excitement; marriage ought to be all calm. Marriage means a home—a family—a place to bring up children in peace and tranquillity, a safe harbor. Love is bohemian; marriage is bourgeois. Love is insanity; marriage is sanity. Love is disease; marriage is solid, stolid health."
>
> (*White Magic*, p. 12)

Phillips lived freely with socialists, writers, and editors, though the latter seem especially to have furnished him with entrée to wealthy homes certainly containing attractive daughters. As early as his "Alice" period he had admitted to himself that he was most comfortable with people raised in literacy and material circumstances like his own. *White Magic* clearly reflects his ruminations as he pondered his own future and the expectations of others. His tendency, as in passages of *Old Wives for New* and his soon to be released *The Husband's Story*, was to conceive of himself as shopping for a wife who would answer all his human needs. *White Magic* reflected his awareness that he needed more, that he could never give up his search for love.

His concept of the artist, too, was a contribution to an American esthetic. In his withering, but almost certainly overenthusiastic essay on the artist Robert Reid, he protested: "Why this cowardice of foreign opinion—of the critics so often caught approving absurd fakes from the European factories?" ("Painter of the Joy of Life," p. 484).

Reid seems to have been distinctly pedestrian, even in the illustrations with which Phillips provided his friend Little. Yet there is vigor in Phillips's overview of the American artistic scene, even before the dramatic and programmatically different outburst of art in the years following Phillips's death:

> America has already contributed some of its most renowned names to art. I suspect that one of those names will some day be written higher than some un-American Americans would, perhaps, now admit. If Robert Reid had lived abroad instead of in America, perhaps the pitiful intellectual snobbishness of our class that professes an interest in art would have discovered that the few foreign painters who through coming here have had the chance to view his work are right in regarding him as indeed a master, a leader and a teacher. But he stays at home and he paints at home—the home things. And he exhibits only at home. Our pitiful, pitiful snobbishness! Of how much pleasure it deprives us!
>
> ("Painter of the Joy of Life," p. 487)

Nevertheless it is likely that *White Magic* offers little to a modern reader not concerned for the details of his century. Nothing would be settled, Phillips had asserted, until the woman question was settled. It had been his intention in *White Magic* to put his mind wholly on the vagaries of love, as distinguished from the other themes in his novels with which he had mixed his man-woman relations. But whereas business and divorce and politics resolutely overlapped into the future, the love theme was wholly confounded by the mighty forces of World War I. Thereafter it would be possible to contrive tales of every kind, from tales pointing to the details of sexual urgency to tough-guy sagas which provided their own versions of love.

What would not be possible, except in debased sentimental forms, was to posit a world of beautiful women and splendid, handsome men somehow removed from the shadow cast by mountains of dead, disfigured, blasted, and insane soldiers and civilians. *White Magic* was no confection. Multitudes of young, healthy, good-looking men and women sought and to varying degrees found what the artist and his heiress sought: satisfying other-sex companionship. His treatment, however, failed to cope with tragedy or even the rumors of tragedy, and, compared with the later Ernest Hemingway's *The Sun Also Rises*, seems almost shockingly oblivious to the horrid and undignified in life.

Phillips knew of both, but his awareness is not obvious in *White Magic*. In its own binding it stood as no more than a criticism of a class of romantic fiction for which in its own time there was still much regard.

"I'm glad you like *White Magic*," Phillips wrote Bailey Millard. "I'm toiling at the proofs of it getting ready for the book. Then I'm going to shut myself in and write a novel—a longish one. They tell me a chicken sings before it lays an egg. But not this chicken. I make groaning sounds, no more like a song than the barking of a tonsilitic seal" ("Phillips's Methods," p. 13).

It is not clear which novel Phillips had in mind, for, as seen, he worked over manuscripts variously along the line of his development. Dreiser was able to raise up inordinate piles of manuscript in six months, and Phillips, certainly in first drafts, may well have added to his backlog in similar quantity. It is possible that it was *The Price She Paid* that he was projecting, in view of its distinct change in tone from other of the fiction he left behind. What is amusing is his promise to "shut [himself] in and write a novel"—as though he had not done this over and over again since he had begun his great adventure.

Despite his complaints, he now wrote with an ease and assertiveness such as he had not before revealed. From time to time he set down sharp and even angry comments as he responded to personal memories or his own descriptions of hypocrites or malicious characters. But more often he concluded that human nature, if it did not deserve blanket endorsement, merited compassion, and he could set down its foibles without excessive emotion.

Such was the tone he adopted for the last of his books to employ the first-person style of presentation, the only one of his formidable fiction to do so. But though *The Husband's Story* featured a fictional character, Geoffrey Loring, whose qualities required assessment by fictional standards, Phillips's last novels utilizing the third-person format also saw him riding his tide of self-expression more and more at the expense of the narrative, suggesting changes in his writing purposes.

The Husband's Story lacked *The Hungry Heart*'s intensity, perhaps for the better in the long run, and it proposed itself as a manuscript prepared by someone named Loring (a pseudonym) and put in Phillips's own hands for editing.

To aggravate my situation [Phillips's "preface" continued], in the letter accompanying the manuscript, after several pages of the discriminating praise most dear to the writer's heart, he did me the supreme honor of saying that in his work he had "striven to copy as closely as might be your style and your methods—to help me to the hearing I want and to lighten your labors as editor."

(*The Husband's Story*, p. 2)

On the other hand, Phillips "protested," he would have wished to disclaim responsibility for such a work. But "Loring, being both wise and kindly, never misses a good chance to put another under obligations." And Phillips, having been so put, submitted:

When you shall have read what follows, you may utterly reject my extenuating plea that any and every point of view upon life is worthy of attention, even though it serve only to confirm us in our previous ideas and beliefs. You may say that I should have repudiated my debt, should have refused to edit and publish the manuscript he confided to me. You may say that the general racial obligation to mankind—and to womankind—takes precedence over a private and personal obligation. Unfortunately, I happen to be not of the philanthropic temperament. My sense of the personal is strong; my sense of the general weak—that is to say, weak in comparison.

(*The Husband's Story*, p. 2)

The Husband's Story, then, was to be truly a novel—an anonymous work to be read and digested. Loring chose his reader pointedly:

I am tempted to begin with our arrival in Fifth Avenue, New York City, in the pomp and circumstance befitting that region of regal splendor. I should at once catch the attention of the women; and my literary friends tell me that to make any headway with a story in America it is necessary to catch the women, because the men either do not read books at all or read only what they hear the women talking about. . . . They tell me and I believe it, that our women abhor stories of middle-class life, abhor truth-telling stories of any kind, like only what assures them that the promptings of their own vanities and sentimental shams are true.

But patience, gentle reader, you with the foolish, chimera-haunted brain, with the silly ideas of life, with the ignorance of human nature including your own self, with the love of sloppy and tawdry clap trap. Patience, gentle reader. While I shall begin humbly in the social scale, I shall not linger there long. I shall pass on to the surroundings that entrance your snobbish soul. You will soon smell only fine perfumes, only the aromas of food cooked by expensive chefs. You will sit in drawing rooms, lie in bedrooms as magnificent as the architects and decorators and other purveyors to the very rich have been able to concoct. . . . Patience, gentle reader, with your box of caramels and your hair in curl papers and your household work undone—patience! A feast awaits you.

(The Husband's Story, p. 3)

A deep flaw thus appears at the outset in the book, if it is to be considered as reading for a period later than Phillips's own. That different eras may follow different chimeras may be granted; but Phillips's constant harping on boxes of caramels and hair in curl papers raises questions of obsolete interests which can trip readers working to follow the story line. And yet it was a strong line which dealt with significant people of Phillips's time, some of whom could have imaginatively been transmuted into representative characters of later decades.

Loring is portrayed as a self-made man, born in Passaic, New Jersey, when it was no more than a village. His father had kept a "dejected little grocery," and the family had lived in a dingy frame cottage, a story and a half in height, two rooms deep. Loring was not like his wife Edna, who had the humorless but useful gift of forgetting whatever it was she wished to forget. Loring did not regret his boyhood; he had enjoyed it. He was glad to get out of it, to make money, to engage in vast projects which the money had allowed him to enter. Loring had passed up through every class. He was not a rich man; in his own estimation he was a *business* man, at the top of a system that began with shoe-shiners and elevator men, and even less. Loring, in fact, was naive; he had no conception that much of his democracy was cant. And if he practiced it more than many of his fellow financiers, it was because he was an extraordinary man for the situation being displayed.

So merciless was Loring's attack on the American woman that Dr. Cooper negated it with praise:

[It] is the type of book that we have long had the right to expect from Mr. Phillips. . . . Like all of this author's best work in the past, it is a study of a marriage that failed. And the reason that it is a better and a bigger book than any of his others is not because of its theme, but because of its workmanship—the thing is better done, and its underlying structure, in its working out of details, in all that goes to make up good technique. The whole intimate drama of a pushing, climbing couple, who start from sordid beginnings . . . and end up in a Fifth Avenue mansion, is given from the husband's point of view with a grim and unsparing irony. It is a ruthless indictment of a certain type of American woman to undertake the duties of a wife and mother and home-maker; but at the same time . . . and this is the point that a great many readers miss—it also shows, between the lines, that while the husband throws all the blame upon his wife, the fault is as largely his as it is hers. If she has been cold and calculating and dishonest in her social life, he has been cold and calculating and dishonest in his business life.[12]

In a separate review Cooper dared a further bit of interpretation: Loring secretly loved the social prestige Edna sought, although he would not lift a finger to help her get it. This was simply inaccurate, as any attentive reader could say; and there were many other points of a like nature intended to dampen the force of the indictment. But more important was Cooper's effort to establish Loring and his wife as being special and insignificant types of Americans: mean, snobbish, dishonest.

For one thing, Phillips definitely respected the Loring kind of industrialist. Years before, in a pen-portrait for the *Saturday Evening Post* (28 June 1902) of Beveridge's friend George W. Perkins, whom he called "the right hand of Pierpont Morgan," he had answered Queen Elizabeth's "ignorant sneer at the commercial and therefore civilized Dutch" with the statement that "we know now that the men of trade and commerce and finance are the real builders of freedom, science and art." Loring had become rich by sharp dealings—but then, what industrialist had not? Loring, in fine, was the typical American success; and in one of Phillips's scenes he told how Loring had come to do something which was not merely wit, will, or hard work, but— sharp. How could he look his wife and child in the face with that on his conscience? He went to Edna for spiritual support, and she demanded that he go ahead and protect her rising social ambitions.

Had she urged him to keep straight, he would not have become a millionaire many times over; he might have become something else. And Edna would never have become a princess.

A typical American success: the poor boy grown rich, intelligent, hard-working, capable, and one with fine insights, circumscribed as he might be by his place in the world. He takes part of the blame for Edna's development. His head had been cluttered with nonsense about the spirituality of women and their moral superiority to men. Phillips's treatment of the subject brought joy to some of the vital people of his time, for example, Mrs. Annie Nathan Meyer, active in education and other causes. In her letter to the *New York Times Literary Supplement* (29 January, 1911) she praised the author's range, characterizations, and steady view of reality:

Into one tradition after another he has charged with his gall-steeped pen. The woman is no home-maker, only a brazen schemer to achieve a more and more costly environment of discomfort. She is no mother; she knows nothing about the real needs of children, she is keen only for their worldly success. She is not the inspirer of her husband; she likes to pose as such. . . .

And finally [the author] boasts that "he has pricked the bubble of the American woman's pretense of superior culture." This undoubtedly took more courage than anything else he has done. Strangely enough, women are not so ashamed to admit they are poor wives, and worse mothers; but when you take from them the glory of upholding the tradition of refinement and culture, then the blow hurts.

Granville Hicks called Edna a "silly woman," missing her enormous will and steadiness of purpose and the shoddy nature of some of his *New Masses* female readers. Her snobbish goals as such are water over the dam. It is helpful to sustaining a critical sense beyond a book's era to compare Edna with Sinclair Lewis's Fran in *Dodsworth,* and to ask what if anything sustains it any more than *The Husband's Story.* Lewis had a fine ear for Babbittry, but his account of 1920s businessmen and their wives contrasts almost startlingly with the greater assurance and sophistication of those who in time subscribed to *Fortune* and the *Wall Street Journal,* book clubs, and the *New York Times,* and showed numerous other signs of awareness of the nuances of society.

Lewis's Fran was more addled than Loring's Edna, and in some ways less a person. One point in Lewis's favor was that he did not challenge the reader to match his social ideals and life styles with those of the Dodsworths, as Phillips had demanded in connection with the Lorings. Still, in 1978 there was an interesting question as to just what made *Dodsworth* memorable, and also *The Husband's Story* not. If that was the case.

There was more, much more, to the book. Phillips gave his reader a glimpse, a bare glimpse of the lawyer Norman—Frederick Norman; he was to have his own book in *The Grain of Dust.* Susan Lenox appears as a name, a guest of Mary Kirkland at a weekend on Long Island. Mary Kirkland's brother first opened Loring's eyes to what had happened to his family while he had been absorbed in business; and later Loring married Mary.

Loring mentioned that he was reserving what he had seen and heard in South America for another volume. Did Phillips plan a sequel to *The Husband's Story,* or perhaps a nonfiction book? "One of a different kind," Loring had called his projected volume.

"I forgive you, gentle reader. Go in peace."

So ended the last of his books Phillips was to hold bound in his hands. Those were great days. The Republican party was in a process of split. The Progressives were aligning. Beveridge joined them in the face of deep Democratic unrest in his own Indiana. A new party—a party of the people! Phillips's fervid work for Beveridge hid his fear that Beveridge might be repudiated by his electorate, as in fact he was. Phillips's posthumous sketch of a novel, *George Helm* (1912), suggests that he died a Progressive, aware that "the people" were subject to fickleness and foolishness, but believing that they continued to carry within them the seeds of renewed democracy.

His own life now had the lineaments of peace and satisfaction. Every day, he wrote one of his sisters sunnily, life had more meaning for him. There seems to have been little overt drama in those days. Although he looked as young as ever, he looked forward to settling anew in his program. From forty to forty-five, he observed, a man begins to reap what he has sown. He is less adept at experiment, his heart and brain begin to lose their facility and lightness; character shows through.

How his would have responded to the new world taking shape under the establishments with which he had coped, it is impossible to judge. The Progressives, with their demand for more freedoms, more open dialogue, more self-assertion, had opened doors they had not anticipated. Soon there would be a youth explosion which would produce a dazzling array of talents and eccentrics: precursors of the new time which would have no use for Phillips. What would he have made of Randolph Bourne, of Van Wyck Brooks, of Max Eastman and Edgar Lee Masters and, of course, of Sinclair Lewis? And what could they have made of him? Many Progressives of his generation, though out of the headlines, found things to do, but few were able to grow with the changing times.

There had been a small scare of serious-sounding crank letters. Threats upon Phillips's life. Anonymous mail. Carolyn insisted that Phillips inform the police, and he did call Central Office to report the matter. Then the somber letters stopped coming.

Later the police sergeant asked Phillips about it.

"Oh, I guess that crank has forgotten all about me," Phillips told him. "I haven't heard from him in months."

Phillips did not know that a young man was living across the street on the top floor of the Rand School of Social Science, and that his purpose in renting the room had been to have Phillips's apartment in constant sight. The young man's room was at the back of the building. He had nothing particular to do with the socialists, but he was nevertheless noticed to be mildly queer, though apparently good-natured. On pretexts of conversation he often visited those who had front rooms, and would look across Nineteenth Street. Sometimes he would forget his host and stare out of the window silently and without moving. The occupants thought him a pest, but harmless.

13

Murder in Gramercy Park

Phillips thought of his personal life as his own affair. Not for him the well-publicized exhibitions of D'Annunzio. There were interviews with correspondents and others, but a Phillips interview tended to become a discussion of ideas, of methods of work, of national and international problems. It was Phillips's contention that these were the important aspects of a man's life. But if he appraised himself so, others did not. The fact that he was a bachelor was often noted. His persistent habits of work were all but notorious. Did he really work *every* night? We have seen that Phillips lived more richly in his routine than vainglorious seekers of the strange and exotic. He read, traveled, attended plays and social functions, all of which failed to appease those dissatisfied with his personality and ways.

His height, his elegant clothing, the sense of control and achievement he exuded made a sharp contrast with his severe prose, his persistent walking, his common sense and scorn of casuistries, all of which seemed a direct criticism of others who were not like him. Their interest was compulsive and verged on the nosey. It was, for example, known that he took three and four showers a day, at a time when it was suspected that too many wettings were not good for the health.[1]

Most threatening to some people, not all, was the fact that he foisted his views on others. Characteristic is the last reminiscence of Anna Strunsky Walling, friend of Jack London, wife of the distinguished socialist William English Walling. Phillips had accompanied her down to the street from his sumptuous apartment. He stood there at the curb while Mrs. Walling arranged herself in her automobile and warned her at length against overindulging in car riding. It would not only separate her, slowly but surely, from the people on the sidewalk, Phillips insisted—he seems to have feared the automobile was creating a special class of aristocrats—but it would affect her health.

Phillips took too seriously the questions of life, thought friends and others who were not friends. Furthermore, he harbored undesirable views. The *New York Times*, following his death, deplored in its editorial comment his "wild thinking," but added, probably in an effort at graciousness, that he had been changing his views.[2] Some of his ideas seemed more appropriate in unshorn socialists, at least as average people then conceived them to be, than in a well-favored and successful man of letters. Indeed, not a few verbal socialists of the time who held to the inevitability theory—that socialism was bound to come by itself, nothing could stop it—saw no reason for putting themselves out in any way. Phillips himself was inclined to think that socialization of key industries at least was on the way; but he resisted the more drastic tenets of socialism in the interests of his democratic and individualistic heritage.[3]

None of this helped make Phillips more acceptable to those of his time who were active and consequential in its affairs, but who needed psychological assurances he would not provide. Lincoln Steffens exposed criminal facts about party bosses who had toughs and killers in their entourage, but who did not so much as dare to threaten Steffens thanks to the sheath of public sympathy and visibility which protected him. Phillips stood alone, as a literary man and as a public figure, his one protection his individual determination and his belief that the public needed and wanted courage in its conspicuous figures.

He was cantankerous, but he was far from humorless. He read his Zola and Tolstoi and retained his modesty. He was a spokesman for a business civilization, and his work would have validity if it did. He was not only capable of jokes, but of practical jokes. The *Times*, later on scraping up anecdotes to his memory, recalled that he had, at a party of wealthy acquaintances, urged them to mingle with the masses and learn what their reputation was among them. He actually arranged to have them board a Fifth Avenue "rubber-neck" bus with a guide to comment on the millionaires who owned mansions on the street. The guide had not only been witty, but had made critical comments upon the members of the party by name. They were said to have accepted good-humoredly the later revelation that Phillips had cued the guide on what to say.

With January of 1911, Carolyn later recalled, the demon of work entered into Phillips anew. Night after night he stood tall at his black drafting-table and mulled over his stories, articles, dramas, and the larger works. A fine frenzy seems to have possessed him. He had decided to release *Susan Lenox* at last, and with that decision it was as if he were releasing some part of himself. It was his masterpiece, he told his sister; but it was more. It was far and away the most dangerous work he had prepared. And it was everything that had motivated him since he had first gone into journalism almost a quarter of a century before to learn what it was a novelist ought to know.

The moral passion which Edwin Markham "so keenly felt" in his last talk with Phillips, the latter's feeling that he would write little more fiction, his mounting interest in the drama, and—most significantly—his new interest in science which prompted striking passages in his yet unpublished *The Grain of Dust,* all these factors foretold some radical change operating within him. *The Price She Paid,* and various new articles and sketches, were written not with the enthusiasm of youth, but in a manner of summation. Other interests beckoned him, a large world for a man full to the brim of love of life and experience, almost ascetic in his devotion to it.

"Everything was finished when Graham went to bed that last morning," his sister said afterwards, "everything to the last sheets of the last short story. For weeks he had been working with feverish energy, not wasting a day or an hour, as if he knew that his time was short."

Not everything was "finished," in fact. And yet perhaps as Carolyn Frevert willed to believe, everything. . . . As was his habit, Phillips continued to sleep through the small hours and part of the morning, to "breakfast" with Carolyn, and then to walk out upon Nineteenth Street, over to Irving Place, and up the half block to Gramercy Park, which he circled, passing The Players and other well-known club houses on his way to the Princeton Club on the other side, where he picked up his mail and exchanged hellos with acquaintances.

On Sunday, January 22, at eleven o'clock in the evening, Phillips set himself to a night of work, and it was seven o'clock in the morning when he left his desk. He slept briefly and well, washed, and prepared for the day. He and his sister ate together at the National Arts Club, and then Phillips remembered to call Charles Frohman, the producer, to tell him he had completed three acts of *White Magic,* the play he was preparing for Billie Burke. It was to be Phillips's second play on the boards, and it meant much to him. He saw playwriting as a challenge and had taken to heart the failure of *The Worth of a Woman* because, he thought resentfully, of the truth it had told, not its inadequacies. This time, perhaps, New Yorkers would not be shocked by the morals of an old-fashioned American.

That day Phillips had received another threatening letter, one of a number of similar messages of recent date reminiscent of those which had disquieted him some months before. Strangely, it was addressed to him, but signed with his own name. "This is your last day," it read. Such things were never pleasant. Phillips put the letter into his pocket.

At half-past one o'clock Phillips prepared to stop in as usual to the Princeton Club for his mail before visiting publishers. He placed the manuscript of his story *Enid* inside his breast pocket and stepped out into the brisk, sunny afternoon.

The Princeton Club faced Gramercy Park's high, exclusive gates from the north. Newton James, a broker, and Frank Davis, a mining engineer, came leisurely out of the club walking west. They saw Phillips striding toward them some hundred feet away, and, leaning against the iron railing of the Schuyler Schieffelin home, a man who had been loitering about for some time.

Phillips was approaching them. His fellow clubmembers had just recognized him when the man beside the fence began to shoot. There were six reports, then they heard the man cry, "There you are! I guess that does for you."[4] Phillips stopped in his tracks, hardly yet realizing pain, perhaps. The stranger turned the gun to his own head, and added, "I'll finish the job now."

He walked to the curb and pulled the trigger, and his body rolled dead into the street.

Only a fraction of time had elapsed. A passerby hurried up to Phillips, who had staggered back to the fence and was trying to keep from falling. "I'm shot," he said, "get a doctor." He turned partway around and looked at the dead man lying face upward in the street. "My God! How could he do it?" he groaned, and then, "How long does it take that doctor to come?"

The man sustained Phillips against the iron railing. Blood was seeping through his clothes and falling. James and Davis ran up.

"Graham," cried Davis, "what has happened?"

"He shot me in the bowels," Phillips articulated. "Never mind him. Get a doctor."

He was now suffering intensely. The three men carried him into the club reception room and laid him on a rug. . . . Not so much in the bowels as in the chest and elsewhere. Phillips waited in pain, and gathering rather than lessening consciousness. At last the ambulance from Bellevue Hospital swung up. He was strapped into the stretcher and lifted slowly into the car, and as he was passed in he whispered to the attendant, "Do not tell my mother. She is old and this will kill her. I am young, and I may live yet."

Somewhere—perhaps in *Victory*—Joseph Conrad tells us that it is only in our moments of crisis that we know what we are. Phillips's were the words of one who had long since made up his mind on basic questions of the world. So, wounded, he set a seal of reality to his life work.

For hours the assassin lay on the pavement in the afternoon sun. Later his body was removed to the morgue.

Fitzhugh Coyle Goldsborough was of "good" Washington and Baltimore family. Even as he fired his revolver, his sister was scheduled to marry the United States consul at Nottingham, England, William F. Stead. Goldsborough was thirty-two years old, had attended Harvard, and was a musician. He had been a queer boy, had written good verse, it was said. He was a trained violinist, having studied under excellent teachers in Washington and Vienna. Stories were told of his eccentricities.

He had made no career, achieved no eminence. A dreamer with poetic illusions, he had settled to nothing. He had played in orchestras which had included the Pittsburgh Symphony Orchestra, had compelled a colleague to listen to his verse, and forced criticism of it. And not liking the criticism he had in a rage broken a violin over the man's head.

He was a failure and brooded. He entertained dreams of grandeur and weakly excused his inability to achieve it. Somehow, in the gray fog of his unhappy thoughts, the wraith of Phillips took its place, as prominent men and women figure in the dreams of thousands as friends and lovers. . . . Goldsborough hated Phillips.

But Goldsborough was not only envious, not only dissatisfied with his own life and accomplishments. He was sick. Aberration at one point had forced him to spend time in a sanatorium. Normal impulses became accentuated and realities confused. He too was a great writer, a great man. He studied Phillips's works not as the ordinary reader did, but with every personal reaction. And he dreamed. . . . He had written that scene, created this character. He *was* the character. . . . Again, Phillips's castigations of weakness and vanity stung him like a lash. The dissections were personal reproaches, expressions of a directed contempt. Goldsborough writhed in anguish and humiliation.

He may even have seen Phillips in Washington—so it was later suggested. Phillips visited the capital often. Sight of his independent figure could well have fed the maw of Goldsborough's jealousy.

But when Goldsborough read *The Fashionable Adventures of Joshua Craig* something closed in his mind. The book was without the shadow of a doubt a personal attack. It was he, Goldsborough, and Goldsborough's family whom this boor was insulting. Phillips had entered the soul of his family and here distorted it and lied about it. . . . The fires of envy and self-disgust leaped skyward, fed by an ever-intensifying insanity. It was not Phillips who was the great writer; it was he. Phillips filched his stories, capitalized upon his ideas, and in return mocked and affronted him.

A weak fantasy, George Sylvester Viereck's *House of the Vampire,* was then circulating. It told of an intellectual vampire who absorbed the genius of all with whom he came in contact, as Shakespeare or Homer might have done in their own time. This formed the inspiration for what became Goldsborough's one obsession. Phillips was a vampire and he himself was the helpless victim.

This was not to be borne. The wretched man felt himself beset. Fate would not free him. He was no failure, no, not he. Phillips rent him, tore away his strength. In self-defense he wrote threatening letters to Phillips and even sought out Mayor William Jay Gaynor to complain of being annoyed. Strangely, he found occasion to mention, but almost impersonally and without animosity, that Phillips had attacked him in print. And yet not strangely, for a certain cunning protects illusions in the layers of the human consciousness. The mayor's secretary heard Goldsborough out and noticed nothing suspicious. He suggested that the next time Goldsborough had reason to feel he was being hounded, he might inform the precinct chief. Goldsborough never accepted this suggestion; the police would not understand. Evidently he would have to settle with fate himself. Phillips was becoming bolder and more arrogant. . . . The evidence of the diary Goldsborough kept, as spread across the newspapers, is that he believed Phillips to be drawing more and more recklessly upon his mind.

How much of himself was Phillips? Was he Phillips, or Phillips he? Hence the letter he sent the novelist and signed with the latter's name.

In this way Goldsborough spent the last weeks, meanwhile acquainting himself with Phillips's movements and making his tortured diary in which he included ideas for poems, scraps of verse, notes for short stories—and above all notes about Phillips, Phillips, Phillips.

At Bellevue Hospital they prepared Phillips for the operating table while outside the news swept the city and was flashed throughout the country. David Graham Phillips had been shot and was fighting for life! Even those who had most disliked his ways seem to have been momentarily stopped in trying to fathom this thing that had befallen him. Acquaintances like Will Irwin carried the shocking news to acquaintances like Booth Tarkington. Carolyn Frevert was busy in the marketplace buying food for a dinner she had scheduled for that evening. At the butcher's she ordered meat.

"You're not having a dinner tonight, Mrs. Frevert," said the butcher gently.

"Oh, yes I am," she answered lightly.

"You're not having a dinner tonight," he repeated. And she looked up and into his eyes, startled. . . . Later, she sat holding her brother's hand in a ward of Bellevue when Arthur Little came. Little found Phillips very pale, very still, "but his eyes flashed recognition, and we all three remained for what seemed a very long time, but which was probably not more than ten minutes, in silence."

At about 5:25 in the afternoon Phillips went under the knife and for an hour surgeons, notably Dr. John Baldwin Walker, worked over him, trying to prevent the spread of infection from wounds in his stomach and chest. Then he was permitted to rest. . . . Phillips's brother Harrison, a journalist, had stepped from a western train to see Phillips and his sister in time to hear the incredible news being shouted in the street. Now Phillips looked up beside his bed and saw his brother miraculouly there.

"But how could you have got here in time, Bill?" he murmured.

The surgeons announced that Phillips had stood up to the operation remarkably well, and that he seemed to be in good condition.

We meet the fate that suits our character, says Aldous Huxley. The metaphysical phrase poises itself on reality. Phillips would have denied it, but here was a fate that had threatened him for years. He had challenged the major tenets of his age, in working politics and business, true, but even more in the principles, the expectations which lay under the day's getting and spending. The madman's hatred of Phillips, his need for disposing of him was deeper than the need of others to stop his discussions of Senate activities, for it was Phillips's character and brains which were unbearable to Goldsborough. It was not for "The Treason of the Senate" articles that Phillips was shot, but for the weave of a novel.

The day dragged on. Beveridge hurried from Washington, and when admitted to Phillips's bedside it was to learn with relief that the wounds were under control and that Phillips would recover. Self-absorbed as he was, as usual, he would have stayed, had any doubts been suggested. So he left word to be kept informed and hurried back to Washington.

Throughout the day of January 24, Phillips moved in pain. His stomach wound particularly troubled him. The anesthesia of the previous day nauseated him now, and he could retain no food. It was a long siege, and Phillips fought unafraid. Life, as he knew, was only a process of development; and he had written that no sensible man ever worries about his own death, for "when I shall die, I will not be here."

Yet life was sweet. He turned his back on death. Up until eight o'clock it seemed that he would live. He asked his sister to distribute available mementoes to friends, if he should fail to recover. He was momentarily amused at the thought that his publishers were acquiring much more publicity than they would voluntarily buy. Then the tide turned. An internal hemorrhage began which could not be controlled. Phillips became perceptibly weaker, and it was clear that death was imminent. Fully conscious, Phillips struggled on, but it was he who finally saw that hope was futile.

"I could have beaten two bullets," he whispered, "but six were too many."

They had fought a good fight. There was nothing more to do. Phillips remained conscious until twenty-five minutes before the end. After that they waited, his brother and sister and the surgeon, and at 11:07 p.m. he died.

Arthur Brisbane called at the hospital. Robert W. Chambers called. George Horace Lorimer, Samuel Blythe, and Alfred Henry Lewis all called. Lewis, an emotional man, all but found the situation unbearable. Arthur Little found a note for him at the hospital, from which Phillips's body had been removed. Beveridge came north in response to Harrison Phillips's telegram to arrange for the funeral.

Phillips was dead; the news was broken. With the quick adjustments of true journalism, the papers prepared their obsequies, and then—what more was there to say?

On Friday afternoon services were held in St. George's Church about which, years before, Phillips had written so intelligent and alive a chapter of his private Americana for a magazine.[5] Now he lay there in state attended by Beveridge and Chambers, by Joseph Sears and Arthur Little, and others. The streets outside swarmed with people. Bishop David H. Greer would have liked to officiate, but a train delay prevented him, and as a result (in Little's recollection), "a minister who had never known Graham, or been known by him—a minister without personality, with artificial intonation of delivery—a minister who had to read what he had to say and who apparently could not say anything that he could not read, intoned a service which Graham would have hated."[6] Little thought Phillips's sense of humor would have prevailed over his sense of disgust, and he thought Phillips would have liked the ballad the well-known Negro baritone Harry Burleigh sang.

There was talk of returning the body to Indiana, but Carolyn certainly found that personally intolerable, as well as inappropriate; later she would lie beside her brother in the earth. Phillips had, of course, remembered his home town with affection, and idealized it in his writings. But New York—vast, complex, exciting—had given him his best years. It had helped him to find himself, had been his citadel for work. He loved New York.

So Carolyn left him nearby in Valhalla, New York, and over his grave she had written: *Father, forgive them, for they know not what they do.*

14

Afterglow

"David's death left everyone speechless," wrote Adele Lewisohn to Charles Edward Russell,[1] and indeed his numerous friends and acquaintances found little to say to the world, and less and less as times changed and dimmed their own contemporary importance.

"For two days Phillips's death was the sensation of the papers. The third day the front page news was of the disappearance of Dorothy Arnold."[2] It was tragic that so cold-hearted and unimaginative a *bon mot* could be recorded in a publication meant for enduring instruction, with no offense being felt by the humanists who were expected to use it.

In the echo of those stunning revolver shots, it is with some sense of the vindication of life that people other than such posterity as the above could learn that all had not ended with Phillips's death. Several articles by Phillips greeted the readers of magazines, with their author scarcely removed. And the week following Phillips's death serial publication of *The Grain of Dust* began. Anna Strunsky Walling, reading it, felt impelled to write of him in the *Saturday Evening Post* (October 21, 1911) and express her sense of loss:

> I thought how natural it was to his big, direct nature to go out to master America, to learn her by heart, inspired by the task of expressing and interpreting her, and to do so in the sledge-hammer method she herself employs, caring only to be true to the truth. I saw how the courage of his work rose from the courage of his character. . . . I should have realized how there was a leap in his power which bore out the feeling he himself had, that he was just learning, just beginning, that his years of sustained and concentrated effort were beginning to fulfill themselves.

She recalled his modesty and earnestness. "Before I die," he had said, "I want to learn the secret of Tolstoi and Dostoevsky." She remembered their last twilight talk in a garden in Paris:

He told me that he was engaged on a novel of which he had already written about four hundred thousand words, and in which he showed that the respectable men and women of society were literally responsible for the horrible degradation of the barter in women. "The public will not soon forgive me this book," he said.

But before *Susan Lenox* was released, other writings, unattended by the author, were to fall into a welter of changing times. *The Grain of Dust* was a tour de force of concept and execution, freely and boldly expressed. The reader who could not learn from it had nothing to learn from Phillips. The infatuation which precipitated the wealthy corporation lawyer Frederick Norman from his comfortable and secure cubbyhole in the gilded system of finance into rudderless insecurity was told with a sweep and style marking Phillips's complete mastery of his intentions.

All for love adequately describes what happened to Norman. This time it is the man who is victim of white magic, but with fictional results less equivocal than before. Norman, at the top of the legal profession while yet young and in his prime, engaged to an heiress, desperately requires the most insignificant of his office staff. *Nouveau riche*, talented young men and even more mature, more sophisticated elements of triumphant America did this, and would continue to do it in defiance of good sense and social pressure. And yet how trite a subject: stenographer marries employer.

But a book like Phillips's must be separated from the silly or lugubrious yarns which succeeded those of Progressive times, though having the shadow of their themes. Their basic fault was a consistent ignoring of the material facts of life. Such writers never knew what motivated men and women besides the unqualified "love" they touted, the senseless bravery of their characters, and their freedom from all human needs and reactions. Their stories approximated the insubstantial fantasies of the silent millions of Americans. In the twentieth-century American novel, there was an ascendant stage in fictional themes which resulted in novels like *The Grain of Dust*, *Jennie Gerhardt*, and *The House of Mirth*, but these themes decayed and became impotent in talented hands, to be supplemented by other major themes capable of directing mature craftsmanship.

Phillips at no stage of his novel had illusions about Norman. Neither, for that matter, had Norman. He knew he was an important corporation lawyer because he, better than others, could maneuver law to the benefit of great financiers. Why lie? When the world was a better place he, or his successors, would do things more beneficial to society.

Dorothea Holloway was not a stenographer in the common sense of the word. She was the daughter of a great and most impractical scientist who, when he might have sold his talents profitably to corporations interested in manufacturing gadgets, preferred to putter with the basic problems of science and life. Naturally, he was poor. Norman had his moments when he felt small beside this vague and bemused thinker. But this was the twentieth century, and a man who could not make his way was, in one sense at least, a fool.

The devilish thing, so far as Norman was concerned, was that Dorothea was her father's daughter. She revered his work and ideals, and had no awe of Norman. In fact she disliked him in a quiet, inexperienced way.

What shines as clearly from Phillips's pages as a swift-moving narrative can permit without interfering with the story line is that Norman was drawn to Dorothea because his soundness of character pulled him away from the trivial life to which his wealth led him. Norman did not *want* Dorothea. Reason told him that he would be done with her after the briefest intimate acquaintanceship. But then, if he could have had her so casually, she would not have been Dorothea.

Norman compromised his engagement with his heiress. With too careless a disregard of consequences he strove fatuously to bind Dorothea to him by helping her father. The engagement ended violently—the heiress's father took his lucrative business away from Norman's firm. Rumor had it that Norman was losing his grip. And when the scientist died, Dorothea was done with Norman—and told him so—and Norman felt the hollowness within, which can make going on intolerable to those who are deprived and have no hope of acquiring some fancied essential to living.

Later, when Norman had gone close to the bottom—he drank, business left him, he moved to smaller quarters, he saw friends shy away from him—he analyzed his failure as having failed to lay in a supply of money to tide him over bad times. But had Norman had the money—had he made a vested interest of himself—he would never have come the way he had in the first place; and he would have somehow consoled himself for the lack of Dorothea. In due time he stopped his descent, not alone, and with a sort of negative assistance from Dorothea. After that, being Norman, he regained something of his place in the business world.

Those who must hurry to discover the social and political implications of the tale will find them more involved than a casual glance
might suggest. For Norman is, in essentials, no better or worse than he
had been before. He is still a corporation lawyer, though one probably
requiring fewer Wall Street scalps than formerly to satisfy his ego,
now that he spends time at home and avoids the Uptown phase of a
successful lawyer's life. Norman is like Phillips in despising foreign
marriages and idle men and women. On the other hand, his law work
is for corporations, and his range of active social sympathies probably
limited. Did he vote for Taft in 1908? What *were* his social views, and
what expression did he give them? These and other conjectures are
useful as they touch the individual reader.

But first he has the opportunity of enjoying the simple humanity
of Norman and his Dorothea, and the friendly commentary of Phillips.

From *The Grain of Dust* to *The Price She Paid* was a step from
warmth to a cold plunge. The writer had many moods and approaches
with which to nettle the public and its critics. And the approach of
The Price She Paid was not the story-teller's approach. Payment of a
price was a way of thought which had been with Phillips all his life.
One paid for everything he got. What hurt Phillips was the blindness
and futility of much human anguish, the poisoned sleep of the millions, fettered to jobs and fellow-sufferers. As another Progressive said:

> Not that they starve, but starve so dreamlessly,
> Not that they sow, but that they seldom reap,
> Not that they serve, but have no gods to serve,
> Not that they die but that they die like sheep.[3]

So Phillips hardened his heart, crushed down his pity, and spoke his
version of the truth. He spared no illusion, no excuse for failure. *The
Price She Paid* hurt, hurt as no "objective" study did. It would not let
the reader sleep.

No extenuating circumstances, Phillips said clearly, can lessen
the facts of bondage and discontent. And basic to these was economic
bondage. Like Emily Bromfield of *A Woman Ventures*, Mildred Gower
was left penniless on the death of her father. She could do nothing,
and straightway felt the effects of her condition. Her brother's contemptuous references to her unmarried state and dependency, her
mother's sordid remarriage, and the frank insults of her stepfather,
who demands that she be off, put her on the rack.

Mildred marries a wealthy man and now feels the chains of married dependency. Whatever the relevance or irrelevance of her social condition to later American circumstances, there can be no questioning the reality of her own anguish. She walks the very fringe of sustenance, and knows that as much as she needs food on any terms, she must give something in return, if she is to live.

> It is more than the very X-ray photography of truth [says a Phillips enthusiast in one of the few memorable passages of his largely myopic work], warped and disguised in a welter of human meanings . . . it is a virtual vivisection of human motives. . . . It is sordid and revolting in some details at first. Later it is less and less brutally compelling, more and more intellectually satisfying and fascinating. . . . Finally the book becomes illuminating and ennobling . . . according to the capacity of the reader to bring much or little to the reading of this modern masterpiece.[4]

That Phillips dealt in part with a social condition which mocked democratic ideals one can debate. That Phillips impeded the story at every turn with his comment, no one should care to deny. What is impressive is that the characters nevertheless live, weighted down as they are with the shackles of Phillips's interpretation. Donald Keith, an alter ego of Phillips's, who opens Mildred's eyes to her self-deception about her seriousness and determination to succeed as a singer, is as cold and inhuman as life itself can be when one is bereft of support. The reader cries out against his justice untempered by mercy, to say nothing of love.

Phillips's implicit answer is that Keith loved Mildred, and that his violent approach to her was his way of showing her the faults which prevented her from becoming independent and successful. But why must everyone be successful? Those who care might follow the question through the book. Esthetically, the truth remained that the novel was not whole, that the story-teller's impulse, though not in a shallow sense, had been inhibited.

Phillips, with his constant revisions, might well have chosen to do more with *The Price She Paid*, had he lived. Still, his method shows through in the tale, indicates that he wished to use the fiction as a vehicle for ideas rather than narrative. Several other of his last works issued posthumously contain similar traits. For readers not committed to a particular theory of fiction, this development in Phillips is a challenge rather than a puzzle. The bottom question in the book is whether dependency and independency are of sufficient interest to late twentieth-century Americans to warrant steady attention, even to overstatement.

Degarmo's Wife and Other Stories collected three of Phillips's short-long, or long-short stories, the best, in fact, of his shorter works. Most of Phillips's brief pieces were, as Frank Harris remarked, too sketchy for depth. Phillips required leeway for best results. But the three stories of this book were all made up of a hundred pages or over—not closely spaced—and gave him some necessary room. Their tone was quite similar: thoughtful, unexcited. "Degarmo's Wife" added a chapter to *Old Wives for New*, giving details of the married life of Murdock's daughter, with the quick, affectionate references to Sophy and Murdock which an author will give, to whom his characters are meaningful.

The base of Phillips's story was the old idea he had sketched twenty years earlier in *Harper's Weekly* under the title of "The First Born." Similar phrases and thoughts were actually used, whether consciously or unconsciously. "Degarmo's Wife," however, fleshed out identical scenes with detail which made its predecessor seem forlorn and pathetic indeed.

"Degarmo's Wife" echoed dimly something of the drive in *Old Wives for New*. "Enid," the second story in the book, written in the three parts of "Courtship," "Marriage," and "Love," seems almost static in comparison. The characters of Walter Prescott and Enid, presented as youth and maid, then as husband and wife, and finally as sweethearts, all but stand still while Phillips cogitates over them as man and woman. This story Ludwig Lewisohn offered in an anthology as furnishing a synopsis of Phillips's style and work. His judgment seems inadequate because he did not indicate any awareness that Phillips's outlook and self-expression had to be discerned within a spectrum of disparate works.

"White Roses and Red," the last of the three stories, best tells us that Phillips was moving away from his old self. What motivated its writing? It told in deep tones of a man who had gone into his forties, who had not accomplished much in life besides experience and amusement. He meets a veritable child, Georgina Bristow, whose mother he had known years before Georgina was born. She becomes enamored of him in terrifying fashion. Fenton nervously finds he cannot laugh away her quite evident feelings for him by pointing to their disparate ages. . . . The reader suddenly recalls that Phillips had created Degarmo as years older than his wife.

"Why do you always insist on your age?" Georgina asks earnestly. "I—no one—ever thinks of it. A man is—just a man. And a woman likes him or she doesn't. Usually she doesn't if he's young and silly" (*Degarmo's Wife and Other Stories*, p. 315).

But Fenton cannot bear so much of her youth and fire; he finds himself too often in discussions involving ideas and ambitions, and—

" 'Getting ready,' he repeated the words thoughtfully. 'Yes, I used to think that. But I either waited too long or never really intended to go down. Now my sword is rusted to the scabbard, and—' he sighed. He looked up and found her eyes sympathetically upon him" (*Degarmo's Wife and Other Stories*, p. 279).

Fenton cannot support such a mockery of his life. He cannot have her; she cannot have him—there is nothing left to have. The fact strikes her to the vitals. Her roots, carefully sheltered in a convent, are not sunk deep enough for her in life to enable her to rebuild her dreams among others.

So ends the final and perplexing story of the last significant book issued before *Susan Lenox* burst over the horizon of Phillips's work.[5]

15

Susan Lenox:
An American Odyssey

For several years after his assassination, talk persisted about an enormous novel Phillips was known to have left unpublished. His reputation, as Upton Sinclair wrote bitterly, had already been put in his grave. Still, there was his unpublished novel. Some critics assumed that it was one of those which had already been issued posthumously—*The Grain of Dust*, perhaps, or *The Price She Paid*. *Bookman*, however, which was better informed, called Phillips's publishers a number of times to ask about the novel which Phillips had worked over for more than seven years—the figure varied—and which had been ready for release only weeks before his death. *Susan*, he had thought of calling it, or possibly *A Girl of the Streets*. He had gone over its 400,000 words four times in pencil, and had given up revising it with the reluctance of a man who hardly knows whether he can give it more or not. It baffled his powers of self-criticism, he said.

At last, in June of 1915, it began in *Hearst's Magazine*—*Susan Lenox: Her Fall and Rise*—and the editors streamed above it the words, "America's Greatest Novel." Criticism, which had so often borne with equanimity the appearance of greatest American novels, stiffened and prepared for battle. It was soon evident that Phillips had left a book vibrating with sensation. It was impossible to get additional copies of the magazine. Censorship made ready to take steps against the forthcoming book as obscene; and when, after nineteen months of agitated serialization, *Susan Lenox* came to an end, it was issued in two volumes. Then the storm broke over it.

It was scarcely a battle. It was, coincidentally, just about this time that Dreiser's *The "Genius"* was released and also denounced as obscene. But Dreiser had H.L. Mencken and legions of others to fight for him, to carry on a campaign among literary people and others of public influence—a campaign which closely marshalled hundreds for

Dreiser and enabled him to enter into the 1920s as a groundbreaker and master in literature. And this despite the fact that The "*Genius*" itself gained no particular status as seminal or memorable fiction.

For Phillips's book there was no such fate. Calumny and derogation was poured on it and its author from every side. There was hardly a good word for it anywhere. The Society for the Suppression of Vice had no difficulty in forcing its withdrawal. The entire first edition was ordered removed, and it disappeared from the stores, not again to be reissued in its original form until its presence among a torrent of futile reprints in a reprint era subsidized by the government gave it some place in a few libraries.

"It would have been better for Mr. Phillips' reputation and the reputation of American letters if it had never been published," the *New York Times* opined on February 25, 1917. The *Boston Transcript* (March 3, 1917) called attention to the Robert W. Chambers preface to *Susan Lenox*, the keynote of which was Phillips's honesty of purpose: "Despite the attempts to prejudge Mr. Phillips' posthumous novel by frantic claims [sic] as to its high moral purpose and sincerity, it seems impossible for an unbiased reader of fiction to view it otherwise than as an extremely offensive addition to the literature of pornography." The *New Republic* (March 10, 1917) kind of intellectual, heavy for Dreiser, talked in a derogatory vein of Phillips's "humorously romantic view of prostitution." And the *New York Sun* noted that Phillips was "not merely less selective than Flaubert; he is positively less selective than Arnold Bennett."

The campaign, strangely synchronized, continued, subsiding to a degree with the issuance of the expurgated edition. After that a kind of calm prevailed—such a calm as dictates that only the best need be spoken of the dead.

There had been a rage of books on sex and social disease back in 1912 and 1913. Outstanding among these had been the highly competent, uncreative *The House of Bondage*, by Reginald Wright Kauffman. The novel demonstrated the thesis of economic determinism in the making of prostitutes. Those who did not know the circumstances under which *Susan Lenox* had been written commented on Phillips's "uncanny" ability to foretell tastes in fiction. A few, however, knew that the germ of the story had been conceived early in the 1880s when young Phillips had witnessed an unforgettable scene:

A young woman, no more than a girl, had been accused of having "fallen," something which in all innocence she did not understand.

To blot away her shame, she had been forced to marry a backwoods lout. Graham had seen the girl sitting defenseless on a wagon, waiting to be carried away to her new home. He had seen the rough husband to whom she had been assigned, and read the tragedy in her face. The blighting of so young a life by ignorance and cowardly pressure Phillips had never been able to forget. It had attained greater meaning as he grew older and better understood the role of women, especially in the impersonal cities, condemned almost en masse to suffering as they readjusted themselves to changing conceptions of their role, and particularly so in America. Phillips had learned the horror of statistics, which were able to foretell in advance what percentage of girls would become prostitutes. He had determined to make clear why prostitution occurred.

But it was not prostitution as such that was the theme of *Susan Lenox*, any more than insurance had been the theme of *Light Fingered Gentry*; it was not even marriage. It was the basic influence of sex in the lives of men and women in American society. Phillips had been a muckraker, but—this can never be too often repeated—he had been first and foremost a novelist. He made inquiry into native customs and ideas involving sex as they were affecting his times and being affected by them. To do this he was forced to question everything that had happened to the American way of life since he had first observed those customs and ideas in operation.

The world from which Susan fled at the age of seventeen because she was unwanted, dominated American life. It combined a mystical reverence for women with harsh conventions that stifled their possibilities for growth. The world into which she ran, the open, anarchistic world, was founded on insecurity. If it made no fetish of virtue in a woman, as Susan's family and community had done, it could even less afford her special consideration. She had to make her place in it as a man did, expecting no quarter, and depending only on her own wit and resources.

But even while Susan fought for independence, insecurity—a product of social and economic change—was beginning to attack such communities as the one which had rejected her. And as insecurity became more widespread and acute, the most unthinking of people were faced with the realization that respectability, which had so long united them and given them opportunities, *was no protection*, that they too must fight for their lives with whatever weapons came to hand. One result of this condition was the tremendous reform upheaval of the 1900s. It was less obvious that old fetishes of morality were becoming less potent and were being frankly disavowed by a second generation which had no stake in them. The youthful vanguard, in the 1910s, went bohemian. Disillusioned in the Twenties, it inclined against all thought and, helped by adult middle-class permissiveness, considered itself emancipated. Later, coming to grips with economic depression, it turned radical and believed that it had at last discovered freedom.

But neither of these successive, short-lived generations was quite so free as it thought. The burning requirments—sex, food, security— produced hasty conventions of various kinds, sometimes contradictory ones. Women could vote now and follow careers, but girls who in the 1930s hardly knew how long their jobs would last plotted desperately to marry safely; "free love" fell out of favor as impractical. So, where Susan's flight from respectable, if prejudiced surroundings originally seemed to critics the height of looseness, in post-World War I times it began to look more like an arrogant, priggish, even impossible adventure. Those who in the Twenties read Joseph Hergesheimer's *Cytherea* and were excited by his vision of enticing femininity lolling in splendor on an emerald shell, saw little need for less sophisticated fiction. But in the Thirties they were more serious; some heard of Karl Marx and could criticize Susan for not having stayed in the box factory into which chance had thrown her. Others, whose dewy youth had contained traces of sexual experience, now pointed out that Susan had never contracted syphilis in her career as mistress and streetwalker.

It would have been vain to remind her critics that many of the women who had, in earlier days, managed to make their way through prejudice and malevolence to success had had to run the gamut of disease, pregnancy, defenseless loneliness. There had been adventuresses in America earlier than the time of Susan Lenox. Adah Isaac Menken and Victoria Woodhull among numerous others had actually made lives somewhere between outlaws and bohemians on one side and respectable people seeking diversion on the other. At one point Menken, abandoned and pregnant, had tried suicide. It would have been just as vain to point out that a ruling female aspiration of Susan's time had not been labor leadership. Those who understood Susan's flight did not sympathize with her ambitions, which were provokingly plain: to do useful work, and to be free to do whatever she liked.

Those who allowed her this did not care for her manner, its old-fashioned idealism and honesty. Those who appreciated her manner did not understand her methods, which made even streetwalking preferable to a secure if unsatisfactory relationship.

Susan Lenox, in a word, told too much; and the hectic years which followed World War I were years of great confusion. *Main Street* was clear; *Cytherea* was clear; James Branch Cabell's *Jurgen*, with a little imagination of sorts, was reasonably clear. They were clear even in the Thirties, though they were not always read during those years. But *Susan Lenox*, in the 1065 pages of the original edition, was as turbulent as its era. Theodore Dreiser's novels, by contrast, and his prewar novels in particular—*The Financier, The Titan, Jennie Gerhardt, The "Genius"*—made no conjectures; they simply stated as a final, unquestionable fact that the dreams and ideals of the nineteenth century were dead. *Susan Lenox* assumed that the old ways had nothing more to offer, and plunged into the issues the reforming 1900s had raised—into a thicket of situations involving economic freedom, moral attitudes, and business approaches. It did so confidently, certain that further reform would make its message of earnest individualism clear—and unaware that war was soon to discredit reform and make the times that had engendered it unfamiliar to a new generation.

Those who later experienced Mencken and the youth ideologue Floyd Dell, Van Wyck Brooks and Edmund Wilson, the psychologists and revolutionists were necessarily wiser than Susan could ever be. But did they necessarily achieve as much? A Susan, when she emerged from her jungle of tragedy and desperation, had, as Phillips claimed, learned to live. As an actress she would be real, substantial. She could remind the younger women and girls that their problems were not superior to hers for being different; that if their lives were in constant danger through catastrophes of sex and economic dilemma, she too had been near death; and that, finally, they must be strong in themselves and in nothing else, since nothing could substitute for inner strength.

"Be strong," advised Burlingham, whose friendship started her in life, without whose first guilding instructions she might not have begun:

> You'll find that you were right at first when you thought only the strong could afford to do right. And you'll see that you were right in the second stage when you thought only the strong could afford to do

wrong. For you'll have learned that only the strong can afford to act at all, and that they can do right and wrong as they please *because they are strong.*

(*Susan Lenox*, I, 240)

It is a hard thing when a man can foretell, as Burlingham could, Susan's inevitable relationship to life. Those who have no imagination are not forced to dare greatly, are not required to feel the full impact of universe and society. They need not challenge them. Susan, who was not born of the desperate poor, who could ignore respectability, but who was of the middle class, of a house founded on respectability, came naturally into opposition with everything traditional in American life.

From the day Susan was born dead—and, being illegitimate, better dead—with her mother lying dead in the next room; from that day on which the doctor, hating to give up so perfect a little body, cleared space in the center of the room and whirled the small corpse round and round like an Indian club—round and round until the room was a blur before his throbbing eyes, round and yet round until the sweat streamed from his face, until the tiny figure cried out in protest, and lived—from that day until the day that womanhood presented itself as a special problem, Susan was unconsciously being prepared for the tragic life before her. Whom would it interest? Her introduction to life offered a legitimate test: it was an extraordinary scene of life defying death, and one a new generation of readers might sometime wish to revisit and compare for reality and use with scenes in the fiction of a Henry Miller, a Norman Mailer, a Saul Bellow.

She was a child; there was not much that could be done to a child who did not push herself into snobbish traps. She was healthy and self-sufficient. But she was illegitimate, and there would have to be a day of reckoning. Had she been less intelligent, less courageous, the social modes would soon have impressed upon her the stain of her inferior position. She might have found humble status in Sutherland, Indiana.

But Susan knew nothing of illegitimacy, could not conceive it or fight it. The events that made it clear to her that she was unloved of aunt and uncle and cousin with whom she had lived taught her only that she could not stay with malicious, unsympathetic people. She did not yet know the significance of money; she did know the significance of character. And when she sat at last as the wretched child had sat whom Phillips had seen in his youth, on a wagon, waiting to be saved by marriage, Susan faced the inescapable proximity of existence, the need for conquering it or being conquered.

One can imagine what happened to the other Susan, condemned to social death at the hands and will of a man made strong by social approval. But Susan, after her nightmare wedding night, ran away. Had she then known all the possibilities of hunger and drudgery and debasement that confronted her, she might have preferred to die rather than go on against impossible odds. It was ignorance that saved her, Phillips believed, as it saved so many neophytes who could not believe the world could be the hideous prison it sometimes is.

Still they pursued, trying to find her and return her to her lawful wedded husband. Society was no passive thing; it was aggressive and determined, so much so that it was hardly worth trying to escape its mandates. There was no tolerance; there was, apparently, no logic. Susan had quickly to supplement her courage with experience, or die.

Were it not for the helping hand which now and again thrusts out, suddenly, even miraculously as it seems, there would be few people of high earnestness and maverick individuality who would survive to do their work. Rodney Spencer met Susan before failure coarsened him, Burlingham long after failure had made him a philosopher. Without the intervention of such people, who either liked her for what she was or helped her to help themselves, there would have been no Susan Lenox.

Yet Susan was beautiful, even as were many fiction heroines. The fashion of a later realism became to paint the drab details of feminine imperfection, as though that made for an intrinsic esthetic virtue. But Susan was beautiful not through the forgery of unimaginative writing, but because Phillips offered details portraying her as beautiful. Her attractiveness did not lessen the sufferings she endured. Frank Harris refused to believe this: Susan, he asserted, could not have walked a dozen feet down Broadway without being discovered. So much for Harris! Phillips believed, however, that Susan's charms and superior talents could not substitute for experience. Neither could they sell themselves; she would have to learn to sell them. This was years and years before Hollywood demonstrated with palpable armies of "lovelies" desperately trying to earn a living the blinding fact native "romance" had resisted: that Susan's face and figure would not help her to live *as she wanted to live*. They would make more difficult her preservation of character. Her character would not help her—nobody wanted character. Nor kindness, honesty, talent. They were a glut on the market. They were not commercial.

Susan was never a streetwalker in the sense of a woman broken to a mean work. She was an artist, as bent on an adjustment in which she could express herself freely as Phillips himself had been when as a boy he had gone into journalism. Susan, observed Harris sourly, was portrayed by Phillips as a sort of second-rate actress. Harris had no wish to respect a woman who had conquered life on its own terms and who could look at him as an equal, perhaps more. A Susan who had learned to use men as they had used her was no prey to lechery. So she must be second-rate.

But Susan was no more a second-rate actress than George Brent, the love of her life, was a second-rate dramatist. That is, Susan being a fictional creation, we cannot tell whether she was or was not. It is true her life did not show a budding and irresistible genius from early childhood, in the way of sentimental novels about "artists." But she had been raised in Sutherland, Indiana. She had been desperately on the go ever since. And, most important, she was a woman, and women who were really artists—not pleasant landscape painters, not parlor singers—were a peculiar breed.

A knowledge of the American stage in its historical phase better suggests the place of a Susan in its annals than does Harris's ill-natured observation.[1] For the rest, it is evident that Susan brought to the stage an experience compounded of everything real.

It is worth noting that nothing like *Susan Lenox* had ever before appeared in the lists of American fiction, and that, when it came, no effort was made to grapple with the problems it posed. Europe had some books dealing with feminine success, either through opportunities derived from high birth, or through or despite the limits allowed women, that is, the passions. But ways had been well prepared for such women. There had been a Nell Gwynn, a Madam Pompadour, a Catherine, a Rachel, a Sarah Bernhardt—a history of more or less extraordinary women who had walked a tenuous road between courtesanship and respectability.

Susan Lenox had no such road for her prepared in America. A harlot was never more nor less than a harlot. Virtue was no social value to be bought and sold according to an adjustable scale; it was absolute. A woman possessed virtue, or the reputation of virtue, or she did not. Susan, to whom her first commercial sex experience was only an urgent means for making money, not for herself but Burlingham, who lay dying in a charity hospital, did not understand this mandate which herded women into one anonymous mass. She had to be taught that having fallen, she was in her generation forever condemned, not only in ignorant eyes, but in educated, intelligent, even kindly eyes. She had to learn that she must make her own standards of right and wrong and must fight for them with all the energy and self-appreciation she could muster.

There was *nothing* in American fiction like *Susan Lenox*. Tenement conditions, factory horrors, political corruption, virtue, vice, were seen for the first time through the eyes of a woman—a lady born, as so many people reminded her in the early stages of her adventures. Susan saw them as little and as much as she had to. She became no labor organizer, no social worker, and for the same reason that prevented capable organizers and investigators from becoming actors and actresses. Phillips's gallery of female portraits contained wives, journalists, businesswomen, and their adventures tell us as much as we care to know regarding the "woman question" which at all times concerned Phillips. But it was with Susan Lenox, the most desperate of them, that Phillips laid most bare the heart of his society as he had found it.

Because Susan was open and honest, she was dangerous to associate with. Sensible, established people naturally avoided her. They recognized her only when she could force their recognition. They were attracted to her when she no longer needed them. She won her long fight. Her victory added one more person to the few who could be forthright and individual and not be destroyed. Susan Lenox made the road for her successors not easier, but more bright. The problem remains why her, and her creator's, services were not better acknowledged.

There are no doubt readers today who would be tempted to break up the story into sections punctuated by Susan's descents into prostitution. Such readers would be behind Phillips who, once for all, put it into its place in Susan's life. The crime of prostitution was not hers, but society's. Prostitution might have ruined her morally and physically, but so might factory work have done that, or any of the other enslaving means of livelihood Susan encountered. None of them did; and if prostitution played a larger role in her odyssey than did factory work, it was because the cesspool of injustice it represented reflected the weaknesses in the American social structure more glaringly than did a native economics with resources to squander. Susan aimed higher than she knew by striving for mere freedom and independence; no wonder she fell so far.

Some things discerning readers can miss in the austere pages; for example, the failure of ecstasy in Susan's life. Through all the horrors which, as the *Boston Transcript* critic idiotically put it, "she deliberately sought," she had barely the opportunity to know joy as it can sometimes come, freely, consummately. In several passages she hints of her sexual responsiveness to her pimp and lover Freddie Palmer.[2] But in general, there was no pagan in Susan; life was far too serious and difficult—it was impossible for her to forget that it depended absolutely on the possession and the continuing possession of money. The daring that can make young life and love an adventure, the simple joy that can ignore fine clothing and position, that can take the chance with food and shelter—these things are missing completely from her life, and separate her from many of the women who before World War I and after expanded their possibilities for life and associates. And though she loved her art fiercely, it was not balanced by that lightness which makes for healthy irreverence and experiment.

Still, considering the fearful catastrophes which overtook the artistic movements of the Twenties and Thirties, is it still possible to say that the material viewpoints which drove Phillips, and Susan, had no roots in reality?

There are problems in *Susan Lenox* not yet solved, which will not be solved merely by reference to the peculiar conditions of life in an earlier America. Sociology is not art. A mature critic quotes a representative passage in the novel:

> The house was exhaling a frightful stench—the odor of cheap kerosene, of things that passed there for food, of animals human and lower, of death and decay. On her way out she dropped a dollar in the lap of the little girl with the mange. A parrot was shrieking from an upper window. On the topmost fire escape was a row of geraniums, blooming sturdily. Her taxicab moved up the street, pushed out of place by a hearse—a white hearse, with polished mountings, the horses caparisoned in white netting, and tossing white plumes. A baby's funeral—this mockery of a ride in state after a brief life of squalor. It was summer, and the babies were dying like lambs in the shambles. In winter the grown people were slaughtered; in summer the children. Across the street, a few doors up, the city dead wagon was taking away another body—in a plain pine box—to the Potter's

Field where find their way for the final rest one in every ten of the people of the rich and splendid city of New York.

(*Susan Lenox*, II, 367)

The critic comments:

> If this impassioned protest strikes our ears as embarrassingly emotional, if it is too strongly reminiscent of Dickens to be in fashion, it may be that the matter which requires determination is whether or not we are uncomfortable in the presence of candor concerning the consequences of the impersonal relationships that are one of the common aspects of life in a great city.[3]

A younger critic, a student, labors to define the artistic problem of *Susan Lenox*. He observes that it is

> a leap from the prose of Henry James to that of David Graham Phillips. Phillips's style seems crude in comparison. . . . At the same time the jump is from the ordered situation of the highly controlled and rarefied atmosphere of a too special artistic selection, to the raw and untidy world of things, chaotic human society and experience in a period of American flux. One tends to believe that this America is our heritage more generally than the America of James' sketches.

He goes on to struggle with Phillips's narrative: "There is the 'gasp, gasp' technique when Brashear is dying, that describes, but does not convey the emotional referents of the scene." He worries over Phillips's discursive habits of comment, which tend to "sermonize" rather than "embody." He struggles with the sheer thickness of narrative, as the vast novel moves from a small town in Indiana, to Cincinnati, and on to New York, where depths of poverty, vice, and the world's work from sweatshop to brothel to the theater become vehicles for Susan's wanderings and journey. He cannot give it perspective by himself. Nor can any one author.

If the novel took more than seven years to write, it took a quarter of a century to develop—the crucial quarter which determined the strength and national scope of the great pre-World War I reform era. Still the years continued to pour wonders upon each other. The book was published in 1917. What does 1917 mean to us? The Ohio, Indiana, and New York which Phillips portrayed have changed many times over. And yet, seen more closely, they are not, after all, unrecognizable. It is only that we have dropped them so entirely as to lose our full capacity to relate them to ourselves, and so to assess them accurately. *Susan Lenox* was part of their saga and will gain from our renewal of the arts of criticism.

16

Phillips:
Queries and Conjectures

It is evident that Phillips did not, any more than did his era, take into adequate account the powers of weakness, the vital factor of irrationality in human affairs. This was the notorious "optimism," the positive thinking of the Reform era. Phillips had Fred Norman analyzing his fall from affluence and status: "I used to imagine that brains were the best, the only sure asset. I was guilty of the stupidity of overvaluing my own possession." Brains are a mighty good asset, his friend responds.

> "Yes—and necessary. But a man of action must have under his brains another asset—*must* have it, Billy. The one secure asset is a big capital. Money rules this world. Some men have been lucky enough to rise and stay risen, without money. But not a man of all the men who have been knocked out could have been dislodged if he had been armed and armored with money. My prodigality was my fatal mistake. . . .
> "Why, I built my fort like a fool. It was impregnable except for one thing—one obvious thing. It hadn't a supply of water. If I build again it'll be around a spring—an income big enough for my needs and beyond anybody's power to cut off."
>
> (*The Grain of Dust*, pp. 291–92)

Phillips himself spent his money freely on the things and activities he preferred, confident of his powers to replenish it as needed. He saw realism, not only in economics but in life. He probably put down the Harry K. Thaw Madison Square Garden shooting of the architect Stanford White—before whose home he himself was shot—as a mere aberration in society. He sought realism in perspective, refusing, for example, to subscribe to the myth of a glorious American past. Learning from John Bach McMaster, he turned impatiently from a history of narrow-minded, ill-living ancestors and hailed a new world being born of enlightened and progressive-minded contempories. His difficulty was McMaster's, that he believed in progress and could not take seriously the blunderers who wanted praise, the incompetent who thirsted for honors, the Fitzhugh Coyle Goldsboroughs who hated courage and human dignity as a reflection on themselves, and a bit of whom resided in the general population.

"My God! How could he do it?" Phillips had groaned in his agony. He would have been wise to have asked the question earlier, as he built his career on what he thought were the firm foundations of hard work and self-control—foundations Goldsborough was able to tear down in the seconds it took him to fire his bullets at Phillips. No one during that time thought to defend Goldsborough or to express sympathy for his illusions. Even the *New York Times,* which had turned off esthetic appreciation of its erstwhile colleague, wondered in its editorial at the strange end of one they termed "so harmless, sincere, and progressive" a writer. It did not occur to the editorialist that in deeming Phillips's criticism of false living harmless, that is, ineffectual, he was indirectly aiding the cause of those who, like Goldsborough, were (as a later phrase had it) trying to tell society something of their point of view.

Phillips understood the compulsions of love, and he expressed compassion for the weak and appreciation of their art or deeds when it appeared due. But that was a different matter from expressing endorsement of their personalities, in Dreiser fashion. And it was far, far from sparing regard of any kind for the diabolic in life which would win attention and interest in later decades. Phillips made a first premise of health, which he equated with social usefulness. For sickness and disease he recommended—even predicted—the hospital or, when necessary, the prison. He could not foresee that a Charles Manson would in time actually attract the sympathy not only of a Jerry Rubin, bent on imprinting an antisocial view on society, but of many other more casual respondents who were fascinated or intrigued by Manson's efforts at self-expression. A world which accorded a Manson anything more than horror and disgust could not use, did not want a Phillips.

The argument that society itself was responsible for the sickness, the destructiveness of its wanton personalities Phillips, and others like him, accepted to a degree. It was, after all, Phillips's Progressive era which gave Clarence Darrow his major career, freed Big Bill Haywood from the shadow of the hangman, though he was almost certainly an accessory to the assassination of ex-Governor Frank Steunenberg of Idaho, and saved the McNamaras from capital punishment though they had confessed their role in the bombing of the *Los Angeles Times,* with attendant deaths.[1] But Phillips saw such principles as reflecting social disorder, not as guides to a future, not heroes to emulate. The future, to Phillips, lay in individual fortitude, and cooperative gestures and ideals. And love of country. Phillips could not understand an internationalism which dignified treason. He would not have grasped John Dos Passos's bitter response to the Sacco-Vanzetti executions in 1927: "All right then we are two nations"—a response not apologized for even after it had been demonstrated that Nicola Sacco probably had participated in the robbery-murder, and that Bartolomeo Vanzetti knew it.

Such matters were hidden as seeds in events of the Rooseveltian era which Phillips could not have, in his writings, uncovered. But neither did Dreiser penetrate into them in his very different writings. The truth was that both Phillips and Dreiser were victims of cultural lag. A number of stereotypes blurred the public vision, making it all but impossible to adjust the Indianans' views for the best use in the unfolding twentieth century decades. Thus the *Saturday Evening Post* in post-Progressive years was seen as ridden with shallow and worthless writings. Its actual distinction was no better perceived in the 1970s than it had been by such avant-garde figures as F. Scott Fitzgerald in the 1920s (see page 68). Babbitt was still imagined to be the "Babbitt" of popular understanding, something, incidentally, the original Babbitt of Sinclair Lewis's creation had not quite been. Mental adjustments were urgently required to account for the intellectuals of the business magazines, the world travelers of industry, and the numerous students of finance who directed the work of cities and national government—though, to be sure, little of this clarified artistic goals.

Phillips's search for the truth about American life was not only the opposite of Dreiser's; it contained problems within its own premises. After all, Phillips, in building his style and vocabulary, had made choices which were not everybody's choices. He had focused on the rich, the well-born, the strong. True, he had judged them according to a scale of values he thought basic to a working society. But in his effort at forthrightness, he could have profitably considered the difference between rudeness and candor. He had himself long tempered his honesty with expediency in his dealings with such masters as Pulitzer and Lorimer. It would have done something for Phillips's presentation to have been more tolerant of those less intelligent than himself, less courageous, less ambitious, who also yearned for comfort and self-esteem.

Phillips had fought and won, but he had no battle plan for those locked in ghettos, in industrial slavery, in changing family structures. He offered too little to those who could not pull themselves up by their own bootstraps in the old way, and whose only hope lay in some sort of cooperative effort with others like themselves.

Phillips, by concentrating as hard as he did on domestic conditions, failed to take into adequate account the Marxian dream which was spread loosely about the world of thought, and which had a mighty future in coming decades. His "socialist" novel, *The Conflict*, was no more than the tour de force of one who did not live the life he read about in *The Appeal to Reason* or got word of second-hand from such friends as Charles Edward Russell and Anna Strunsky Walling. *The Conflict* was a rationalistic statement which did not probe the realities of the "working men" who were presumably the human base of the new world coming. Phillips foresaw, in a general way, social planning and labor-industry mediation. He did not foresee the passion and readiness to violence which would produce not only socialism but "national socialism," not only the Lloyd Georges and Karl Kautskys but the Lenins and Mussolinis. *The Conflict*, based on the reformist campaigns of "socialists" in cities like Milwaukee and New Haven, was as obsolete as were they. But the more intense dedication of such Americans as Haywood, Emma Goldman, and William Z. Foster, not to mention much mightier revolutionary symbols abroad, insufficiently affected Phillips's outlook.

Dreiser could appeal to or be better respected in principle by revolutionists because his books constituted a criticism of American life, evidence that it had inwardly decayed and was doomed in the new world being born. Phillips had nothing to offer the ideologues of a new society and those who would view cynically the vision for which Woodrow Wilson asked them to fight in World War I. Those to whom Phillips would have expected to appeal, the progressive industrialists, the social workers and educators, were themselves to lose status. Samuel Gompers, who bestrode American labor for fifty years, became a lost figure in American lore, vaguely recalled as a "labor faker." Jane Addams, John Dewey, Robert M. La Follette—these became sentimental memories, when that, and not immune to criticism for having allegedly done too little, too late.

Henry Ford, in declaring to wholehearted general agreement that history was bunk, could as readily have added fiction. And indeed by the 1970s fiction was in deep trouble, competing ineffectively with reality, if reality was the statement of life to be found on television and in the declarations of challengers of the Establishment in Berkeley, California, in Belfast, in Lebanon, and, of course, in Moscow and Shanghai.

But even with adjustments made for time and tide, there were questions to ask of Phillips's social program as reflected in his fiction. Phillips idealized a middle class which earned its bread if not quite by the sweat of its face, in Lincoln's phrase, at least by steady, productive labor. Phillips did not have to cope with the perplexities of mass production, the assembly line, "service" industries which too often provided little service—the kinds of problems which would flesh out Elmer Rice's *The Adding Machine* (1923), John Howard Lawson's *Success Story* (1932), and Arthur Miller's *The Death of a Salesman* (1949). A new middle class admitted to drinking, fun as a social goal, something less than loyalty to spouse and family, and other tenets which had not been readily practical in Phillips's time. Dreiser himself lived rakishly during the Progressive era and not only suffered little by the fact, but accreted a loyal and energetic following. Later he became not exactly obsolete, but old-fashioned and no longer a living force. In 1977 it appeared likely that a reconstructed criticism might be willing to treat several of his works as classical. The question was what could be done intelligently and informedly with Phillips.

Partially, the problem was with criticism, which had evaded the question with specious generalizations. It deemed Phillips, among others, not only a digression from main currents, but irrelevant. This, it suggested, was the age of specialization; you could not deal in detail with everybody who happened to have written books. Even literary historians had to be selective in writing literary history.[2] Anyhow, the question of Phillips had been long settled, by one or another satisfying article. Time had told the tale.

Time had also recorded the fact that 1977 was not a vintage year for any American fiction, and that there had not been vintage years for some time. At stake, therefore, was not merely Phillips's quality, but anyone's; and in addition, there was the question, asked anxiously in literature departments, of what the literate public and its children wanted, if anything. In an election year there had been talk of integrity, of whom one could trust, of licentiousness, how it could be or ought to be defined. There had been debate over the proper limits of social welfare, of the equality of races and of sexes. But above all there had been a recognition of the expedient: how drastic unemployment could be diminished, rather than wiped out; what expression of opinion about "ethnics" would or would not gain votes; which posture toward Russia or China—Tibet was not mentioned—was most realistic, whether moral in the strict sense or not.

Phillips, and for that matter Dreiser, could help little directly with such questions. Dreiser could not help with any attitudes which required energy, resolution, a grasping for the ideal. He could help with respect to a sense of realism about the nether side of American human nature. After all, his admirers had been right to praise him for telling a portion of the truth about the drift and eddies of Americans struggling between impotence and fantasy. The intelligent, the alert, the thoughtful could pause in reading his plodding pages, and tone down their hopes for universal peace and happiness. Dreiser was a good and instructive antidote to extravagant American hopes.

But no nation could live indefinitely on cynicism and apathy, varied by wild explosions of unrest. Could the nation use a more "optimistic" approach, try for achievement rather than confusion or fatalism? Phillips had never promised sweetness and light, only a fighting chance. The "criticism" which did not notice this distinction, for example, in *Light Fingered Gentry* or *Old Wives for New*, deserved no attention or respect.

Susan Lenox seems at the end of her long saga to be accepted in society as a distinguished actress, having successfully hidden her sordid past. But O. Henry paid blackmail money through most of his meteoric career—which ran almost parallel to Phillips's—as a short story writer to someone who knew he had served time for robbery in the Columbus, Ohio, federal penitentiary. Susan Lenox is an American success, by luck, by tenacity. What is the meaning of her story? How useful is it? Critics would have to match their arts with those of the *New York Times* book review critic who, in its February 25, 1917 issue thought it would have been better for Phillips's reputation if the book about Susan had never been issued, because it was false to life on three counts.

And now, the three counts. First, Susan was represented as a person of intellect and character, and such a person "does not go down into the depths." Second, if she did, she could not emerge among respectable people, and "still be pure." Finally: "The story is grotesquely and conventionally false to life in its dependence upon that long-ago-exploded fabrication of the muckrakers of economics, that a woman can get nowhere except through sexual dependence upon man." The *Times* writer did not explain what was false in the theory, or how it had been exploded, but at least he had assumptions on which he founded his summary view that the book was "repulsive" and somehow different from what Balzac, or Zola, or (he added in strange combination) Alphonse Daudet would have made of the story of Susan.

He thus denied the fact which succeeding years would bring ruthlessly forward, that licentiousness had indeed helped some actors and actresses to advance as public figures. A more intelligent criticism would cope with the fact and match it against Phillips's treatment of it. It would cope with the question of art and journalism. Phillips, in rigidly concentrating on Mildred's "voice box" in *The Price She Paid,* seemed journalistically heartless in his time, unromantic, commonplace. Yet his determined honesty had directed attention to quality, in art, in life. Was the search for quality in American pursuits, in American protagonists, a valid literary theme? It was for criticism to answer this question, to take scenes from *The Price She Paid* and from other Phillips fiction, and show something: how it compared with past and present reality, what Americans were or wanted to be, whether Phillips's characters moved on their own or seemed puppets of the author's will—anything which might show that criticism could do more than respond to new fads or vague fancies.

Ultimately, Phillips would be lost, or found, as a novelist. He would indeed serve some simon-pure journalist-historians as having been a figure in journalism. And he would serve other historians through his *The Treason of the Senate.* But as an entity he would rate, one way or another, through his fiction. He had given it his best and built his life to serve it. The problem in estimating it lay in the fact that fiction had exploded in the 1920s far beyond the Progressive horizons. Phillips had been viewed invidiously, but such others of his time as Cather, Wharton, and London had also lost their incandescence. They were diminished further by the rise to eminence of such

Thirties talent as Dos Passos and James T Farrell, answering the needs of Depression-haunted Americans.

Following World War II the uses of the novel had diminished generally, so that by the 1970s even novelists wondered about its future. Their opinion was in part defined by their reading public, which appeared to find them dispensable. The last word, then, would be said by readers.

If they should rediscover the uses of fiction, as readers of *The Jungle* had once discovered them, as readers of John Steinbeck's *The Grapes of Wrath* had, then there was a future for other novelists as well, and for Phillips at least an assessment not based on the absurd grounds of *The Great God Success*. Those readers would be mostly middle class, unsure of their "self images," torn between desires for security and for adventure, struggling with the implications of family, rights, and obligations. They could find comparable puzzles in Phillips's "upwardly mobile" characters. Men could match their aspirations and feelings with those of a Fred Norman, a Horace Armstrong, a Burlingham, or, for that matter, a David Graham Phillips. Women could assess a Courtney Vaughan, an Edna Loring, or the Murdock women. There was everywhere in Phillips's fiction consideration of business, law, civic life, and art for any reader to match with his own views and expectations.

One thing was certain: the problem was one for readers, not for Phillips. He, in his dreamless sleep, was as independent of their decisions as he had been in life.

Bibliographic Note

The bibliography of Phillips is so inadequate as to require consideration of its problems before it can be profitably redirected. Its primary
fault has been esthetic: an inability of commentators to note any varia-
tion in Phillips's prose. This has maintained a grotesque attention to
Phillips's very first sketch of a novel, *The Great God Success* (1901),
with no attention being paid to the personality and point of view it
revealed. From such beginnings no good could come, and none came.

Phillips's own times promised to do better, noticing in reviews at
least his increasingly complex themes and treatment, though dis-
mayed by his increasingly aggressive display of themes and personalities. The rise of Theodore Dreiser, and the deterioration of the themes
both Phillips and Dreiser worked in the hands of writers like Fannie
Hurst, reflected badly on the audience Phillips had once hoped to
reach, and had reached in brave Progressive times.

Criticism of Phillips thereafter all but disappeared on the academic level, and became a criticism of Progressivism elsewhere. It has
already been noted that "pro" Phillips writings like Ludwig Lewisohn's *Expression in America* (1931) were simply passed over. Attempting to deal with the distortions of such critics as Granville Hicks
and the flip-flops of H.L. Mencken becomes an exercise in futility. It is
more profitable to read Phillips himself and go on from there.

And here it seems wise to recognize that Americans, for whatever
reasons, have preferred to read something else. The fact that they have
read badly at times, making an incredible cultural hero of Henry
Miller, for example, is neither here nor there. At other times they have
honored Sinclair Lewis and Dreiser, and still do, to a degree. In short,
there is a mixed record, in which Phillips plays little part.

But this does not mean he always will. A new time can be expected to cope with the author of "The Treason of the Senate" and of
Susan Lenox as myth and as reality. To repeat, the available critical
record has been such that I leave it, for those interested, to two avail-

able bibliographies, one which left the rails of judicious inquiry through overenthusiasm, the other which never got on the rails at all: a duty bibliography intended to turn academic wheels to no end. One wonders what its collaborators read for fun. The first is Abraham Feldman, "David Graham Phillips, His Works and His Critics," *Bulletin of Bibliography*, May–August, September–December, 1948. The other is Frank L. Stallings, Jr., comp., "David Graham Phillips (1867–1911): a Critical Bibliography of Secondary Comment," *American Literary Realism, 1870–1910*, Winter 1917.

Phillips figures in my *The Muckrakers* (Pennsylvania State University Press, 1976), *Appointment at Armageddon* (Greenwood Press, 1976), and *Progressivism and Muckraking* (R.R. Bowker Company, 1976). My views of Phillips criticism appear in "The Reputation of David Graham Phillips," *Antioch Review*, Winter 1951–52. I provided introductions to Phillips's novels *The Cost* (1969), *The Deluge* (1969), and *The Grain of Dust* (1970), all published by Johnson Publishing Company, the last being the only novel by Phillips displayed in esthetic terms and published at my request. Other Phillips reprints, published in a torrent of reprinting which did nothing for cultural standards, appeared as cultural artifacts rather than literature. It has been an odd phenomenon how academics presumably concerned for literature have been more at ease with such works as T.S. Arthur's *Ten Nights in a Bar-Room* than with writings as human endeavor.

The root of such troubles began, strangely enough—though it was doubtless inevitable—in Phillips's own home, with the myopia which permitted his sister Carolyn Frevert to turn for aid and comfort not to literary folk of quality but to a friend, Robert W. Chambers, and to a new friend, Isaac F. Marcosson, who appears to have been an amiable person, but scarcely one whom she should have dowered with all her shrewdly garnered wealth and her brother's heritage. It gives some measure of how much of herself she had given her brother, how little his passing left her, that she could find no better harbor for her psychic life than this almost incredibly shallow man.

Yet the fault was not wholly hers. She saw Phillips's posthumous works through the press and put part of his reputation into flammable films. Albert J. Beveridge added little if anything to her efforts. Nor did Charles Edward Russell, though he esteemed himself a literary man and critic, and received some public recognition on that score. In one opinion Russell expressed to me, he made it clear that he could have nothing to do with any venture which involved Frank Harris's opinions, as though being a rascal necessarily meant that someone was untalented. Yet Harris, in his *Latest Contemporary Portraits* (1927), crude though his piece was, probably did more for Phillips in dubbing him "the greatest American novelist" than Russell who, in his several writings involving Phillips, made no distinction between his journalism and his fiction. Russell had fine qualities, but they were limited esthetically.

It is a demonstrable fact that the most rarified criticism presupposes some real or imagined human being behind the literary artifact; and it is a sad heritage which has portrayed Phillips as an unprincipled scribbler. It thus helps to make contact with the true Phillips, through such fragments of his days and ways which have survived the maceration of so much of the Progressive heritage. I have not here used all the bits and details which I have picked up in the Library of Congress's Beveridge Papers, Charles Edward Russell Papers, and other papers, in the Lorimer Papers of the Historical Society of Pennsylvania, and elsewhere, because it does not suffice to rehabilitate Phillips's character. The primary aim of a legitimate consideration of his work must be art, and only art. However, for those interested in the personal side of Phillips's life, and of related lives, *American Literary Manuscripts: A Checklist of Holdings in Academic, Historical and Public Libraries in the United States* (1960), containing a brief section on Phillips holdings, though far from satisfactory, provides a start for those interested in this aspect of Phillips.

But, for the last time, the final test of his validity lies in his writings: the logic of their development, their connotative overtones— everything that gives savor and meaning to words. Their qualities vary; even more, their relevance to our affairs varies. I do not offer final judgments on his works. I do suggest that several of Phillips's substantive writings preceding *Susan Lenox* should be read before it is; and that it should then be taken whole and pondered for its overall philosophy and human principles before being examined in parts.

The following are my own hard core of preferences at this time; ultimately, many of Phillips's "lesser" writings could aid us to construct a Phillips canon useful to our times: *A Grain of Dust* (1911); *Old Wives for New* (1908); *The Husband's Story* (1910); *The Price She Paid* (1912); *The Hungry Heart* (1909); *The Fashionable Adventures of Joshua Craig* (1909); *Degarmo's Wife and Other Stories* (1913).

Notes

Introduction

1. See, for example, R.E. Banta, comp., *Indiana Authors and Their Books 1816–1916* (Crawfordsville, Ind., 1949), which no more than "condenses" an acccount of Phillips from Stanley J. Kunitz, ed., *Authors Today and Yesterday* (New York, 1934), pp. 523–25, a scissors-and-paste item.

1. Hoosier

1. "Who's Who—and Why," *Saturday Evening Post*, 27 April 1907, p. 17.
2. Walt McCaslin, "Historic Architecture Marks Indiana Town," *Dayton Journal Herald*, 20 March 1974.
3. Charles A. Beard, *The American Party Battle* (New York, 1928), p. 57.
4. The entire article merits review as a point of departure. B.O. Flower, "David Graham Phillips: A Novelist with Democratic Ideals," *Arena* 31 (1904): 236 ff.
5. For comparisons, see my essay "A Tale of Two Authors: Theodore Dreiser and David Graham Phillips," Ray B. Browne et al., eds., *New Voices in American Studies* (West Lafayette, Ind., 1966), pp. 35 ff.
6. Phillips to Bobbs-Merrill Company, n.d., The Lilly Library, University of Indiana.

2. The Higher Education

1. These and other details are from the Archives of DePauw University and University of Cincinnati records.
2. An exception was Charles Macomb Flandrau's *Harvard Episodes* (1897), a group of tales told with consummate control, a heritage of the Progressive era, but unlike Phillips's tales not reflecting a democratic bias.
3. J.W. Piercy to the author.
4. Albert J. Beveridge to Phillips, n.d., Beveridge Papers, Library of Congress, hereafter L.C., for this and following quotation.
5. Wilbur G. Kurtz Papers, DePauw Archives.
6. Vera S. Cooper, Librarian, DePauw University, to author; Piercy to author; DePauw Archives; Claude G. Bowers, *Beveridge and the Progressive Era* (New York, 1932), p. 162.
7. I.F. Marcosson, *David Graham Phillips, His Life and Times* (New York, 1932), p. 23.
8. See p. 199, n. 13. Phillips's affection for Princeton blurred that distinction in his thinking, and gave him a rapport with Wilson's ideals which would have been qualified, had Phillips lived to observe his Presidency. Arthur S. Link et al., *The Papers of Woodrow Wilson* (Princeton, 1975), XX, 372.
9. Marcosson, *Phillips*, pp. 51–53.

3. Midwest

1. "Phillips's Methods," p. 6; for a variant version, "Literary Folk," p. 14.
2. Theordore Dreiser, *A Book about Myself* (New York, 1922), p. 37.
3. W.A. Swanberg, *Dreiser* (New York, 1965), p. 37.
4. In one of Phillips's pseudobiographer's more grotesque gaffes, he had Phillips as a journalistic acquaintance of Hearn's, for whom Phillips had an "unbounded admiration." Hearn had left Cincinnati ten years before. I.F. Marcosson, *David Graham Phillips, His Life and Times* (New York, 1932), pp. 81–82.

4. "That Damned East!"

1. Quoted in Phillips, Sr., to Beveridge, April 11, 1891. Beveridge Papers, L.C.
2. The tale is set down in I.F. Marcosson, *David Graham Phillips, His Life and Times* (New York, 1932), pp. 104 ff. Phillips himself recounted the incident in his *The Great God Success*, pp. 20 ff.
3. Ml Collection, Miscellaneous, Newberry Library, for this and following paragraph.
4. Charles Edward Russell, "The Message of David Graham Phillips," *Book News Monthly*, April 1907, p. 511. Phillips employed the episode in his *A Woman Ventures*, pp. 88 ff. For further comment on Phillips's treatment, see page 00.
5. Phillips, Sr. to Beveridge, March 16, 1891. Beveridge Papers, L.C.
6. Frank M. O'Brien, *The Story of The Sun* (New York, 1918), p. 331.
7. Gerald Langford, *The Richard Harding Davis Years* (New York, 1961), p. 187.
8. Richard Hough, *Admirals in Collision* (New York, 1959); Captain Geoffrey Bennett, *By Human Error: Disasters of a Century* (London, 1961), pp. 100 ff. For Phillips's international "beat," Marcosson, pp. 148 ff. This is taken, without acknowledgment, from Phillips's own account, "The 'Beat' on the Victoria Disaster," *Saturday Evening Post*, 26 May 1900.

5. "Alice"

1. Arthur Bartlett Maurice, *The New York of the Novelists* (New York, 1916), pp. 139–41, provides details of Phillips's tragedy, though with none of the circumstantiality Phillips himself provided. A photograph of the house in which much of the tragedy occurred appears opposite page 130 of Maurice's book. The following quotations, with comments by himself, are all from *The Great God Success*.

6. A Brilliant Failure

1. "The Story of the City Daily," p. 11. This was one of three articles by Phillips on the subject.
2. Beveridge was willing to reciprocate, if not to Phillips, who made a point of avoiding asking favors, but to Phillips's brother and cousin, whose qualities Phillips's father described; Phillips, Sr. to Beveridge, March 11, 1892, December 3, 1896. Beveridge Papers, L.C. There is a scattering of Phillips-Beveridge correspondence in the Beveridge Papers from 1891 into the new century. Several strategic passages will be noted in their due place.
3. Letter to the author.
4. Charles Edward Russell, *Bare Hands and Stone Walls* (New York, 1933), p. 241.
5. L. Filler, ed., *Late Nineteenth Century American Liberalism* (Indianapolis, 1962), p. 56.

6. I.F. Marcosson, *David Graham Phillips, His Life and Times* (New York, 1932), p. 206.

7. For details, W.A. Swanberg, *Pulitzer* (New York, 1967), pp. 222 ff.

8. Phillips to Beveridge, January 25, 1899. Beveridge Papers, L.C.

9. Claude G. Bowers, *Beveridge and the Progressive Era* (New York, 1932), p. 121. John Dos Passos made this speech notorious by quoting it in his novel, *42nd Parallel* (New York, 1930). Beveridge's later turn away from imperialism to such humanistic causes as child labor has been less appreciated.

10. Bowers, p. 141; Phillips to Beveridge, March 15, 1901. Beveridge Papers, L.C.

7. Venture in a New Time

1. Edmund Clarence Stedman's *An American Anthology 1787–1900* (Boston, 1900) strove strenuously to be fair and full, but printed appalling verse as well as durable poems in fewer number; see also Robert H. Walker, *The Poet and the Gilded Age* (Philadelphia, 1963).

2. Ernest Lacy, *Plays and Sonnets* (Philadelphia, 1900), p. 169.

3. Lacy, *The Bard of Mary Redcliffe* (Philadelphia, 1910), p. 194.

4. Lacy, *Plays and Sonnets*, p. 206.

5. Introduction to Stephen Crane, *Collected Works*, ed. Wilson Follett (New York, 1926), X, ix–x.

6. For the Crane-Conrad empathy, stirred by Crane's reading of Conrad's *The Nigger of the 'Narcissus,'* and Conrad's admiration for *The Red Badge of Courage*, R.W. Stallman and Lillian Gilkes, eds., *Stephen Crane's Letters* (New York, 1960).

7. For Norris's conscious search for method, see Lars Ahnebrink, *The Influence of Emile Zola on Frank Norris* (Uppsala, 1949); idem, *The Beginnings of Naturalism in American Fiction* (Cambridge, Mass., 1950).

8. W.A. Swanberg, *Dreiser* (New York, 1965), p. 142.

9. Ibid., p. 145.

10. John Tebbel, *George Horace Lorimer and the Saturday Evening Post* (New York, 1948), p. 9.

11. *Saturday Evening Post*, December 1975, p. 62 (a reprint).

12. See George Horace Lorimer, *Letters from a Self-Made Merchant to His Son* (New York, 1970 ed.), introduction by Lawrence Grauman, Jr. and Robert S. Fogarty, for analysis of Lorimer's style and cultural impact.

13. "I'm leaving the World [sic] Jan 1 to adventure a little in the 'literary' way—vaguely, timidly, not over hopefully—But I cant bring myself longer to delay an experiment I should have made ten years ago—Ive been waiting to get rich or famous by accident—And I feel I cant afford to wait any longer—" (Phillips to Mrs. [   ] Wolcott, December 25, 1901. Special Collections, Lockwood Library, State University of New York at Buffalo.

14. Granville Hicks, "David Graham Phillips, Journalist," *Bookman* 73 (May 1931): 259; John Chamberlain, *Farewell to Reform* (New York, 1932), p. 166.

15. For an examination of the conflict between escapist and realistic fiction, Filler, "Romance and Reality," in *Appointment at Armageddon* (Westport, Conn., 1976), pp. 284 ff.

16. Left unfinished at Crane's death, the novel was completed by his friend and fellow journalist Robert Barr (New York, 1903) and reissued in 1926 in Crane's *Collected Works*, with an introduction by Thomas Beer.

17. Ima H. Herron, *The Small Town in American Literature* (Durham, N.C., 1939) describes aspects of the changing town, as in its comment on William Dean Howells's *The Lady of the Aroostook*, like so much of Howells's and others' fiction infirm in texture and yet profitable in parts for the student of literature, as in the following quotation from Howells's character: "Their children have gone away; they don't seem to live; they are just staying. When I first came there I was a little girl. One day I went into

the grave-yard and counted the stones; there were three times as many as there were living persons in the village."

18. Upton Sinclair, *My Lifetime in Letters* (Columbia, Mo., 1960), p. 50.

19. Letter to the author.

20. Beveridge to Phillips, February 13, 1902; Phillips to Beveridge, December 25, 1902; Beveridge to Phillips, January 17, 1903; Phillips to Beveridge, n.d. Beveridge Papers, L.C.

8. Success Story

1. An interesting comparison can be made with Thomas Wolfe, who much more than Phillips sought untrammeled self-expression. Yet Wolfe's attempt at a play, *Mannerhouse* (New York, 1946), suffused with "southern" idealism, was, more than Phillips's, shackled by what might be called stagey language unworthy of the author's best.

2. Fairfax Downey, *Portrait of an Era, as Drawn by C.D. Gibson* (New York, 1936), p. 110.

3. Beveridge to Phillips, November 27, 1903. Beveridge Papers, L.C.

4. Phillips to Beveridge, n.d. Beveridge Papers, L.C.

5. Flower, "David Graham Phillips, a Novelist with Democratic Ideals," *Arena* 31 (1904): 236 ff.

6. Ibid.

7. Bobbs-Merrill Papers, Ms. Department, Lilly Library, Indiana University.

8. Sinclair, letter to the author.

9. Introduction to Charles Macomb Flandrau, *Sophomores Abroad* (New York, 1935), p. 24.

10. Phillips to Lorimer (two letters), n.d. Lorimer Papers, Historical Society of Pennsylvania.

11. Mark Schorer noted, in his *Sinclair Lewis* (New York, 1961), p. 518, that *Dodsworth* was "in a number of ways" suggestive of Phillips's *The Husband's Story*, but lacked the wit to notice the intrinsic similarity of texture. More foolish was his view, supposedly freeing Lewis from the imputation of plagiarism, that by 1929 "the Phillips novel was largely forgotten"—presumably by profound literary historians as well as by the fly-by-night public. The fact was, of course, that Lewis and Phillips were contemporaries, and that Lewis almost certainly saw and read *The Husband's Story* when it was published.

12. A file of materials is among the Bobbs-Merrill papers, Ms. Department, Lilly Library, Indiana University, including also the following quotation.

13. Owen Wister, *Roosevelt, the Story of a Friendship* (New York, 1930), p. 257.

14. John Chamberlain, *Farewell to Reform* (New York, 1932), pp. 164–65.

15. Henry Miller, "Marie Corelli: A Recommendation," in "The Guest Word," *New York Times Book Review*, September 12, 1976.

16. *Bookman* 21 (June 1905): 342.

17. Originator of the phrase was the political boss of Pennsylvania, Matthew Quay, whose letter advising a collaborator that, given certain legislation, he would shake the plum tree inspired Phillips's concept. Those who were puzzled by Phillips's interpretation of the incident could have profitably studied Quay's career, among others. In the closing year of his life, Beveridge called upon the old man, now frail and haggard. Sitting at the window looking out, Quay said, as the younger man was taking his leave: "I shall be dead in a few months, and the papers will say, 'Matt Quay, Boss, is dead.' Had I lived my life differently, they would say: 'Death of Matthew S. Quay, Statesman.' Take warning by me, young man." Then taking a copy of "Peter Ibbetson," he wrote upon the fly-leaf the enigmatic words, "Dream true," and gave it to Beveridge as a parting gift. (Claude G. Bowers, *Beveridge and the Progressive Era* (New York, 1932), p. 207). Quay died before the publication of *The Plum Tree*.

18. *The Reign of Gilt*, pp. 159 ff. Phillips entitled his chapter "The Compeller of Equality."

19. For further comment upon it, Filler, *The Muckrakers*, pp. 171 ff.; *Appointment at Armageddon*, pp. 335 ff.; and my introduction to *The Deluge* (New York, 1969).

20. *Review of Reviews*, December 1905, p. 756.

21. Frank Harris, *Latest Contemporary Portraits* (New York, 1927), p. 28.

9. Fiction and the Senate Blast

1. *Bookman*, March 1911, is particularly useful in this revaluation of Phillips's work as literary man and socio-political writer, and is the source of later unfootnoted details. It was aided by Bailey Millard's and other reminiscences. Despite its conservative bias, *Bookman* may well prove strategic, among other publications, in cultural assessments of the Progressive era, simply because of its persistent emphasis on literary factors.

2. A new edition (Lexington, Ky., 1970) seeks to see it as "social history," but its introduction by John D. Hicks misses the fact that a literary critique was necessary so that it could be discriminated from other writings by Progressives. Their era patronized White, but it also patronized his betters.

3. Letter to the author.

4. Millard, in a letter to the author.

5. For an interesting defense, revealing the viewpoint of one of the accused, see Appendix B of George E. Mowry and Judson A. Grenier, *The Treason of the Senate* (Chicago, 1964), pp. 226 ff. In the course of his defense, Senator Joseph W. Bailey called on La Follette to corroborate that he had cooperated with Bailey on Indian lands legislation, which La Follette did. In his last article Phillips reproved La Follette, as he had others for less innocent reasons, for having honored "senatorial courtesy," which he saw as generally involving trickery and fraud.

6. Phillips to Beveridge, July 31, 1906. Beveridge Papers, L.C.

7. Phillips to Beveridge, May 29, 1906. Beveridge Papers, L.C.

8. Phillips to Beveridge, August 11, 1906. Beveridge Papers, L.C.

9. Beveridge to Phillips, April 18, 1906. Beveridge Papers, L.C. "By the way," added Beveridge, "talk about radicalism, what have you to say now about his courage and sincerity in view of his inheritance tax proposition. If that speech don't [sic] make you a Roosevelt man I don't know what will."

10. As noted before (see page 00), the best authors of that era kept pots boiling in ways later decades did not require. Thus Jack London freely explained how, once his name was before the public, he took advantage of the fact to unload upon editors everything in his desk, good, bad, and puerile.

11. For Peck, see my introduction to his *Democrats and Republicans* (New York, 1964).

12. I.F. Marcosson, *David Graham Phillips, His Life and Times* (New York, 1932), p. 226.

13. Woodrow Wilson, fighting his last battle as president of Princeton in behalf of a democratic elite, gave an impassioned speech on the subject, not too well received by the Pittsburgh alumni he addressed. Phillips was inspired to write him, without solicitation or response; in a letter dated April 19, 1910: "Dear Sir, Your Pittsburgh speech makes it impossible for me longer to resist the temptation to write you a letter of thanks. . . . /I of course hope you will be able to make Princeton the university of the present and the future, instead of a mockery of mediaevalism. But whether you are permitted or prevented there is, in the broad, of small importance. Your ideas can not but prevail, and I am sure that their force is already being felt in scores of colleges./If by chance there should ever be any way in which I could give you the least help, I shall be proud to get the opportunity." Arthur S. Link et al., eds., *The Papers of Woodrow Wilson* (Princeton, 1975), 20: 372.

14. Back matter for Phillips's *Light Fingered Gentry* (New York, 1907).

15. Phillips to Lawrence Chambers, editor, Bobbs-Merrill Company, n.d.; Phillips to Merrill, January 25, 1908. Bobbs-Merrill papers, Ms. Division, Lilly Library, Indiana University.

10. Harvest

1. One such tale, which failed to bring its talented author the response he needed to continue his fictional campaign, involved the unfortunates in New York City hospitals: Frank Leonard's *City Psychiatric* (New York, 1965). The novel was honored with an introduction by the investigative reporter John Bartlow Martin.

2. Montrose J. Moses and John Mason Brown, eds., *The American Theatre as Seen by Its Critics* (New York, 1934), p. 163.

3. Ludwig Lewisohn, *Expression in America* (New York, 1932), p. 327.

4. "Other Books by David Graham Phillips," back matter from Phillips, *The Fashionable Adventures of Joshua Craig* (New York, 1909). D. Appleton and Company arranged a standard format for Phillips's books which was maintained until his death.

5. Dreiser, *A Book about Myself* (New York, 1922), pp. 156 ff.

11. Legends

1. In a letter to Bailey Millard, "Phillips's Methods," p. 13.

2. Phillips to Beveridge, January 10, 1908. Beveridge Papers, L.C. It was a low moment; Phillips emotionally signed it, "Your old and eternal Friend."

3. Phillips, *The Second Generation*, p. 332; *Old Wives for New*, p. 448 et seq.; *The Husband's Story*, pp. 452–53.

4. Phillips to F.A. Duneka, May 3, 1902. Clifton Barrett Waller Library, University of Virginia.

5. Ibid. An earlier letter (April 24, 1902) regrets that Duneka had not made a more detailed criticism of the Phillips ms: "It would have helped me in rewriting the [illegible] in these chapters which, as I think I told you, I was too dissatisfied with to let go as they were."

6. J.A. Sears to the author.

7. Phillips to John O'Hara Cosgrave. Clifton Barrett Waller Library, University of Virginia. This was apparently written from shipboard on one of Phillips's trips.

8. Hamilton Holt to the author.

9. Alexander Kaun, *Maxim Gorky and His Russia* (New York, 1931), p. 571.

10. Ghent to the author.

11. Arthur W. Little, memoir of Phillips addressed to I.F. Marcosson; ms. copy in author's possession.

12. W.A. White to the author.

13. Phillips to Beveridge, n.d. (two letters). Beveridge Papers, L.C.

14. Ibid., 1908? See also Phillips to Beveridge in which he tells him "for the millionth time that the distribution of property . . . is the burning question." n.d.

15. Little ms.

16. For a glance into the sort of affair possible and fairly common in well-appointed New York circles, Arthur Rubenstein, *My Young Years* (New York, 1973), pp. 181–82.

17. Phillips to Beveridge, 1908? Beveridge Papers, L.C.

18. Little memoir.

19. Phillips to Beveridge, August 11, 1906; idem, n.d. Beveridge Papers, L.C. He was even more impertinent in a letter (ibid., n.d., 1909?) which threatens that Bev's "insane" ideas on health will leave him "a seamed, wrinkled old hulk, no longer mama's delight and everywhere called 'old man Beveridge.' One look at your [illegible] and people will say 'Why, he's a back number—Might as well ask us to dig up Wash or T. Jeff.' "

20. Phillips to Beveridge, four letters, one dated October 15, 1908. Beveridge Papers, L.C. Another letter, of June 10, 1908, read: "When my mother told my little niece that there was no Santa Clause [sic]—she put her fingers in her ears and said 'Leave me my Santa Clause'—They tell me there is no love no friendship—that it is all lies—'True' I say 'but leave me my Beveridge' [.]"

21. *Bookman*, March 1909; review under name of Firmin Dredd.

22. "Phillips's Methods," pp. 12–13.
23. Phillips to Beveridge, n.d. Beveridge Papers, L.C. In a letter for December 25, 1909, he noted: "You think you're it, you know," and went on to cite some complimentary letters which had come his way. "All demand a *sequel.*" See also letters of January 16, 1909, November 15, 1908, and n.d. letters of 1909.

12. Art and Social Change

1. A fictional work of no talent, but one which expresses 1920s attitudes—such as the dazzled discovery of sex as a thing in itself rather than as part of life concerns—is W.H. Speckman, *Heyday* (New York, 1953).
2. R.W.B. Lewis, *Edith Wharton* (New York, 1975) uses her secret journals to describe her extramarital adventure.
3. A commonplace academic, Fred Lewis Pattee, was consistent enough in his reading to note the obvious relations between Phillips and Lewis; as he said, with random inaccuracies, in his *The New American Literature* (New York, 1930), p. 338: "The successor to David Graham Phillips as fictional critic of the American social regime has been Sinclair Lewis. . . . The change in literary tones and methods wrought by the twenty years which separate the two men is more radical than often is caused by the evolution of a century. To read one of Phillips's novels, say 'The Cost' [Pattee's lack of discrimination may be noted] after 'Main Street' and 'Elmer Gantry' is like sitting for tea in a Victorian drawing room after a matinée session with the 'talkies.' Lewis was reared not at all on Victorianism, and there was in him no childhood impress of Puritanism."
4. John Dos Passos to Mark Schorer, February 18, 1959, in Townsend Ludington, ed., *The Fourteenth Chronicle* (Boston, 1973), p. 618.
5. Frederic Taber Cooper, *Some American Storytellers* (New York, 1911), p. 133.
6. Ibid., p. 134. Italics added.
7. F. Scott Fitzgerald, *This Side of Paradise* (New York, 1920), p. 36; see also p. 55. The novel gives a good sense of changing à la mode collegiate reading.
8. Thomas Wolfe, *Look Homeward, Angel* (New York, 1929), p. 160.
9. Upton Sinclair, *Mammonart* (Pasadena, Calif., 1925), p. 355.
10. Holograph letter by Phillips, preceding his article "Beveridge the Man," *Pearson's* (October 1910).
11. Phillips to Lorimer, n.d. Lorimer Papers, HSP.
12. Cooper, p. 136.

13. Murder in Gramercy Park

1. This fact, as recorded by the present author in article form, was actually used in a strange article which found evil and neuroses in "Progressive" manliness, and a combination of horrors in Phillips's life, all on the basis of conjecture; James R. McGovern, "David Graham Phillips and the Virility Impulse of Progressives," *New England Quarterly* 39 (September 1966): 334–55.
2. The major details following having to do with the assault on Phillips and his death have been culled from the *Times* news columns and commentary.
3. This chapter in earlier form was read by the late Algernon Lee, in Phillips's time head of the Rand School of Social Science and a socialist intellectual. He protested that few true socialists were brash enough to circulate in general society "unshorn" and that the inevitability concept did not affect the majority of socialist workers.
4. Six reports were recorded in the press, but obviously, Algernon Lee noted, there must have been five, since the assassin saved one for himself, and had used the conventional six-shooter.

5. "The Business Organization of a Church." For what it was, standing beside once-delightful Stuyvesant Square on the East Side near Fourteenth Street, see Elizabeth Moulton, *St. George's Church* (New York, 1964).

6. Little memoir.

14. Afterglow

1. Ca. March 16, 1911. Russell Papers, L.C. An interesting letter in the Beveridge Papers, L.C., is from Phillips's old Pulitzer editor, William H. Merrill, famous as a genius of "yellow" journalism, January 25, 1911. In curiously stiff prose, Merrill urges Beveridge to write of his friend for the "edification" of readers, describing Phillips as one who had grown from "a man of fancies and ideas almost without discrimination, to one who had "conquered *self*" in the interests of a patent success ("yes, even victory"). Phillips had tried to help Beveridge's 1910 campaign with an article in *Pearson's,* stipulating that it was to be for love and not pay. Beveridge was not able to marshall words in behalf of his dead friend.

2. Granville Hicks, "Phillips, David Graham," in Dumas Malone, ed., *Dictionary of American Biography* (New York, 1934), XIV, 539.

3. Vachel Lindsay, "The Leaden-Eyed," in *Collected Poems* (New York, 1923), p. 70.

4. John Curtis Underwood, *Literature and Insurgency* (New York, 1914), pp. 244–45.

5. This study does not deal with his posthumous *The Conflict* (1911) which, in the context of Phillips's development, makes the book more useful as a comment on the socialism of his time than on his development. Also not treated is his short novel— probably no more than an early draft which he did not develop—*George Helm* (1912), which is, strictly speaking, not a novel at all, but a long informal essay illustrated by a story, and intended to reaffirm Phillips's conviction that "the people," despite their tendency toward confusion, were ultimately indomitable, had the heart of the matter, and would support realistic but sound statesmen when they should appear.

15. Susan Lenox: An American Odyssey

1. Harris, *Latest Contemporary Portraits* (New York, 1927), p. 24.

2. *Susan Lenox,* II, 194, 492. Arthur Little tells of conversations with Phillips regarding Susan's character: "You know, he was a bit crazy on the subject—used to talk about her as though she was a real person. Once, sitting just where you're sitting now, he became dreamy, then he said, 'You know, Arthur, Susan *liked* to f—.' " (Little to the author.)

3. John M. Harrison, "Criticism of David Graham Phillips's Novels," ms.

16. Phillips: Queries and Conjectures

1. Filler, *The Muckrakers,* chapters xvii, xxvii.

2. So Robert E. Spiller told the present writer before publication of his collaborative *Literary History of the United States* (1948). My own views are embodied in introduction and essays by various hands in *A Question of Quality* (Bowling Green, O., 1976).

Index

Adams, Henry, 23, 24
Adams, Samuel Hopkins, 33, 83
Addams, Jane, 138, 185
Aldrich, Nelson W., 77, 99, 100
"Alice" (Phillips), 40 ff., 131, 146
Anderson, Sherwood, 4
Armory Show (1913), 111
Armstrong Investigation (1905), 109, 116
Arthur, T.S., 192
Atherton, Gertrude, 88

Baker, Ray Stannard, 60
Balzac, Honoré de, 104, 188
Beard, Charles A., 8
Beer, Thomas, *The Mauve Decade*, 50
Bellamy, Edward, 12
Bellow, Saul, 3, 176
Benét, Stephen Vincent, 68
Bennett, Arnold, 172
Berkman, Alexander, 55
Beveridge, Albert J., and Phillips friend-
   ship, 16–18, 20, 33, 53, 76; and imperi-
   alism, 59; introduces Phillips to Lor-
   imer, 67; on *The Master Rogue*, 79, 84;
   praises *The Plum Tree*, 86, 89; and
   "The Treason of the Senate," 101–2;
   praises *Light Fingered Gentry*, 109; cor-
   respondence, 125, 128, 129, 131, 132;
   and *The Fashionable Adventures of
   Joshua Craig*, 135; Progressive defeat,
   154; and Phillips's death, 162, 192
Blythe, Samuel, 102, 162
Bourne, Randolph, 153
Brisbane, Arthur, 58, 162
Bryant, William Cullen, 23
Burke, Billie, 157
Burleigh, Harry, 163

Cabell, James Branch, 61, 68, 72, 175
Cable, George Washington, 27
Cahan, Abraham, 27
Carnegie, Andrew, 55
Cassatt, Mary, 111
Cather, Willa, 68, 188

Certain Rich Man, A (W.A. White), 97
Chamberlain, John, 88
Chambers, Robert W., 129, 142, 162, 172,
   192
Chatterton, Thomas, 62
Churchill, Winston, 88, 103
Cincinnati, University of, 15
Cleveland, Grover, 56
College of New Jersey. *See* Princeton Uni-
   versity
Conflict, The (Phillips), 185, 202 n. 5 (Af-
   terglow)
Conrad, Joseph, 65, 68
Cooper, Dr. Frederic Taber, 133–34, 138,
   139, 150–51
Corelli, Marie, 88
Cosgrave, John O'Hara, and "The Treason
   of the Senate," 95; as Phillips friend,
   126, 128
Cost, The (Phillips), 15 ff., 81–83, 92, 95;
   compared with *A Certain Rich Man*
   (W.A. White), 97, 110
Crane, Stephen, 27, 33–34, 36, 41, 64, 68,
   72, 124
Curtis, Cyrus H.K., 67

Dana, Charles A., 23–24, 32–37; and *The
   Great God Success*, 70
Darrow, Clarence, 183
Davis, Richard Harding, 33, 50, 64, 124,
   128
DeForest, John W., 16
"Degarmo's Wife" (Phillips), 36
Degarmo's Wife and Other Stories, 169 ff.
Dell, Floyd, 175
Deluge, The (Phillips), 91 ff.
Demos (George Gissing), 21–22
DePauw University, 8, 14 ff.
Depew, Chauncey, 86; and "The Treason
   of the Senate," 98 ff.
Dewey, John, 185
Dickinson, Emily, 62–63
Dos Passos, John, 138, 184, 189
Dowson, Ernest, 119

Dreiser, Theodore, 2, 4, 9, 10, 69, 76, 103, 112, 117, 122, 136; journalism, 25–26, 30–32, 39, 41; *Sister Carrie*, 65; and documentation, 115, 121; *tempo* in his fiction, 145; writing methods, 148; *The 'Genius,'* 171; philosophy, 175, 183, 184, 185, 186, 187, 191
Duer, Caroline, 131
Dunne, Finley Peter, 3
d'Utassy, George von, 98

Eakins, Thomas, 111
Eggleston, Edward, 27
Emerson, Ralph Waldo, 3, 12, 34

Fairbanks, Charles W., 86
Farrell, James T., 189
Fashionable Adventures of Joshua Craig, The (Phillips), 93, 132 ff.; and Phillips's assassination, 160
"First Born, The" (Phillips), 36, 169
Fitzgerald, F. Scott, 68, 136, 142
Flandrau, Charles M., 84
Flaubert, Gustave, 172
Flower, B. O., 9, 80, 89
Fortune Hunter, The (Phillips), 103–4
Frederic, Harold, 27, 33–34
Frevert, Carolyn Phillips, 10, 15; and David Graham Phillips, 26–27, 28, 67, 76, 125, 131; leaves husband, 53; friend of R.W. Chambers, 129; and Phillips's death, 155 ff.; role in his reputation, 192
Frohman, Charles, 157

Galsworthy, John, 68
Garland, Hamlin, 80, 125
Gautier, Theophile, 27
George, Henry, 12
George Helm (Phillips), 153, 202 n. 5 (Afterglow)
Ghent, W.J., 54, 127, 128
Gibson, C.D., 124
Gissing, George, *Demos*, 21–22
Goebel, William (Phillips's article), 86
Golden Fleece (Phillips), 78, 117
Goldsborough, Fitzhugh Coyle, 159 ff., 183
Gompers, Samuel, 185
Gorky, Maxim, 127
Gorman, Arthur Pue, 100
Grain of Dust, The (Phillips), 76, 152, 157, 165 ff., 171
Great God Success, The (Phillips), 4, 40–41, 65–66, 69–70, 117, 189; absurd status among critics, 191
Green, James A., 25, 26, 28

Halstead, Murat, 23, 24, 25, 26
Harland, Henry, 61
Harris, Frank, 40; on *The Plum Tree*, 88; on Phillips's characters, 93–94, 112, 169; view of Susan Lenox, 177; as critic, 192–93
Harris, Joel Chandler, 27
Harte, Bret, 68
Hay, John (*The Bread Winners*), 21
Haywood, William D., 183, 185
Hearn, Lafcadio, 27, 196 n. 4 (Midwest)
Hearst, William Randolph, 7; and Pulitzer, 57–58; and "The Treason of the Senate," 95 ff.
Hecht, Ben, 3
Hemingway, Ernest, 3, 136, 147
Her Serene Highness (Phillips), 72, 103, 105, 126
Hergesheimer, Joseph, 174
Hicks, Granville, 95, 152, 164, 191
Hill, David B., 75
Homer, Winslow, 111
Housman, A.E., 88
Howe, E.W., 16
Howells, William Dean, 11, 21, 61, 80
Hughes, Charles Evans, 115
Huneker, James, 66
Hungry Heart, The (Phillips), 85, 136 ff., 148
Hurst, Fannie, 191
Husband's Story, The (Phillips), 78, 85, 108, 146, 148 ff., 198 n. 11 (Success Story)

Ibsen, Henrik, 113, 139
"Interests, The" (coined by Phillips), 100
Irwin, Will, 161

James, Henry, 27
Jennie Gerhardt (Dreiser), 66, 136, 165
Jewett, Sarah Orne, 27
Johnson, Tom, 86
Journalism, pre- and post-Civil War compared, 23 ff.; New York, 30 ff.; *Victoria* disaster, 38–39; literary aspirations, 53 ff., 60 ff.; and magazines, 61; Phillips's articles on, 71, 74; Phillips's magazine work, 86

Lacy, Ernest, 61–63, 64
La Follette, Robert M., 59, 86, 96, 101, 185
Lawrence, D.H., 145
Lawson, John Howard, 186
Lawson, Thomas W., and *Frenzied Finance*, 83; and *The Deluge* (Phillips), 91 ff., 95
Lewis, A.H., 3; as friend of Phillips, 127–28, 162–63

Lewis, Sinclair, 68, 138; and Phillips, compared, 85; *Main Street*, 137; *Dodsworth* and *The Husband's Story*, 152, 153, 191, 198 n. 11 (Success Story)
Lewisohn, Adele, 164
Lewisohn, Ludwig, 119, 169, 191
Light Fingered Gentry (Phillips), 117, 118, 144, 187; as Phillips milestone, 109 ff.
Lindsay, Vachel, 167
Little, Arthur W., 127, 130, 131, 145, 147; and death of Phillips, 161
Lloyd, Henry Demarest, 12, 55
London, Jack, 3, 6, 80, 155, 188
Long, Huey P., 59, 86, 88
Lorimer, George Horace, on Phillips, 6; his editorial program, 67–69, 77; and *The Master Rogue* (Phillips), 79; and *The Mother Light* (Phillips), 85, 99; friendship, 126, 184
Lowell, James Russell, 34

McMaster, John Bach, 182
Madison, Indiana, 5 ff., 110, 163
Mailer, Norman, 3, 137, 176
Main Street (Sinclair Lewis), 137
Manson, Charles, 183
Marcosson, I.F., 19, 192, 196 n. 4 (Midwest)
Markham, Edwin, 2, 61, 95, 157
Marlowe, Julia, 62
Master Rogue, The (Phillips), 79, 84, 89, 100, 116
Masterson, Bat, 128
Melville, Herman, 2
Mencken, H.L., on Phillips, 7; and poetry, 63–64; on Veblen, 90; on Dreiser, 66, 171, 175, 191
Menken, Adah Isaac, 174
Meyer, Annie Nathan, 151
Millard, Bailey, 7, 135, 148; and "The Treason of the Senate," 95 ff.
Miller, Alice Duer, 131
Miller, Arthur, 186
Miller, Henry, 88, 176, 191
Morgan, J. Pierpont, 32, 151; Phillips on, 86
Mother Light, The (Phillips), 84–85
Muckraking, 11; "The Treason of the Senate," 95 ff.; and fiction, 109 ff., 116
Myers, Gustavus, 98; on "The Treason of the Senate," 99

New York Times, Phillips writes for, 71; approves *The Plum Tree* (Phillips), 87; deplores his "wild thinking," 156; denounces *Susan Lenox*, 172, 183, 187–88

Norris, Frank, 27; outlook and method, 65; and the *Saturday Evening Post*, 68; 80, 89; and Phillips, 97

O. Henry, 187
O'Brien, Fitz-James, 27
Old Wives for New (Phillips), 116 ff., 146, 169, 187
Older, Mrs. Fremont, 98
Olney, Richard, 56

Parkhurst, Rev. Charles H., 30
Peck, Harry Thurston, 104
Perkins, George W., 59; Phillips on, 86, 151
Phillips, Carolyn. See Frevert, Carolyn Phillips
Phillips, David Graham, Sr., 5 ff., 34, 35
Phillips, David Graham, youth, 5 ff.; education, 14 ff., 20 ff., 106, 158, 199 n. 13 (Fiction and the Senate Blast); Cincinnati journalism, 23 ff.; New York, 30 ff.; his reading, 34; *Harper's Weekly*, 35–36; London assignment, 38–39; "Alice," 40 ff.; and '90s issues, 55 ff.; magazine journalism and early fiction, 60 ff.; and Dreiser, 65–67; "John Graham," 69; and Beveridge, 76; and the drama, 77–78; articles and fiction, 78 ff., 103 ff.; success, 83 ff.; and Sinclair Lewis, 85; *The Reign of Gilt*, 89 ff.; "The Treason of the Senate," 95 ff.; *The Second Generations* as transitional, 104 ff.; changes publishers, 108; major fiction, 109 ff.; views of art, 110–11, 146 ff.; views of love, 112–13, 131, 145 ff., 165 ff.; happy endings, 115; sense of humor, 123, 156; his established round, 124 ff.; health attitudes, 132, 155; changing times, 136 ff.; changing style, 148; Progressive, 153; assassination, 155 ff.; posthumous publications, 164 ff.; assessments, 182 ff.
Phillips, Wendell, 12
Phillips, William Harrison, 10, 14, 98, 161
Piercy, J.W., 16, 33, 58
Platt, Tom, 87
Plum Tree, The (Phillips), 86 ff., 95, 113
Poe, Edgar Allan, 27
"Point of Law, A" (Phillips), 77
Pound, Ezra, 2
Price She Paid, The (Phillips), 74, 148, 157, 167 ff., 171, 188
Princeton University, 20 ff., 106, 158
Pulitzer, Joseph, 23, 37, 39, 52, 184; democratic campaigns and Phillips, 55 ff.; on *The Great God Success*, 69

Ralph, Julian, 33, 36
Reid, Robert, 146–47
Reign of Gilt, The (Phillips), 89
Rice, Elmer, 186
Richardson, Henry H., 111
Richardson, Samuel, 105
Ridpath, John Clark, 15
Riis, Jacob, 33
Rockefeller, John D., 11, 12, 32; and
    Wealth against Commonwealth (H.D.
    Lloyd), 55; Phillips's article on, 60, 86
Rogers, Will, 68
Roosevelt, Theodore, 75; on Phillips, 102
Rubin, Jerry, 183
Russell, Charles Edward, 34, 127, 164,
    185, 192; cultural outlook, 35; Phil-
    lips's journalistic associate, 54; and
    muckraking, 83; and "The Treason of
    the Senate" idea, 95

Sacco-Vanzetti case, 184
St. George's Church, 75, 163
Satterlee, Herbert, 128
Saturday Evening Post, 67–69
Schurz, Carl, 76
Sears, Joseph H., 85, 126, 129, 135, 163
Second Generation, The (Phillips), 97,
    110, 111, 113, 117, 118; as transitional
    novel, 104 ff.; compared with *Light
    Fingered Gentry*, 112; compared with
    *The Fashionable Adventures of Joshua
    Craig*, 132
Serling, Rod, *Patterns*, 79
Shaw, Albert, 93
Shaw, George Bernard, 78, 113
Sinclair, Upton, 1, 2, 96, 127; on G.H. Lor-
    imer, 68; *The Brass Check*, 71; and
    McClure's, 75; *The Jungle* and Phillips,
    83–84; T. Roosevelt on, 87; on fiction
    length, 144
Sister Carrie (Dreiser), 65, 66
"Social Secretary, The" (Phillips), 84, 89,
    91
Socialism, 127, 156, 185
Sparge, John, 127
Spencer, Herbert, 32
Steffens, Lincoln, 3, 30, 156; and
    McClure's, 75; Phillips visit, 76
Steinbeck, John, 116, 189
Stendhal, 109
Sterling, George, 68–69
Strindberg, August, 113
Sullivan, Louis, 111
Sullivan, Mark, 7, 95, 98
Sun, The. See Dana, Charles A.
Susan Lenox: Her Fall and Rise, 1, 4, 74,
    107, 112, 127, 129, 130, 171 ff., 187–88,
    191; and the dilemma of independence,

25; lack of critical canon, 70; Phillips
    decides to release for publication, 157
Swinburne, Algernon Charles, 35

Taft, William Howard, 128, 167
Tarbell, Ida M., 75, 76, 96, 138
Tarkington, Booth, *The Magnificent Am-
    bersons*, 105, 161
Thaw, Harry K., 137, 182
Tillman, Benjamin R., 101
Tolstoi, Leo, 3, 66, 156, 164
"Treason of the Senate, The" (Phillips), 1,
    4, 6–7, 55–56, 95 ff., 115, 130, 162,
    188, 191
Twain, Mark, 9, 61, 109

Veblen, Thorstein, 60, 90–91
Viereck, George Sylvester, 160

Wallace, George C., 86
Walling, Anna Strunsky, 155, 164–65, 185
Warhol, Andy, 111
Watson, Tom, 86
Wealth against Commonwealth (H.D.
    Lloyd), 12, 55
Weaver, Gen. James B., 12
Wells, H.G., 127
Wharton, Edith, 93, 132, 137, 188
Whistler, J.A.M., 111
White, Stanford, 111, 124, 125, 136–37,
    182
White, William Allen, compared with
    Phillips, 96–98; reminiscence, 128
White Magic (Phillips), 145 ff., 157
Whitlock, Brand, 3
Whitman, Walt, 35, 61
Wilde, Oscar, 119
Wilson, Edmund, 175
Wilson, Woodrow, 20–21, 67, 185, 199 n.
    13 (Fiction and the Senate Blast)
Wister, Owen, 16, 75, 87
Wolfe, Thomas, on Phillips, 142; com-
    pared with Phillips, 198 n. 1 (Success
    Story)
Woman Ventures, A (Phillips), 73–74,
    117, 126, 167
Women as major Phillips theme, 116 ff.,
    137 ff. *See also Woman Ventures, A;
    Light Fingered Gentry; White Magic;
    Grain of Dust, The; Susan Lenox: Her
    Fall and Rise*
Woodhull, Victoria, 85, 174
World, The. See Pulitzer, Joseph
Worth of a Woman, The (Phillips), 77, 157

X Club, 127

Zola, Emile, 16, 31, 65, 156, 188

DATE DUE